Connecting The Dots To Shangrila:
A Postmodern Cultural Hx of America

Joseph D. Reich

Fomite

Burlington, VT

Copyright 2016 © by Joseph D. Reich

All rights reserved. No part of this book may be reproduced in any form or by any means without the prior written consent of the publisher, except in the case of brief quotations used in reviews and certain other noncommercial uses permitted by copyright law.

ISBN-13: 978-1-942515-50-0
Library of Congress Control Number: 2016939862

Fomite
58 Peru Street
Burlington, VT 05401
www.fomitepress.com

Cover image: © Slidezero | Dreamstime.com - Town In Sepia Colour Photo

"Few great men could pass personnel"
-Paul Goodman

Contents

I.	Residence	1
II.	The Study Of Hollow Objects	15
III.	domestic,Violence	67
IV.	Scenes From The Ventriloquist Convention	87
V.	A Tourist Guide To Nodding-Out	165
VI.	Bally's: scenes from the overground	215
VII.	When Flash Gordon Called Groucho To Tell Him The Market Had Crashed: how to make ends meet	245
VIII.	The Railroad Flowers	255
IX.	The Bones Of Buddha	285
X.	A Reenactment Of Waking Life: stanzas of the season and notes of a misanthrope	295
XI.	Melancholia: scratch & sniff prints for the upcoming apocalypse	343
XII.	A Fragile Childhood Strung Together By Chicken Bones	373
XIII.	Sometimes They Make You Feel So Alone	411
XIV.	Character Analyses: How Juvenile Delinquents Sleep Like Creatures In Hibernation	457
XV.	A Bundle Of Blues	497
XVI.	Suburbanization: a wasteland of illusions	519
XVII.	Assembly Not Required: naked psalms	537

XVIII. On The Hx And Deleterious Effects Of Advertising:
      101 principles in psychological stanzas   561
XIX. Those Final Stages Of Growth & Development
      Eric B. Erickson Failed To Mention   587
XX.   The Drug Trade   605

About the Author

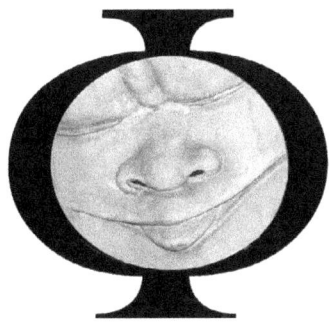

Joseph Reich has been published in a wide variety of eclectic literary journals both here and abroad and is a six time Pushcart Prize nominee. His most recent books include, *A Different Sort Of Distance* (Skive Magazine Press), *If I Told You To Jump Off The Brooklyn Bridge* (Flutter Press), *Pain Diary: Working Methadone & The Life & Times Of The Man Sawed In Half* (Brick Road Poetry Press), *Drugstore Sushi* (Thunderclap Press), *The Derivation Of Cowboys & Indians,The Housing Market: a comfortable place to jump off the end of the world and The Hole That Runs Through Utopia* (Fomite Press), *Taking The Fifth And Running With It: a psychological guide for the hard of hearing and blind* (Broadstone Books), *Scenes From the Dynamite Stand* (Bedlam Press), and *The Rituals Of Mummification* (Sagging Meniscus Press).

I. Residence

12:00

Working the graveyard at the schizophrenic residence
they listen to *tom & jerry* all night up in the balcony
and cracking-up as if watching it for the very first
time and in many ways with thought patterns and
impulsivity and short-term memory very much are
hearing tom screeching and pans being slammed
over rival top hats and tails…seems about right

1:30

And to keep myself a float, groggy, bleary-eyed, listen to albums
from childhood…springsteen's, "the river" nirvana's, "nevermind"
neil young, "harvest" grateful dead, "workingman's dead" and so on

2:00

Supposedly kerouac didn't like any the rock & roll bands
from the sixties but when his friend ginsberg introduced
him to bob dylan he was one of the few artists he really liked
a lot and thought had talent…think if he had made it and was
around just a little bit longer would have really appreciated and
loved bruce's first couple albums as they came from such similar
backgrounds; he also too wasn't a huge fan of broadway as most
likely due to his down-to-earth nature couldn't stand the histrionics

2:25

You find yourself mildly shocked as that actor you really liked a lot
always been quite fond of was found dead with a syringe still stuck
in his arm in his bethune street apartment in the west village section
of new york one of those damn fine character actors who was not
mainstream at all and always played fairly odd and eccentric and
endearing roles were totally able to relate to and sentimentally

and solemnly think back to your days in new york,
a solitary soul, restless and anonymous and that's
what it was all about so guess not so much about
being shocked anymore, never really was, but
straight-up sympathetic, little heartbroken
which becomes a conduit and secret tunnel
and labyrinth to the natural instinct of compassion

4:00

You fall back into the sofa, eyes bloodshot
after a cat-nap, dog-tired, watching james bond
007 muted in technicolor and true *nobody does it
better* fighting off all those haters and villains which
does seem like the classic metaphor for human nature

4:35

You start to hear the floorboards above you
creaking and pacing back and forth and will
soon have to measure and pour the bleach
for her for the old lady with the o.c.d.
who won't stop cleaning and if you
don't give into her instantly when
she keeps on making demands
on the spot or don't pour out
the dirty water for her will have
meltdowns and slam doors and start
going off abusively and threatening
and cursing and yeah she started off so
nice and kind and charming and manipulating

why i could never stand that expression honeymoon period
as takes a phase of existence so hopeful and innocent
and just sullies it like her like she clams she isn't

4:35

As an aside when you bring this
to the quote on quote managers
they'll pretend to be listening
and giving their token dose
of validating but are clueless
and have no idea how much
this is feeding into her pathology
enabling and doing the exact opposite
and absolutely nothing to help her
clinically matter of fact backfiring

4:36

What it means to have that blunted flat affect
how you're taught to measure and assess and
diagnose or that look to look tragically alone
completely empty and vacant and lost in the
world totally disoriented and in constant conflict
with the self and soul profoundly and precisely
all having that psychotic break somewhere at
the start of early adulthood as if the chemicals
in the brain decided to revolt and it all goes
downhill from there no longer knowing
why or where or who they are anymore

4:45

Ghosts wrestling ghosts…

4:52

You sometimes like to wonder or pose the intellectual question
if they have any remembrances before they had their psychotic break

5:00

While all the schizophrenics
are snoozing like mad kids
in the evening after all
the episodes & meltdowns
& explosions & hallucinations
after their p.m. meds have been taken
& cigarettes smoken & rants ranted
in frozen feeling-no-pain fences
backed-up against the back of
bleary-eyed railroad station
whose brilliant shrill scream
suddenly comes streaming
from smoking silhouetted
chimneys of ancient new
england antiquity from
the beautiful & bleak
anonymity of deep
blessed nothingness
& muffles
all the madness
for the moment
all the hellish howls
& hacking coughs
from the jaws of
out-of-control
& impulsive
insane lions
without a home
returning back to
the safe & secure
darkness where the
growling belongs
& goes blowing
& bellowing
& blasting
& barreling
full-throttle
fast-forward
ahead then
vanishes

into thin air
into the blissful
bones of long-gone
oblivion evening
with steaming
steam whistles
& wild whispers
spitting orgasmically
through all the false
truths & lies i get to thinking
all the borderline girlfriends
i somehow fell for were like
real-life killers in *constant
commotion* in constant
chaos & crisis trying
to drag you into their
craziness & dangle
you over the cliff
with constant
crimes (against man)
of passion, relentless
& romantic making you
their savior & the next day
arch-nemesis staying forever
embedded in your consciousness
as if somehow, somewhere suspended
between their dream & your nightmare
becoming something of a muddled
& mangled & miraculous vision
whose head pops up intermittently
like some strange blissful trigger
every so often without warning

5:25

Looking at your computer like some sort of beacon
to give you solace and keep you going you get to thinking
that your partner the girl you married gets to know you intimately
like that dude at disney world all squooshed into his goofy costume

5:45

You think about your boy…boy you love so much
dreaming the saint that he is in his bed and me just
sitting there in that chair weeping like jesus in the
fluorescent window with flakes starting to fall past
the lamplight of the platform with a view to the back
of the silhouetted movie theater and just those bare
phosphorescent escalators climbing up to nowhere
to the blank beaming lights and you be like that stranger
from *the myth of sisyphus* just riding it up and down up
and down with my head bowed down in vacant reflection
somehow in this ridiculous routine and ritual contented
making a little liberating sense and feeling redemptive

6:00

Trains which rattle and rumble and pump and prattle
and disappear into the night and think you actually
miss them when they are gone and how much you
loved their presence for the moment (maybe like
brilliant rare instance and sensation of fucking?)

6:12

How they never ever stop and just zoom past your window
like some illusion from *the twilight zone* and those idiot
commuters never getting off but thinking all the better
and how much more you prefer this romantic image

6:15

A young brando howling at the top of his lungs
at the bottom of the banister in *streetcar*…

not coincidental a little later on when he got older
hollering under the streetcars of the metro in paris

both great towns, both great performances

both sick of it all of the bullshit of it all drained from living
from the obstacles and injustices and inequities of being

dawn…what a strange and shallow and deep fragile thing

"love exciting and new" these days seem all the cruise ships crawling
in with passengers puking from some sort of bacterial food poisoning

things aint the way...

"keep on pulling me back in!"

6:21

You wonder if there will ever be that final calm that
sane psalm settling self-soothing otherworld paradise
and kingdom after all the deceit and betrayal and
bullshit and brainwash double-talk from devils

you wonder if even then will it really matter?

6:25

A love letter to your wife who's so kind
and good and innocent and how much
don't deserve her and if she only knew
how much i suffered on a daily basis
and how i have to try to justify my life
with all the assholes i am surrounded
by and just cannot and never relate to

6:30

I miss you
i wish i was dead
and had money
and could give
it all to you
and dylan
willie loman
slash social worker
slash that 'smart jew
carl solomon' naturally
dying of natural causes
in the chair by the window
in the spotlight of the lamp post
of the platform when that train
goes naturally whizzing by
and casually disappears
as if nothing happened
like kerouac's cantos
and choruses and
in fact nothing
did happen

6:39

I need just one of those plain sandwiches
i used to get under the plane trees of nice
when i was wandering alone contented

free with simple fresh hunks
of mozzarella little vinegar
and pesto leaves on le pain

had no one just the cactuses
and palm trees and sea and
couldn't of been happier

6:46

I think they should have a special verdict
for innocent *and* guilty for in fact deep
down inside (on a very shallow and
fragile level) existentially and nihilistically
aren't we all constantly guilty for feeling innocent
and absurdly innocent in feeling persistently guilty?

6:52

Feeling like some sort of constant thief
under the microscope trying to whittle
my way out of the snow globe clawing
my way and always finding myself just
short of finding my way back home

7:00

Property matches automatically appear
from a long time ago (which seems like
the only person, place, or thing reliable)
when we desperately tried to sell home
and nomads and did not no where to go
happened to be in the big and wonderful
i mean the big and bad i mean i got that
wrong all down in the land of texas and
got these cattle ranch gates which lead
to a great plot of land and plantation home
with all this space to roam and be your own
proverbial version of the pearly gates heading
to final farewell heaven place to call your own

7:12

When you do your skeleton stretches in the middle
of pitch-black room you look out the broken shutters
like brando in new orleans and think of your sleep-in
colleague who gets to 'cause she's got seniority and
she's young and she's shy and think may have married
her high school sweetheart but has a ton of issues and
attitude and a big butt to boot and just once want to
give a slight rap at her door and she'll just let me in
without saying a thing and will simply spoon her
for the remainder of the evening 'til it's time to
give the clients their morning dosing of lithium

7:30

When you get out of your shift you see all these log cabin logs
neatly piled in a woodpile flush against the red wooden slats
of the depot under the mountains like some strange surreal
still-life as if in after the struggle nothing did ever happen

7:45

A tiny broken attic window
which only a couple are privy to
hidden somewhere between the purply
blue mountains against the constellations
and the railroad station which looks out to
miserable bliss of all this like some secret
subterranean escape tunnel to the heavens
and the owners know it and will never
repair it with all the radiant variations
of seasons and spirits flying through
and why would they even want to?

8:00

You literally follow the icy snowy river
and powdered sugar mountains home
the sweet smell of chimney smoke
almost like brandy and cologne
from the schools and homes
cutting in ribbons across
the mountains and
down steep sleepy
hills into the town

angels & madmen abound...

II. The Study Of Hollow Objects

1

punched,punched black
i am yer punching bag
please don't punch back!

    wherethehell's yaw mask scare yah
                  audrey hepburn

2

h/clinton who looks like one of those insane:dolls
come,to,life in the middle,of,the,night smart,as,a,whip
tough,as,nails & can put:up a good:fight & d/trump who looks
more like some:grownup orange:faced oompa:loompa:monster
who cares more about his hair&reallity:show:make:up&turned
him,self into,a,product &will one dayhonor&tellus about his "terrific" plans
& policies like selling some glossy:cata:logue from one of his properties
the multi:billion:heir coming down waving from his golden,guilded,esca,late
or to announce his presidency&provide:the:panic:ea for the comm:on:man
&if believe that got,a,bridge in brook:land man:sion,in,miami dubai:beijing

3

always wished that that song had gone–
"it's only a paper moon on the sidewalk
of baton rouge" as spent a good:amount
of down:time down there on the bayou
&knowtoo how the semi-tropic/yawl
who,mi,ditty can kill you & fuck you
&haunt you &effect you &influence
your moods&behavior practically
having,hallucinations sweating
it,all,out though the punched-
out portholes of that lonesome
streetcar & that never,ending
piping sweet/smelling scent

of persistent,brilliant,burning
magnolia penetrating every
orifice swear would have
so much more preferred
the expression if it said
"flattery:will:kill:you"
due to fear of success&
self-destructive tendencies
always could never stand
"can trust him about as far
as i can throw him" cuz most
of them who i always ended up
not being able to trust were very little
men&could throw them a country mile

4

they god a war
starting some-
where in "crimea"
4 no rhyme,or,reason
peep,that!like some
twilight,zone,episode
of forgotten film,noir
black&white/characters
don't even know how it
started don't even know
how it big...ended say it's
gonna be another world war
(better:get:out your bread&butter
the new atkins...) don't even need
hitler(propaganda lagangmembers
in afghanistan, have,you,heard,the
one? libya threatens,to,bomb north
korea &you do the hokey/pokey &
you turn,yourself,around...) don't even
need the long cinders of kissinger's cigar
the good bedsidemanner of staticy radio
to gather:round&stare at...geraldo,rivera
&barbara walters (barbra,streisand

18

&ol' dirty bastard bow!bow!bow! u go
hungry! lou gehrig/stevemartin "i'll have
a pancake on my whip cream please!")
something's gotta give mayakofsky,
zukovsky,john travolta...strayed out
the criminal/diaries of gulliver's/travels
compton,california jean genet&jeanpaul
sartre who glanced over the shoulder
of simone dew boo!voire (translated
into second language "i think...there
fore i am" who borrowedwhobawd
him a mandolin&mandarinoranges
hope& to get in his good favor
maybe,even,delusionally,ask,him
to marry her) while blowingbutterfly
kisses&playingpingpong "sarcasm!"
so,says obsessive,compulsive
felix,unger (aweright! propaganda
or plagiarism wisp/spring sweet
nothings during pillow talk was
the:inspiration they werelovers
they wereleftovers how,can,you,
really fault/them... what's really
the difference between the sadistic
punch/line and existential build-up)
fought with the wife all of last night
over,a,rackoflamb&heartpalpitations

  wept with the cheap:carbonated wine
  from price,chopper stead of the pain killer...

5

homes should always
be hung with the smells
of lasagna,pork,chops
and onions and baked
apples and mashed
potatoes red,wine
almond,pleasure

(what it means
to be human)
going straight
to the true,blue
blew heart and soul
and absolutely nothing
nothing in the world
could possibly stop
its path–"hey, you
doing anything
with that?"

6

delicacy:on:delancey
lowereastside siblings
fighting,over,fish,eyes
"hey! who took the pupick?"

7

if you asked me how the:world:began
i would tell you it's when all,the,gods
randomly all,of,a,sudden spontaneously
fainted and bit,the,dust & it all sprang
up from their powerful&sorrowful
&solemn brooding:bodies &when they
gradually/fluttered into the nether:world
somewhere between the conscious
&unconscious world this is when
the world developed all its natural
geological traits&characteristics
&formations&came into:being

that sole:solitary:survivor:explorer:being
standing proudly,stranded,deserted,abandoned
on the edge of the pre:ci:peace looking off to the horizon

winds coming in and soon
will be the blessed rain
all in the shape of...

8

threw the shadows
of,your,blinds you see
moving shadows &dream
they're wild coyotes opposed
to those very psychotic:hostile
perfectly:manicured:pedigrees
of even more passive/aggressive
asshole/neighbors as those lone
solitary:coyotes have always
had so much more,in,common
and can relate to so much
more just minding:their:own
wandering from the woods at
sundown all by their lonesome

school has just begun
and that fake aristo:cracked
psycho:kindergarten:teacher
has just started roaming with
wine:glass around the dead:end

exhibitionist takes off
her clothes in window
to get herself closer
to everything
she has lost
& will
begin
again

9

on the dead end it's my kingdom is better than your kingdom
but when you really get to know them it's pure dysfunction and
damage and damn miserable if you kind of get what i'm saying?

you dream back to your childhood of that river
flowing all the way down past the trains...

10

something of a new psychological theory and
hypotheses: that dreams and nightmares are not
just purely subconscious but the defenses present
as so permeable (compromised and fragile) rather
more so, receptive and awakened and enlightened,
somehow interestingly, become conscious, meaning
the subconscious has become so keenly and profoundly
aware, perceptive and heightened even something feeling
and being 'conscious,' of a very pure and keen 'conscious
unconscious,' heretofore as well in the awakened state of
reality and similarly (or more accurately, contrary) while
following these exact selfsame patterns or believed beliefs
or psychodynamics, we may very well surmise with those
defense-mechanisms so fragile, the conscious or conscious
reality due to too much (of a sensory overload) or a hyper-state
of self-awareness (and brooding and ruminating) may consciously
become subconscious (often playing itself out in an exacerbated
state referred to as magical thinking) and thus these brooding
and ruminating individuals may have to go through certain
routines and rituals (played out as checking rituals to try
and break away from the brutal reality of these frustrating
dynamics) in order to function, thus manifests itself into
obsessive-compulsive and likewise in conclusion we
may see the cognitive, as well as behavioral patterns
or an actual 'flip-flop' of the subconscious and conscious
therefore often playing itself out in dreams (more often than
not nightmares) and consistent (inconsistent maladaptive
patterns) of the reality or disorder of obsessive-compulsive

11

those who i have known with such profound
or severe:cases of bipolar,schizophrenia
even borderline d/o with just a fewcouple
choicewords have said some of the most
keen&perceptive shit i have ever heard
so much so made me stop to think&
(reflect &inretrospect never to forget)
so much,more,so than any of those
supposed very sober,minded,forward
thinking,climbers &up&coming gogetters
the,most blatant&obvious&predictable
motherfuckers i have ever met (who
always left so much to be desired)

12

that period of time (or moment
in time…) is some of the best
exchanging ideas and thoughts
and really getting to know each
other on an intimate basis then
that strange and awkward
unnatural act of seduction
actually going through with
it in many ways like entering
the dark room with all those
emotions of fear and doubt
and anxiety and pain and
pleasure as all that happens
in the moment and what
develops is the eventual
denouement; you leave
her hovel in far better
shape than when
you entered finally
contented which is
having the weight of
the world off your shoulders

as if the world never existed
which is a wonderfully pleasant
baffling & blissful anti-climax
to all these dramatic probing
& feeling-out plays & acts

13

don't you know ghost:stories are really
a certain,sort,of passionate pillow:talk
and pillow:talk haunted ghost:stories
from your past,with,plans you plan
for your lovie/dovie future
& suddenly willing to expose
to some complete stranger you
at,last,finally trust ready,or,not
here i cum! glistening frost
from the streetlamp begins
to glow off the midnight:
window of sleepy:hollow
as you know you got
no:where to go but know
none of that really matters
as somehow feel calm &
comforted by the moment
leftover polenta & romantic
candlelit dinner with dreams
&visions&promises secretly
stashed in the refrigerator

14

somewhere between the inventor of the ship in a bottle
and the first man who walked on the face of the moon
is the true-blue existential nature of man (hysterical
neurotic and nihilistic) and culture and civilization
(the overall patterns of its collective behavior and
character) maybe why have always desperately

found myself just treading water ("keeping your
head above water" j.j. walker kid dyn-o-mite!
florida evans and their misunderstood, stoic
kind and compassionate father and husband
who got murdered in cold-blood in the projects
of chicago) lost and stranded somewhere in
no man's land between that ship (stripped clean
and folded down and out to its bare essentials)
in a bottle and that distant unfamiliar faraway
man just exploring trying to find and figure
it all out the ways and means of the stars

15

wouldn't it be cool if during,an,interview
when they ask you for your references
you say–"i'll show you mine if you show
me yours" and when they remove them
selves from the room you proceed to
move your bowels and wrap,it,up in
a nice little kleenex:tissue and store
it like where's?waldo some:where
in,their,room which when they find
it and got,no,idea what this represents
only proves how much more (in)competent
about the clinical,psychology,field; bart:be
the:scrivener in another room having become
a dope addict due to a situational:depression
and just another depressed,new,england town
goin,down,the,drainnodding back&forth–
"i prefer not to, prefer not to…"

you feeling tired and wasted
like one of those peanut butter
& fluff sandwiches having
gotten way too pungent
your mother made
you in those brown
paper bags for lunch

16

i remember whenever they asked me
what i wanted to be when i grew up
instead of giving all the boring and
obvious answers like a doctor or
lawyer or astronaut or ballplayer
i said i wanted to be a big hairy
yellow gorilla who drives a bus
and to call me butch well i did
in later life coincidentally run
into a number of these kids
who just felt exactly by all
looks and appearances
(and even expressions)
displaced and brainwashed
and lonesome and lost and
sadly enough just your everyday
schmuck becoming exactly who
they said they would (not exactly
sure what they had become) as
had mapped out their exact future
right out of high school and really
did not know who they were anymore
(or what they had suddenly become
in the grownup world) and can feel
pretty confident in my conviction
to know exactly who i am as
that big hairy yellow gorilla
who drives a bus and can
call me by the name of butch

17

how do you become a billionaire?
seems like these days they come
a dime a dozen and that we got
a whole mess of them and don't
seem any more holy or sacred
or for that matter charismatic

than any killer or sociopath
any best friend or girlfriend
who turn their back on you
for no apparent reason
remember reading
the biography of
bernard baruch
and when he made
his first million and
was a real big deal
back then and his
old man simply asked
him how he planned
to spend it or what
he was going to
do with it to
contribute
something
good and
positive
to society and
the environment
don't remember
exactly what
he said or what
was his answer
but do know they
got that really good
college right next
to yeshiva in that
section of town
in downtown
manhattan
i really like a lot
where people don't
really hang out too
much but the sun
slants through
perfectly
at dusk

18

you remember
roz schlomovitch
this fairly insane half-crazed
eccentric and intellectual chick
with a very dry sense of humor
you used to love to hang out
with in the halls of *wurzweiler*
school of social work at yeshiva
during one of those late afternoons
you had nothing else to do but brood
about your future confused not knowing
where your life or existence was heading
to and her happening to mention we should
just bum-rush one of our professors in their
office like *the shining* twins with that haunting
menacing and monotone drone and should
just present to them some of our thoughts
and ideas in that selfsame cadence to try
and see if we could get a rise out of them
don't know what ever happened to her
as was always a pleasure to be around
as a friend but would sort of get freaked
out whenever i tried to get closer due
to her very exclusive and insular issues
with her 'fear of intimacy' and affection
and have some kind of temper-tantrum
or make crazy accusations; she was
a rich girl from the state of michigan
and had this weird and awkward
codependent relationship with her
father who was some sort of surgeon
and apparently never quite cut the chord

19

cold never stand
those of excessive
or even for that matter

ascetic&asshole pride
as in the long run
in my very modest
& humble opinion
from all looks
& appearances
& experience
(or lack there of)
always left so
much to be
desired

like those married to their jobs
"aiii!" (the sound of pirates
of john,paul,george&ringo)

20

thinkpreferred & had so much more
respect for joe,buck&ratzo,rizzo
pacing back&forth a:cross
creaky,lopsided,floors
shivering,to,death
frozen,to,the,bone
teeth chattering
wrapped up in
their blankets in
that,vacant,haunted
burnt,out,tenement
inn the rawbronx
new york listening to
that stray:pawnshop
radio hearing over
&over again that late
sixties advertising
spiel–"orange juice
on ice is nice,orange
juice on ice is nice"
trying desperately
to keep warm &

keep to the beat
& rhythm dancing
to it like some kind
of funeral hymn
repeating it
over & over
& over again
like some sort
of prayer in the
hopes to bereborn
& delivered out of
their hellish nightmare
to the promised land
& fantasy world &
florid hallucinations
of the flora of
the technicolor
of ft. lauderdale,
f-la- florida

21

have damnwonderful triggers
in taking,my,kid out of school
early to the doctor while he was
putting together some sort of news:
print:paper:mache escape,from,alcatraz
mask or another &office was hidden
up there back there up around
the granite pits and cement
trucks and the truck docks
in holy blasts of train whistles
in the far,off,distance high:up
in the mountain:tops in the
moses god:like firmament when
used to work the docks way out
out in portland,or,gone with ex,cons
just let out of jail on,parole always
threatening to kill,each other and
freedom was really,having,absolutely

no one and no place to go accept
a long bridge to walk over,at,dusk
back to the jack:london:hotel
slabs,of,ice and logs,rolling
under bridges down:river
with the hot:springs and
lumber:mills in the hills
freedom an empty
room with a sink
in the corner
a chill pint
of orange
mad dog
40/40
& books
you had
bartered
from the blood
you had donated

22

learned far more from hard-working criminals
than any thief-boss or false father-figure

real truths and lowdown wisdom
than the higher-than-holy repetition

of nauseating behavioral patterns
of agendas and treating people

like pawns and possessions
(even worst of all when coming

from own family members which
ironically is the greatest crime of all)

the actual lay of the land and culture
the small city and big town in america

its geometric configurations
and how they function

its literal mists & fogs & smog
& slouching out of motel doors

at the end of the world
at the end of freight trains

just a little after dawn
already 73 degrees

to try and land a job somewhere
out there in the middle of nowhere

rambling with the tumbleweed
past airports & casinos & suburbs

not knowing a single soul meeting up
not knowing it back then with some fugitive

on-the-run from the reservations out in montana
literally hustling pool halls, whiskey & corndogs

& climbing back on, drunken & disheveled
feeling-no-pain frozen buses of other lost

soulful lost souls
american indians

silent & reflective, strong & sensitive
also seeming to have nowhere to go

not caring if i made it home dead or alive
ironically feeling un/wanted dead or alive

a whole thriving town of very single-minded
driven competitive aggressive go-getting assholes

their coward & conformist herd mentality
narrow-minded mean & malicious expressions

their body language of attitudes & alienations
how young girls always prowled in packs of threes

discovering lonesome to be far better
than ever being 'taken in' or accepted

while in the long-run bringing on
far more issues & conflicts & problems

the senator's son living in a boxcar with a bible
and a sweeping panoramic view of the skyline

razor blades
& a shot of wine

23

but there was that truck driving lady
complete stranger all the way out there

on the outskirts of portland, oregon
(when portland, oregon

was still poor
land or gone

and not some really hip & rich &
kitsch all-knowing gentrified town)

who from the goodness of her heart
relying on the kindness of strangers

on some cold winter's night just gave me her coat
when she thought i was down & out & cold

runaway running trucks up and down the coast
surviving off biscuits & gravy & faith alone

24

*a fine line between criminality
and our perception of heaven and hell
or what we believe to be our good deeds
in contributing something positive to society

25

*i always seemed to understand shit
somewhere between memories
and the madness of it all

26

*one must die several times in order to truly understand life
and if after that you don't or cannot you'll never know why

27

know why those college cheerleaders
close-up look like they're gonna eat
you up & swallow you whole wan
nah be eaten:up swallowed:whole
by sum,college,cheerleader
all parts,of,her,hole then cum
out through her,holiest,of,holes
perhaps when she's doing one
of those sexy:kicks knowing
exactly what,she's,doing right
in front of,the,cameras with that million:
dollar smile ev/en something of a rebirth

28

weird made-up dreams. eternally turning into one of those
thin sticks of bubblegum from a pack of baseball cards. a jew
still hiding out in the haunted holocaust forest. yourself pleasantly
and gratefully murdered at some pitch-black starry campground.
tap dancing while they shoot me up against a brick wall. turning
bullhorn. the bullfrog on myself to once more find my soul. a little
man playing harpsichord in the corner with ice cream coin dispenser.
fangs. and fedora. so romantic being bandit holding up a train
to give all the pretty girls roses. a black man in black face still
not being served at the counter. masturbating while the girl
scouts and vacuum cleaner salesmen show up to my front door.
game postponed. cloned. chimpanzee champagne. see things
in the wasted things. stickie on kitchen counter simply reads
seagulls. feel far more remorse killing a spider than i would
a neighbor. literal snake in the grass who wouldn't think twice
about stabbing you in the back, then frolicking in the grass.
fucken fag. white man's logic. all for the kids. real family man.
really extension of him. a possession. grin. would trust a drunk
far more than a monk. than a hunk. am in a funk. you need
whispers. mantras. prayers. to get you up the stairs. becoming
deeper and deeper a part of the deep shadows. like the deep
hollow hull of the skull of a ship which has entered the shallows

29

falling asleep in the electric chair
waking up dreaming of evolution
from the first seal waddling out
the ocean like chaplin in black
& white fast-forward silent film
san simeon to the last ferry
and buffet and schmaltzy
lounge act band capsizing
in the escape from alcatraz
mythological mediterannean
to the first tulip blossoming
and puckering up in the indian
summer of the shag carpet suburb

to the final cruise of romantic blues
(the love boat soon will be making
another run...) the skull of the king
and the pharaoh not the court jester
and fool who were the real true-blue
philosophers and emperors girl scouts
selling cookies from door to door while
their mothers are whores sneering and
snarling in the distance and neverending
dusk and dawn from all they project and
cannot offer (and now cannot afford) from
stud husbands who bought them for a steal
and will eventually betray them (for girls and
angels half their age) for their rawshack rick
shaw claims of lack of effort and sex appeal
which are their insurance claims that they feel
they truly don't love them. rockettes kicking
themselves out of marzipan rainbow cookie
wedding cakes brought up by con-artists
and false father figures and embezzlers
(who dabbled in the stock market and
sacrificed their first born son) and lived
on the bowery off the vaudeville theaters.
it's fair to say all dreamed of being one of
those dope addict *twilight zone* actors never
exactly returning to the planet earth never up
for an academy re-reading books from darwin
to dostoevsky. daymares of incest of dropdead
cousins who will never, who will always leave
you abandoned, whispering the original sweet
nothings of existence waking up in a motel room
next to your one-night stand, to that gorgeous girl
you always dreamed of and now threatens you with
self-hatred and love. mona lisa *was* a drag queen
was a frightened dove flying away off of fidel's
shoulder, then swallowed you up at the dance
at the meat market in the lightning of boca raton
florida. you thrive off leftovers and black & white
film-noirs lighting up the lamplight in the poverty-
stricken mansions of the madmen of madame
new orleans. the criminals and phantoms know
all burrowing through the escape tunnel from

the netherworld to the devastation of heaven.
guilt is ephemeral (and existential and the
dream of a lifetime, the life & times of moses
before & after he was left on the clothesline
of the nile due to tough times) and stems
from long-term abuse and damage getting
swept up by blissful wildfires in the rain &
the thunder in the back of the movie theater
which takes you away and delivers you to whole
other runaway milk & cookie methadone dimensions

drizzle falls past the blinds of the hygienist...

30

i wonder
if a president
will ever be
considered
in the miss
interpreted
murderous
category
for possible
impeachment
based on
excessive
masturbation
and when he
has to explain it
to the american public
exclaims—"i wasn't
having sex i was
just fantasizing
and fondling
and imagining
and in no way
shape or form
did it affect my
decision making

or ability to reason
or perform the job
at hand matter
of fact it..."
seeing him
give that final
farewell dramatic
wave of the hand
from air force one
heading back home
to independence
maw-zorro...
"boy they sure
did put up a lot
of bodegas and
fortune tellers
in this area
since
i bin
gone"

31

got a brand new all-american idea
which is sure to bring in all,the,masses
just working on:the:patent a fast-food drive-
thru fried:chicken shack where you can make
your order while simultaneously your:con:fessions
and then through the mouth,of,jesus pick:up your
bucket & he tells you if you are forgiven or how
many hail marys&rosaries you gotta say after
your feast of extra-crispy breasts&wings &
drum:sticks and as a condiment and side dish
your choice of either those,convenient,little wet
wipes, blow:up:balloons of,yer,savior or:bite:bullet

32

amazing how they
deported chaplin
& freud on,the,run
from nazigermany
should have seen
that/coming as all
good&decent
prophecies
are simply
really just
keen,intuition
& instincts
from the
barrel
of a
gun

33

son's gonna
be a wild,billy,goat
4 his 3rd grade musical
practicing his lines with him
highlighted in blew/red matchbox
car he traded&got in a trade sticking
out the sty:ra:phone cup advantages
far outweigh disadvantages bringing
me back to my passionate wise,ass
can't,keep,my,ass,out,of,trouble child
hood due,in some sordid historical play
about the american:revolution &crooning
about the first person who happened
to be a black,man who lost his life
and pumping,our,fists in the air
way before les miserables—"who
was the first to shed his blood!
crispus atticks!crispus attics!" (how2
spend your tax,returns sure as hell

not,on,one,of,those disneycruises
so much more prefer one of those
antebellum hanging spanish moss
islands hanging off the coast of
the carolinas) am still/jealous of
jim:carrol for his addictions to heroine
and codeine medicine ,buy the way
what the hell does that expression
really mean anyway—"i was
just thinking out loud..."

34

the shoot:oww! the end of "dog day afternoon"
those hasidic,jews,davening at the wailing wall
(just trying to make it all seem worthwhile) like
junkies stalled,stranded,nodding out on,the,corner
of san,francisco in the tenderloin:district ,dawn need
a cognitive:behaviorist just that gorgeous bitch
of a weather:woman in her form,fitting,dress
showing off her hour:glass:figure&simply
pointing to regions of deepdown,concern

35

concernedtoo much,haiku,written
about persimmon seed&kittens
not enough about the struggles
of everyday:existence making
absolutely nothing of yourself
dropping your son off at his school
in the mountains & when you drive
home through the old ninety-seventies
deck houses closing your eyes singing–
"i went down to memphis where i learned
to talk the jive" planting,your,car in garage
& contemplating through cobweb,window
at the last of the snowfalling in the hills

at the blissful glistening radio:tower
blinking,in,the,distance like a beacon
wondering&thinking&going back to nothing
forgetting how to make scrambled eggs&coffee

36

straydeer,straydogs in,the,garage
what about old,girlfriends?
ghosts&gods?

37

miss the girl with the monstermountains
and the bubblebutt bending,over taking
over sittingonmycock(the one who said
never ever make me have to make a
decision between you and my dogs
and then down the road cried out
i knew they were gonna make you
take off in the long run!) as:well
as the one with the flat chest who
was the best and was a red head
and to die for and so much more
good looking and tragic and damaged
(whose idiot faggot coward boyfriend
in college used to tie her up to a chair
and take pictures of,her,naked) making
love to her in that hidden anonymous
motel (all should be hidden anonymous
motels) off the tick:tock,coast of gloucester

38

nothing quiet smells like the sea
cuz the sea is the sea is the sea
is the sea is the sea is the sea
is the sea is the sea some night might
say a woman's pussy maybe seaweed
forgetting everything and remembering
nothing nothing quite smells like the sea
cuz the sea is the sea is the sea is the sea

"glider rides today..."

39

abstract:

i always loved those b-movie
film noirs where holes got shot
through the motel door and all
you saw was the light streaming
through and wonder if they got
them on the other side as well
or if that was just straight-up
irrelevant and all about pure
empty hollow void of it all

i've decided i just want to live
in the lobby of an old motel
along the side of the road
with all those postcard
carousels and simply
waste away with the
passing of seasons
passing of demons
passing of strangers
of course always
keeping my
distance
cause

aint
that
a lot
a little
bit this life
and existence?

drip drip drip drip drip drip
drip drip drip drip drip
drip drip drip drip drip
drip drip drip drip drip

specifics:

the girls who work
behind the front desk
always like angel orphans
coming off abusive relationships
and the guests well you guessed it...

40

taking her
from behind
her behind
you find
colleen
was like
some
gigantic
pachyderm
but loved
her just
the same
as was
always
all ways
open and
receptive
and connie

just a little
while later
this gorgeous
red head with
the tiny tits
and niblets
but shy
and self-
effacing
and self-
conscious
and loved
her that
much
more
for this
until you
discover
they're
all different
varieties and
specimens and
hybrids of flowers
from the great big
hearty hibiscus
to wildflower
and then there
was madelaine
there was always
madelaine with
the borderline
disorder you
couldn't help
but to love
cuz always
brought
the drama
and passion
and histrionics
and everyday
a different

sort of multiple
personality
disorder
different
sort of
variety
living
and
dying
and
trying
there
was lisa
from around
the corner
who told
you her
life story
they always
told you their
life story
and for that
was always
abundantly
grateful and
appreciative
as felt like
they took
you in
and man
you needed
to be taken
in and always
wanted to try
you on for
size and
experiment
and thus
represented
the ultimate
perennial
or you did

never quite
sure about
any of this
as if
any
of it
really
mattered?

41

we look back at those girlfriends
who were most open and receptive
sexually and intellectually and think
about and reflect back on the most
for the desperate and unquenchable
need and desire to eternally belong

42

remember this one time
   going out with this divorcee
who hadn't had it in so long
   and just took off her
shirt & bra & panties
   and casually commented–
"you held up pretty well"
   and she just started blushing
and cracking-up and know
   deep down inside
sincerely meant it
   from the heart
still don't know what
   i said that was
so wrong and don't know
   guess the difference
between cats and dogs

43

loved that borderline girl
with her skewed vision
(taking that definition
so literal&serious
"absence makes
the heart grow
fonder") what
she thought
love was
was so
hard to
get playing
hard to get
with the
mind
body
&soul

44

foghorn!foghorn!forlorn!foghorn!
slow,motion,sleepyhollow,solong
farewell,got,so,far,got,solong,togo
can't even get out of freak:in:airport
in,laguardia with all that kvetching
watching the plane take off to paris
classic parable to the stagnant male
female/bickering end.of.being relation
:ship being:grounded in that late:night
diner with all those mirrors just to stare
at yourself and wonder where it all went
wrong knowing it all went wrong so long
ago in,the,suburb in the borough,of,riverdale
how denial in the long run will all eventually
become a certain form of detainment
as all you're left with is a doggy bag

the pretty,young,sicilian girl i met on the ferry
at the end,of,summer returning from the south
of france! having worked at some:posh:resort
out there all season and telling me how much
she couldn't,stand,them and missed her family
back in sicily. i happened to strangely be pretty
damn fond of them (and all their symbols and
images and representations of freedom) and
somehow always kind of appreciated them
their pride and their culture or maybe somehow
as well i was on,the,run (literally:running for a
ferry,at,dawn after having just crossed,the,border
on:a:train from nice,to,northern,italy where the
italian:rail:workers were on strike once again
getting there last second one saying *w. africa*
and the other *sicilia* actually thought about it
then went for the latter) from a pretty,bad,break
up with borderline:girl who had driven:me:crazy
!back in the states, and probably in a very zen:
buddhist:fatalistic way didn't give a damn
what,happened,to,me during this colorful escape!
looking forward for the first time (not caring if i
lived or died) to just finally arrive through the holy
mythological mist*and*fog of the mediterannean
for real:life:rollicking adventures while a stunning
bride and groom sweeping,through,cobblestone
of,the,ghetto to get married and myself getting
stoned by street:urchins (mafia:children who
didn't want their pictures taken or how they
were born and raised and brought up or
for that matter not at all!) and attacked
and mauled by some lunging:watch:dog
(very much for the same reasons) with a
peach.basket mashed over his snout where
the horrible,old,hags bawled out loud,widows
or women who had just been cheated on now
hanging their bleached,whitewashed,schmatas
up on the clotheslines etched and silhouetted
by the breath of god:like mountains rising up
surrounding all of palermo but o!the!beaches!

of gorgeous,voluptuous,radiant southern:italian
women and that decadent:carousel in the far:
off,distance with aristocrat,children and parents
turned off lost somewhere between the cactuses
and shore yet it was a lovely escape and journey
and helped me to just forget it all and next time
i saw her at *wurzweiler school of social work*
at the beginning of autumn i was all sculpted
and bronzed and she fell for me once more
and i fell for someone else far younger
and prettier and charming asking her
to marry me which think pretty much
in the long run ended up killing her...

46

miss the state of brooklyn
going to that mafioso:bakery
on the corner to pick up my
fresh hunk of mozzarella
& long loaf of italian:bread
big pepperoni & mushroom
calzone on the other corner
strolling past the social:clubs
& barber with the insane,irish
,brothers leaning back with their
arms around each others shoulders
& in the window strange&surreal
but more than slapstick:a/scene
of the homely older,lady (only
loved&respected&feltcomfortable
&fantasies for these exact same
reasons) stimulating,the,scalps
of delinquents who seemed
under,the,influence with
some sort of vibrator/contraption
&the spirit of that whole mad carpet
of stray leaves skittering up from
the stray,autumn,season up from
the holy merchant,marine,twinkling

twilight,river eventually tumbling
beneath the slapping windy gates
of home:sweet:home brownstone
which really felt like a home all by
your lonesome with your filthy fouton
on linoleum where you took all your meals
&ate it all up looking out to all the rooftops
&watertowers of the world some crazed
insane sci-fi*film*noir showing up on
television when you least expected &
really needed it like planet:of:the:apes
1968 bleak&barren vision&landscape
waking up 3,000 years later chuck
heston's manic&hysterical haunting
laughter thinking am really able to
relate to him&that isolation&bliss
ful zen:buddhist tragic nihilistic
sense of the state of nowhere

47

in,the,end it's all so goddamn dostoevskian
ashes:to::ashes dust,to,dust "you know
major tom's a junkie" major cocktease
weather,women know exactly what
they're doing disco:dancing sweeping
their hands in,front,of rapid,city,omaha
cheyenne,chi-cago all's i ever cared sister
was to spurt*my*gysm all over jackson,hole
casper,wyoming that scene in *my fair lady*
where audrey hepburn tries to become
something she's not taking after doctor
doolittle pathetically balancing books
on her noggen and starts going off–
"the rain in spain falls mainly
on the plain" should have been
a used:car:salesman board:certified
:surgeon jack klugman as that ventriloquist
in that *twilight zone* episode where the dummy
suddenly comes to life&takes on a life of its own

48

i want to knock
out,the,teeth
of the ven:
tril:oquist
with
the,hole
schmooze
&schtick
&leave
him
sense
/less
like
his
dummy
full,of
,him
self
and
shit

49

was,sitting,back at:night trying:to:relax
and catch a good ballgame think it was
the la:clippers vs, the houston:rockets
&got to thinking about the term technical
foul and what the hell was so technical
about it anyway how there was
absolutely nothing technical
about it a matter of fact
quite,the,opposite
and should call it
something like
out:of:control
or impulsive
or histrionic
or dramatic

while that
middle,aged,chubby,pasty
faced,kawcasian iz:screaming
at the top,of,his,lungs practically
or rather,impractically pulling,
the,hair out,his,head &throwing
a tizzy:fit &temper:tantrum
&his ballplayers,laughing
under,their,breath kinda
like a,little,sibling
watching things
selfdestruct&unfold
knowing his older,brothers
can't stay out,of,trouble
even got to thinking
just once wish
the ref:real:calm-
like &dirty:harry-
like just stared at him
with those squinty eyes
and whispered–"you're
team sucks and should
focus more on them
instead of making
me the scapegoat"
shutting him the
fuck up and
walking off
to the sunset

one day want,to,live happily,ever,after and be
one of those hysterical:lunatics doing,one,of
those infomercials on late:night:television
something for like some zap!bathroom
cleanser or flexible,impenetrable,hose
which real chameleon:like always
goes right back to its original
shape&form everything
we ever dreamed of &
live in the land where
they always seem
to be from:from

king of prussia
pennsylvania
wherever
the hell
that is
or maybe
even:kalifornia
in one of those
castles:hidden
in the hills
where they
survive:off
highballs
& pills
or where
the porn
stars live
behind those
perfectly/sculpted
hedges & electric
fences & spend
rest of my
daze living
happily ever
after in denial
developing
a drinking
problem
or what appears
to be the new craze
of the day some sort
of sex addiction which
to me never seemed all
that bad if between two
consenting adults
&will &volition
&dealing,with
the concepts
&principles
of passion
&approval
&acceptance

&happiness
not harming
a single:soul
which is far
mo,i,can,say

50

all i can say, all's i can't say
think they should have one of
those referees with flags flying
in the congress for an *offensive*
foul defensive pass interference
excessive taunting personal foul
&just think what a more positive
&productive place it would be
&think they should even
have a penalty:box straight-up
imagine that & just load them
the fuck up all those fucken god
damn republicans like that trend
from way back in the fifties when
they used to see how many teens
they could stuff in a telephone booth
(no negative campaigning be allowed
too & will be considered in the category
of a breach of code of conduct & actually
have to tell you what they're going to do for
you which will be subject to quarterly review)
& even like you & me like when
they entrap us for 125 bucks for not
making a perfect stop at a stop sign
or point a radar gun from behind the
bushes at the dairy queen when you're
supposed to be picking up speed they can
also nail them with a ticket forced to pay a fee
& eventually if they accrue way too many fines
or penalties may be considered under close scrutiny
due to abuses of power & privilege & entitlement
& poor representation no longer putting the best

interests of the people ahead of them for possible
suspension of sessions until they finally hit rock
bottom & get it & learn their lesson of why
they originally were elected to office

51

had finally,given,up after
years of not having any
of my:prayers answered
and just started making
prank:phone:calls to god
as my sarcasm and acting
out in the past had always
paid/off in,the,long,run,and
most of all by my teachers
saying such stuff like "joey
is a very smart boy and has
great potential but always finds
the need to be the class clown"
the heading from my report:card
in synagogue reading "holocaust"

52

i wish there had been a magritte
                    where there
was just a gigantic,black,crow

        thoughtfully brooding
in the yard
        with a bare treetop
balanced on its skull

                at my funeral
i want it to just be
        my wife & her

                    spiteful girlfriends
blowing spitballs at me

                    like that fly
who didn't quite make it
                    & just made it
to the butter:tray
            in the refrigerator

my fifth grade teacher
who used to read
stories to us
with our

        dumb
founded
        flabber-
ghasted
        ex:pressions

                    seated
                            on the floor

her legs
spread
wide
open

                    for all the world...

all the world's
            just wearing
        those faded
                    tech:nicolor
    party hats

blissful
to muted
home movies
dreaming fantasizing
        masturbating

                to that
                cuban
                bombshell
in the pull-out beds
in the bomb shelter
                    at the end
                    of the jewish
                    dead end

having to be pulled
                    out
of the crystal
        water glass
                at the end
                        of bar-mitzvahs

sobbing sensitively
            after those horribly

                    boring
    sweeping cliches

that they
just wanted
to be friends
        then stuffed back
                    in breast pocket

with matches
        moping
                sent packing

to the safe & secure
white noise humming
of the slide projector
in the deep dark den
time-life collection

53

can't fault me for my addictions
to bagellox&creamcheese honey!
my panic-stricken grief&separation
anxiety&heartbeating when,the,sun
comes,streaming,in threw the isolated
dusty:blinds at the change of seasons
dillpickles&sourcream&onionpotatochips
asking you to stop speaking while,i'm,eating

54

salem alakem
salem witch burning
try campbell's kitchen
broccoli &chicken alfredo

55

wonder if sushi
ever craves us
wonder if in
mid-life crisis
in my arrested
stage awe
development
can whip out
crayon and
start doodling
to,high,holy
blessedoblivion
on the brooding
walls,like,every
thing,must
go,madman
and how cathartic
that'll feel like some

scene from "last tango
in paris" without the butter
wonder if like willie,wonka
or wanda the wild,eyed worrier
from the bronx, ny can crawl
into the tourist cup i got from
the general store with a good
book either wittgenstein,spinoza

56

fucken american:tv literally feeds&bleeds
into your ptsd like that game,as,a,kid
if you flinched&friend would punch
you right in,the,arm dead&numb
wouldn't,give any of these films
a,red,cent of my hard-earned
paycheck as it seems to just
all get computer-generated
(having absolutely nothing
to do with any:real:life breathing
human(s) character development)
who can one-up in this formulaic
recycled crap of special effects
during the end,of,the,world apocalypse
or who can outrun the great balls of fire
being flung up high in the air/silhouetted
then charge you a couple,more,dollars
just to pour this fake pasteurized:jalepeno
cheese over your nachos swear to allah
swear to god would be the exact reason
would climb on a jetliner&become an
expatriate&finally hear myself taking a
great big deep breath (big sigh of relief)
when taking:off from american airspace
rice-a-roni the,san,francisco,treat ?what
happened to those warm/wet towels
they used to let you throw over
your face in those old time
chinese restaurants after

a:feast to relieve you
of all grief&disgrace
&make it allright
all:sane again

57

always loved when you traveled abroad
to places like paris, le sud de france, nice,
sicily, england, the countryside, the cotswalds,
south kensington, and they would play these
very long games, some times last for days
on end, matches of cricket on the green
on those perfectly-cut lawns, would even
take tea breaks, never quite sure 'cause i was
a kid like 3:00, 4:00 british standard time and
now with all the idiot, ridiculous american shit
going down just wonder in the middle of those
brilliant tea breaks one of those players all of
a sudden decided to freak-out or have a melt-
down or tizzy and start smashing the teacups
and saucers over rivals' heads and the tea and
crumpets and clotted cream would go flying
and very old refined ladies in moo-moos in
the stands started cursing demonstratively
and just this image would help to put
american sport, put it all in perspective
watching these very silly serious overpaid
multi-millionaires who get more than any
government official (although like the babe
said these days did have a better year than
any of them) but again when you watch
our heroes knocking out their fiancées in
elevators in atlantic city and then dragging
them out senseless, unconscious in front of
the security cameras or teach their two year
old kids very punitive and dickensian lessons
i like to sometimes think about my travels
abroad, how i was even calmed and self-
soothed as a child and apply this very

absurd, devastating image and drama
and if this would ever happen during their
downtime just taking their tea during reflection
gaining a whole other perspective and impression

58

can't help thinking
with the,seasons,melting
cruising through the shattered
eggshell mountains through the heart
of the heart of crucified heart of jesus
cathedrals the devil is still white,man
country,club,caucasian in his saab&volvo
higherthanholy insincere&hypercritical
passing from generation to generation
that vacant feeling of non/belonging
alienation sob!samsonite:luggage

59

still got miss? hat:tie mc:dan:iel
sitting in the back of the theater
in the segregated,section
the/evening she accepts
the oscar for her poor
tray,yawl in gone
with the wind
and couldn't
have been
more soul
ful so full
of soul self-
effacing
graceful

i remember this black girl forgot what her name was
but really got to know her well and we really started
to hit it off and hang out a lot and vibe in the cafeteria
in between classes at *the new school for social research*
exchanging all these stories of each other growing
up like her telling me pretty modest and humble
when she was young was so depressed and down
in the dumps just for purposes of attention-seeking
and i guess reaching out for help would like lower
bottles on a rope from her tenement window with
suicide notes in them and remember once she
had asked me out and asked me if i wanted
to cut class to see that film forgot what
it was called but about those close-ups
of insects and bugs and little creatures
in the jungle o yeah *microcosmos*...
and we took off to soho or was it
noho really not sure one of those
tiny little art theaters and when
they started to show all these
brilliant close-ups of like these
caterpillars and praying-mantis
and tree frogs and so on how
they survived and got along
and ambulated and functioned
in their natural environment
in the jungle with their
humming and hissing
amplified aloud she just
started all of a sudden
putting the moves on me
and get fresh and whispering
and fondling me in between
my legs while i reciprocated
and started to kiss her neck
and touch her breasts then
go downstairs and finger her
down deep between her legs
while she started to breathe
heavily and moan and groan

and simultaneously showing
all sort of muted and magical
and panning-in with the camera
and doing close-ups of the bug
and insect world in that film forget
what it was called o yeah *microcosmos*
and all kind of ironic 'cause that day
and moment remember i felt the time
i had really learned the most in college

61

listen& to good ol' gangsta rap
by the fire while the absentee
owner tries to insult&make fun
of you in front of customers&
you just started &gotta teach
yourself &starting to pick up
the system &simply decide
the next day not to come
inn& don't know why
she doesn't pick
up pick up why
has the worst
wickedreputation
&biggest turnover
of any posh resort
in the area &sad cuz
all the classy beautiful
tomboys just coming
off abusive relationships
go all out for her &every
time she decides to fly
flybynight once a month
from california to burlington
international,airportinn vermont
starts up this fuckedup&diss,funk
channel cycle once more oivey!
goodlord! you decide to go back
to working the graveyard at the

home&residence for schizophrenics
(&those afflicted,with,tourette's)
as seems more self-soothing
&reality-based& sympathetic

62

as kids we ran threw water
colors & seasons & sea
gulls & rocky beaches
returning home with sea
shells & the ocean
& whole universe
in hour sneakers
falling asleep
coiled in slumber
sunburned snuggled
like that eternal echo
of the ocean stored
& recorded
in the folds
of the folklore
of the fossils
of the conch
shell at
long last
swooning
the history
of the whirled

63

hole
arm
war
stuffed
with
stained

t-shirts
but still
smell
in like
spring
time
straight
out the
dryer
marriage
is to be
grateful
& to have
known one
time what it
felt like to
suffer alone

64

your wife
picks up
kentucky
fried
chicken
boneless
bourbon
benadryl
&pickles

65

you feel guilt
that you are alive
and feel like a liar
but deep down in
side know you're
a soul survivor

somewhere
between dreams
& nightmares &
a damaged reality
somewhere be
tween the sea
& mountains

66

melan
choly
have
i ever
hap
pin
too
men
chin?

III. domestic, Violence

-40

It is a strange and fascinating phenomenon
but places where i was always supposed to be
or feel a part of always felt less a part of and those
foreign less familiar even dangerous far more a part of

-39

Living out here in the suburbs
is like being stuck in the mouth
of a clown not being able to get out

        "i think
          therefore i'm not"

-38

Like getting all prepared
and setting up for the sacrifice
and slaughter at the dinner theater
at the coliseum and no one ever appears

-37

Arguing all the way out to amish country…

grape soda ingredients: citric acid, maltodextrin,
calcium phosphate, salt, artificial flavor,
ascorbic acid (vitamin c), red 40, blue 1

-36

You watch that neighbor as always bawling out her children
literally bent over in that perfect norman rockwell punitive pose
position like a nun wagging her finger finding yourself turned on

-35

Hang gliders crashing all around
and they're still having one hell of a barbecue

Wives getting rowdy off wine coolers and husbands
high off light beer trying to make the moves on daughters

-34

Do you think dracula ever went to the all-night diner had
flapjacks and hash browns to try and cure his melancholia

ruminating about that pretty little red head with the drinking problem
probably pretty good tipper though cuz knew what it was like to suffer

-33

I think if the ten commandments
was just a little bit more descriptive
with a little less budging room to let
the humans bullshit and make excuses
like one of those great big thick endless
fold-out laminated menus you get in one
of those boxcar diners with all those soups
and burgers and side orders of fries and
potato salad and stuffed derma and
biscuits and gravy and the fish of
the day and gyros and meatloaf

and combination platters all
those club sandwiches and
bacon lettuce and tomato
endless choices of cake
and pie from that silver
satiny spinning display
sometimes even
a whole list of
wine and highballs
and beer and martinis
we wouldn't find ourselves
in the shape we're in yet we
just keep on doing the same shit
we're doing with little to no explanation
or conscious or consideration in who we're
hurting like *thou shall not*...yeah you tell me when
was the last time you ever really saw that stop anyone?

-30

That expression you never get a second chance
to make a first impression—well who the fuck
said i ever wanted to make a first impression
or even for that matter a lasting impression
when surrounded by so many goddamn obvious
crude and vulgar snide and smug motherfuckers

-31

You eat ginger snaps at dusk and love
losing yourself watching the weeping
willow through your kitchen window
how it can never stop moving like it
has a life of its own in the setting sun
reminding you of when you used to be
a concierge at a luxury hotel and greeting
all the young pretty puerto rican girls coming
in and out of the doors during change of shifts

-30

A whole string of diabetics lined
up outside the sugarless bakery...

-29

Days like these
seem like good
days to eat warm
muenster cheese
sandwiches maybe
those black beans
straight from the
can saved for just
the right occasion
and i guess bowls
of tomato soup if
you happen to have
tomato soup available?

Would like to see one of those
old-fashioned cereal boxes with
"the well-balanced breakfast"
the food pyramid the 8 essential
vitamins and some dope addict
nodding-out passed-out with his
head collapsed against the table

-28

Often when life's become a fucken broken record
when eyes bloodshot freaken wired and wasted
i like to give myself the third-degree treatment
and shine that bright light right down on me
i got from *ikea* from the boston braintree
branch even slap myself around a bit
which helps to add to the mood

and atmosphere and ambiance
knock a little sense into myself
go where were you on the night?
where were you in your life?
have you treated the wife?
when do you feel right?
when do you feel wrong?
how long since it's been
since you've been long gone?
what do you plan to do once you get free?
what do you plan to do if you can't be me?
it all ends up feeling pretty decent though
like some sort of distorted yoga session
having that bright bulb shining down
on myself in the pitch-black dark room
like when it used to be cool to go down
to florida and it was a vacation and donald
duck wasn't getting busted for groping tourists

i head over to the refrigerator and help myself to
the last of the crab rangoon from the night before

-27

Really admired
those ancient
egyptians

(those
spiritual
magicians)

who wanted
to be buried
side by side

with their beloved cats and dogs
for when they make their fine fateful
return trip back to *the valley of the dolls*

-26

I'm like one of those guys who likes to garden
in the lightning and thunder, be out on the lake way
too long, can't really explain, just the way i always been

-25

Meeting your blind date in the greenhouse in the pouring rain
and turns out you get along real well but got the wrong one
and don't find this out until much later on, get married
and live happily ever after as mistaken identities

-24

You start to think that maybe life is just one big freudian slip
of the tongue and start to think back to your father who was
a dentist out in whitestone, queens a pretty nice jewish guy
and when you were a young adult living in the lower east side
taking the #7 all the way out there to the last stop in flushing
and then a crosstown bus and the secretary who i've known
my whole life long who has seen me grow up calling me in

(always a bit of an awkward dynamic
feeling a certain sense of favoritism
or nepotism i never wanted
almost like a self-loathing
like one of those relatives
in a picture frame you're
not supposed to talk about
who took their life but still
constantly hanging around)

while him eventually casually asking "do you grind your teeth?"
and still at the time having a lot of pride and a little defensive
"yeah, just a bit, but not like one of those ancient egyptians"

not really getting or understanding the reference as their civilization
had a history of really bad gums due to the desert conditions a lot
of sand and wind and as usual sort of shook off one of my bizarre
comments with a concerned half-crazed grin behind thick goggles
and took off his mask and handed me over to one of his hygienists.

i now find myself grilling on my back porch with my pretty wife
and kid and think all i really need in the end is for them to wrap
me up in tinfoil and just drop me off in a nice hole in the sand

and that will be it none of all that grand mummification
ceremonial planning bullshit so what did i say again
about life being one big freudian slip of the tongue?

it was all sort of ironic 'cause years later
my mom found my bite plate which i never wore
like discovering an ancient skull in my night table

-23

Am i becoming that relative who just shows up solely to weddings
and bar-mitzvahs and no one really knows? man i hope so! kind of
like w. wonka in purple plush pimp hat when he first stumbles out
that ominous door of his foreboding abode pretending to be all
mysterious and brooding and what they perceive to be a crippled
freak and then does a neat little somersault magically welcoming
them all. was it brando in *the godfather* who said something along
the lines of–'when was the last time you ever invited me over
to your home for supper?' when in fact in actuality was taking
care and protecting them all. you hear your wife scream at you
while you're in the shower–"get out and put down your dreams!"

-22

Women planning weddings is vulgar
just for that one moment then tossing
the bouquet over their shoulder jostling

for position and that bully from the bronx
with borderline disorder always getting it

not getting it continuing to fuck
up and sabotage her relationships

-21

The bridesmaids
all look like pigs
at the trough

-20

Tacos & fight night
& the husband & wife
go at it in the waning light

-19

Visions of morbidly obese mother-in-law
going down sinking in the bumpa' boats

you can only imagine what the eulogy
would sound like at her funeral

if cotton candy
& corndogs

will be
included?

-18

Later on in the marriage
when things aren't going
just exactly as planned
meeting her romantic
standards and vision
when things become loveless
and he's no longer into her
they will provide (that being
the bridesmaids and parasites)
unconditional support
which comes in the form
of gossip and rumors which
they thrive off of so their lives
may seem a little less miserable
like maybe he's a homosexual
and you should divorce him

When he finally does
she claims he is crazy
and can't get his shit
together for the split
up (says this in a very
histrionic and aggressive
and competitive manner
while breaking down)
and spends 24/7
in the basement
masturbating
turns out she's
got quite the case
of munchausen…

-17

My luck find me guilty of murdering myself
and when they ask me how do you plead
i'll simply respond in a muffled mocking
tone "pretty sure you got the wrong guy"

having been found with my head stuck
right in the barbecue with the shishkebob
a modern day sylvia plath who just gave up
and simply fed-up with the wife and her moods.

as reported i'll have been
found swept in the corner
of the porch while apparently

helped themselves to seconds
doesn't much matter anyway
it all tastes like chicken…

-16

These days feeling caught
between just wanting

to be choked and
choking the chicken

-15

You wonder if the cavewoman ever
gave her man a tantra massage?
how long did it take before
they discovered blowjobs?

after fire after post-coital how
long did it take to smoke the pipe?
tell ghost stories around the campfire?

look up at the stars and contemplate
their mortality developing a cognitive
consciousness of confusion and curiosity?

way before any of the folklore
when did they invent the smore?
when did dog's howl die down over suburb?

-14

Today after being on the lawn all day
pushing my lawnmower in the baking sun
black mulching the roses erica just looked
at me and said you look like a werewolf and
thought yeah so tell me something i don't know

-13

United states
of the puzzle
    america

        gotta
           work on
               my back-

                        hand

   the scent
of autumn
pears

dangling
   through

       living-
           room
              window

this year
is the year
i promise

    my dear
    is the year
    i'm gonna

           make
    my year

               i'm gonna
                    make

                         my tarts

promise to god
to the sea
to tea

    & clotted
cream

love/hate letters
        stained in burgundy

                (in tears, in steam...)

    finger sandwiches
        bees & margaritas
            & avocados & burgers

                        leftover bullets & guacamole

-12

Today i decided to drive through one of those fancy-schmanzy suburbs along the seashore you know the ones with that dense population of *wasps* who are always walking in their higher-than-holy mobs with their pure perfect pedigrees and middle-aged women thinking their still hot and all that and trying to tempt and overcompensate acting stuck-up (front for being kept-down and controlled and oppressed and sexually-repressed not getting their needs met) returning with

their tennis racquets and tennis skirts always way too short as if
they play a real competitive sport from the country club so there
i am minding my own through the wildflower dunes and steeples
'cause i had been secluding myself on my property for just a little
and all of a sudden out of nowhere out leapt one of those half
wild wolves half dogs running alongside the open window of
my car (rich people always seem to have these rambunctious
creatures based on some sort of deep-seated fear or paranoia)
and was like some optical illusion or one of those archetypal
werewolves freud and jung were so fond talking of and heard
myself suddenly say aloud "fuck, i should have been freud!"
but because i was in something of a decent mood as had
just gotten in a good workout naturally went into one of
biggie's old tunes "what kind of shit is that? like they
hustle backwards…" or something to that effect
and disappeared to the horizon. i'm a jew and
disciplined and desperate and my one vice
later on tonight will be to order in take-out
chinese most preferably the sesame chicken
and crab rangoon as have a real hankering and
yearning for my hometown of brooklyn hopefully
too to catch a good ball game like chicago vs st. louis

-11

Later on while i was driving dylan around
i suddenly out of nowhere started to howl–
"when i was back there in seminary school
a person put forth to me the proposition
that you can petition the lord with prayer!
petition the lord with prayer! petition the lord
with prayer! you-uu can-not petition the lord
with pray-errr!" and started cracking-up and
as we drove around from playground to playground
began naturally blissfully hollering aloud–"you cannot
petition the lord with prayer!" while in the back of my head
heard jim morrison's wonderful mournful ruminating refrain
hymn–"can you find me sanctuary, i can't make it anymore
the man is at the door" and thought of all those late-sixties
seventies suburban split-levels surrounded by that beautiful

horrible multi-colored gravel and sleepovers those radiant
old greek guys who owned those restaurants and diners who
looked exactly like their fine crusty layers of baklavah like those
postage stamp lawns at dusk when the light hits them just right

-10

I think the first time we realize life's not fair
is how girls treat or don't treat you (cruel
and with a certain amount of aloof
and absurd brutality) back there
somewhere in grade school

-9

Boyhood felt as brutish and absurd as having to meet for rumbles
after school to protect some sort of shallow and superficial code
of honor which never seemed particularly honorable of course
no one showing up to the battle and all the surreal and dramatic
silly side talk and prattle which preceded that of what each side
was gonna bring secretly gasping a private sigh of relief which back
then seemed to touch on the whole notion and concept of your being
and mortality and fragile identity i guess never amounting to a thing

-8

The beagles have escaped from the pool from the home across the road
and start to run and howl before the rains and crackling lightning and
thunder come down. the girl who used to babysit for us and has turned
into a beautiful woman bends over in her bikini bottom and tank top
on the dead end to retrieve them. she will be going to a good college
in chicago. her younger brother messing around with her best friend

-7

Say they're bringing bob barker
back to *the price is right* again
everything just seems right
in the world again and hope
too in a strange and sadistic
way they bring back those
playboy bunnies who claimed
and made accusations he made
sexual advances or more specific
ultimatums which dealt with the status
of their positions or maybe just said things
inappropriate which made them feel uncomfortable
but oi vey imagine having to work with them everyday
with those great big smiles and goddess figures go figure?
showing off dining room sets and kitchens like surrogate
wives bringing life back to those long blue afternoons
where you got nothing left to do with mad lunatics
on the loose charging down aisles like the running
of the bulls when they hear the catchy spiel
"come on down!" practically ripping out
their hair eyebrows blouses pulling open
curtains and revealing whole living rooms
or more importantly trips around the world

glad they're bringing bob barker
back to the price is right again
everything just seems
right in the world
hearing that catchy spiel
stealing through your home

-6

I want to be just like some chubby old distinguished lesbian
and left the hell alone to water my garden and how come
all these stupid silly little sing-songy botanical poems
written about cats and roses and returning to the earth
and soil and none about a reunion of prisoners with real

stories to tell exchanging pills and punchlines and paybacks
at silver metallic picnic tables in sunken summer courtyard
of celebration and survival after just being let out of prison?

-5

First day of barbecuing season
and you can hear the distant mad calls
of wild seagulls outside your screen door

the rabbits come out of rabbit holes
the helicopters and motorcycles
and stray cat lingering around

your swamp who will
always be welcome
around these parts

-4

I find it just really weird and obscure
in what they consider paying your respects
as from what i have witnessed (in body language
and expressions, power-struggles and getting closure
a natural extension to a very sincere insincere character)
nothing seems further than having anything to do with respect

i mean the postman wasn't even invited!

-3

A new psychological hypotheses: perhaps all this so-called resistance
in adulthood is due plainly to the fact that still subconsciously trying
to live in a dream you refuse to wake up from and just could never
ever really get comfortable with these cruel and vulgar mean-spirited
hypocritical and opportunistic so-called humans? with their culture

(with their horrible behavior and character that has millions upon millions of loopholes in them like one of those film-noirs with the bulletholes in the wall and empty stream of light streaming through)

-2

You got all those psychological phenomenona where you just can't remember, of dementia and alzheimer's and a thing called disassociative fugue where for example you might take a train ride and don't remember how you got there; well do they have something perhaps maybe possibly of a contrarian-like phenomenon where you just remember way too much and can't stop thinking (of) and don't mean all the obvious stuff like your manic and racing thoughts but you know more so something like you just know and remember too much?

-1

Sleepwalker knows more
than all the mean masses

he is romantic, crucified
complex, conflicted

as they consciously choose
to be a bunch of blind conformists

he is quixotic and mysterious
they're obscene and obvious

0

You want to just fall asleep
in the barber chair and
never wake up again

IV. Scenes From The Ventriloquist Convention

Faze 1:

Hospitality

At 5:45 a.m. big brown bags of bread from brooklyn
get dropped off for the continental breakfasts. neat
clean stacks of newspapers like flapjacks are stacked
on the sidewalk. a curb right in front of the polished doors
hosed down leaving an oasis of beaming pristine puddles.
the man in the hot ice truck is passed-out like some sort
of cosa-nostra victim with his engine still running, and all
the pretty young puerto rican girls to die for with mad spirit
and heart sweep in for their housekeeping, while the idiot
doorman goes through his customary ritual and routine
of making small talk and trying to make his big score.
a little later on down the long freshly-vacuumed hall
one can hear echoing through the doors—"i have no
reason for living. i got no purpose to get out of bed
in the morning as all my dreams are out to get me.
i grew up in an abusive, dysfunctional household
to say the least and ain't even sure if i'm coming
or going. i think my kids all hate me and my wife
resents me, or vice-versa. doesn't really much matter
anymore. i look forward to nothing and backwards
for something. and feel like i'm constantly on-the-run
having gone nowhere and don't know what i've done.
i have a drinking problem, an eating disorder, and
can't keep a stable job. i feel like my guilt and
paranoia is getting the better of me once more.
i have constant trouble with authority and they
tell me they got issues with me. i'm sure they're
all out to get me which includes in very specific
order, the government, my neighbors, my boss,
my fellow workers, human resources, and society.
i still don't know my purpose or point for living.
never have and never will..." at 9:29 in the a.m.
the whole pathetic and faceless crowd slightly
shrugs and collectively looks up in utter shock
and disbelief at this lost little man of self-disgust
who has just confessed his whole existence and
being and returns the same ridiculous look right

back at them, as had expected such a better
reception, and from everything he had heard
about these functions, far more support and
validation and manages to utter–"this *is* the
class for the 12-step program, isn't it?" the
convention center audience like a herd of farm
animals appear to all drop their shoulders with
their pasted-on grins and stoic and stoned scowls
whose very driven, single-minded determination
of who-you-know nepotism turns to a similar-like
look of loss and nihilism, as apparently he had
read the signs all wrong and got it all mixed-up
between alcoholics anonymous and this new
sort of brainwash and rags-to-riches rage of
the day of false saviors and fake sages, other-
wise going by the name of motivational speaking
and leaves the bleak congregation of moronic
know-it-all businessmen and smug salesmen
who in many ways are really no different
than him, speechless, and suddenly seem
to take on the demeanor of one of those
one-dimensional, paint-by-number portraits
or paintings one sees hanging in their junior
suites as a team of ventriloquists and dummies
yet perversely and interestingly like some
kind of group therapy session, he ends up
taking on a new heir of confidence, taking
his time to pick out one of those freshly-
baked sweet rolls, pleasantly pours
himself a cup of joe, and heads out
down the hall with a whole new
perspective. they remain seated
role-playing their existence
beneath the hum-drum
consistent hum and bulbs
of the overhead projector

Faze 2:

Gentrification

In the end they're gonna
just turn america into one
big ole convention center
with absolutely no personality
and no character and of course
they'll be no history and no future
and everyone will just be dragging
their whole numb skull life with them
with little pull-out wheels behind them
like cheap chariots with no life to them
or expression (a pull-out collapsible
generation which asks no questions)
all with the exact same uniforms
picked out for them of khakis
and button-down blue shirts
with an absurd and false sense
of pride talking synchronized
and homogenized and zombie-
eyed on their cell phones and
wow what'ya know walking
at the same time and those
big boards in the lobby
will tell them and their
comfortable and cozy
corporation the exact
time and exact direction
and exact rooms they're in
with their overhead projectors
which will supply them their
personified statistics and flow
charts and pie charts and projections
and this dazed and sedated procession
will exit bleary-eyed, pleasantly engulfed
and swallowed by the shadows of that glow-
in-the-dark projector and this is what it will
mean to live happily ever after after all it

was all catered by *dunkin' donuts* and of
course everything for sure runs on dunkin

Faze 3:

The Dunkin Donut Man

There was this guy used to work security
in his trench coat at *the murray hill hotel*
in new york and looked exactly like that
dude from those dunkin donut commercials
"time to make the donuts" and every time
those asshole bellmen saw him used
to try and mock him and play him
thinking they were being so droll
and clever (but obvious as hell)
"time to make the dooo-nuts"
and he was a good sport
about it and would give
a slight and awkward grin
and keep it all in but just
a couple months later
heard at one of those
charity functions or
conventions or real-life
reunions had roughed-up
some guest (probably giving
off the same kind of smart ass look
and expression, but word around
the proverbial water cooler pretty
much minding his own business)
and threw him up against the wall
and frisked him and suppose somewhere
down the line in the long-run shit finally
did just get to him causing him to act-out
or perhaps be impulsive and assert
his identity and position and believe
this absurd and unnecessary incident
is so representative and provides
the perfect analogy and metaphor
of what man has to put up with
on a ridiculous and absurd daily basis
and man's cruelty to man and what they
will do to each other in the most petty

and trivial and mean-spirited coward-like manner
while poor schnook probably had to support some
wife and kid out in queens and now had to suck
it up, all this dumb and obvious male-bonding
stuff far worse than having to pay any union
dues and sure as hell know not a part of any
sort of job description and know they weren't
gonna be there for him when he really needed
them as just once for good reason lost his temper

Faze 4:

The Obituary Which Shows Up Every So Often

S. Mountain Lodge

Compensation: SHIT

If you are interested in the chance of a lifetime . . .
WORK ANYWHERE BUT HERE.

If you want to be treated fairly, like a human being . . .
WORK ANYWHERE BUT HERE.

If you want a career opportunity . . .
WORK ANYWHERE BUT HERE.

But, if you want to be treated like a nobody, be pushed around,
be threatened, bullied, or harassed - BY ALL MEANS WORK HERE.

THIS PLACE DOES NOT CARE ABOUT YOU.
Do yourself a favor and RUN AWAY from this place.

Faze 5:

Ibid/Routines

It's all those things all those nightmares
and dreams all those things which make
us feel conflicted and guilty that aching
bleeding heart and soul all those things
which barely make our lives bearable
and the things we love and wake us up
and hear on the radio at 5:45 a.m. which
get us out the door in the deep dark morning
bums with their hoarse coughing on the bench
on the corner the young classic beauties
waiting at the bus stop where they're
chopping down trees from the dense
forest as you drift into the miraculous
misty woodsy fog through that one
blinking light like a beacon which
makes you feel alive when you're
at your lowest point and heart
won't stop sinking when you
pass the train depot and leave
town down into the matchstick
mountains to the posh resort
to pour coffee for the tourists
the newly married couples
the glowing pregnant mother
the geriatrics the deaf blind
and dumb all just trying
to get by and make names
for themselves wrestling
with their mortality
on a daily basis
divorcées smoking cigarettes
trying to catch a last glimpse
of sun during an indian summer
in the barely blushing *bushy tail*
fall foliage trying for one last
final seduction hoping for just
a little attention a little instant

gratification for one possible
good final fuck to make
it all seem worthwhile
from an anonymous stranger
maybe even perhaps a doorman
or bellman pictures and postcards
included after the pathetic
meetings and metaphors
and how to make a score
in such business like
towns like ithaca
or chicago
which involve
the all so important
traits and characteristics
of aggression and ambition
in the bullshit and blinding glare
of overhead projectors and sales figures

Faze 6:

Rituals

He works as a bellman/doorman
at the very posh e. resort & spa
up in the high mountains of vermont
and dreams every time after his shift
is over at dusk he just picks her up as they
like to hitch (a common mode of transport
out here) and are beautiful and natural and
down to earth and trust and every time he
picks her up dreams it's the first time ever
and a new experience and has never met
her and she never tells him her name and
what she does and just drives down that
long winding country road to her home
and for the lift exchange for each other
sexual favors and finds he even prefers
to give her pleasure (go down to that
warm wet pussy of hers as she closes
her eyes and lifts her head up in pure
ecstasy against the vinyl seats) and
repeat this ritual day in and day out
weeks months even years. when
he gets home kisses his wife
and asks how her day was

Faze 7:

Talk Therapy

The other
doorman
this really
young nice
kid he was
maintaining
a rap with
standing
directly
across
from
some
gigantic
pumpkin
who had
just begun
to lose its
features
to be
come
sunken
with pained
expressions
distorted
lopsided
high up
in the high
mountains
of the indian
summer of
fall foliage
told him that
summer he had read
"the metamorphosis"
by kafka and wept
this was the one
thing and person

and rapport and
moment he was
gonna surely miss
and never forget

Faze 8:

The Tourism Industry

AT "THE EGG INSTEAD BED & BREAKFAST" THEY'RE ALL
FOUND DEAD DUMBFOUNDED WITH GRINS ON FACES;
THE HUMAN CANNONBALL, THUMBELINA, THE TIGHT
ROPE WALKER, THE SWORD/FIRE SWALLOWER DEPEND
ING ON THE MOOD & SEASON, THE BARKER BARKING IN
MIDSTREAM, THE LADY WITH THE BEARD, WHILE EERILY
THEY ALL SEEM TO MAKE THE EXACT SAME REQUEST
DISCOVERED NOT BY COINCIDENCE IN THEIR SUICIDE
NOTES "DO NOT WANT TO BE BURIED IN WICKER" AND
THE ONES WHO SHOW UP FOR THE CEREMONY ARE NOT
THE VETERANS FROM SOME TOKEN LOCAL CHAPTER OF
FOREIGN AFFAIRS BUT THE TOWN WISE ASS DELINQUENTS;
THOSE SUSPENDED SUSPENDED IN TIME & ACTION LIKE
SOME ETERNAL DETENTION FOR THE 21 GUN SALUTE &
DON'T SHOOT ALL REGIMENTED & REVERENT UP IN
THE AIR, BUT SHOOT EVERYWHERE ELSE BUT, AIMED PRE
CISELY, PRECARIOUSLY, AS ALL THAT REMAINS ARE THOSE
PORCELAIN PLATES & BREAK THOSE STAR TREK & STAR
WARS & TOM & HUCK PRESIDENTIAL ONES WHICH FORM
THE PERFECT MOSAIC IN A MISH-MASH MULTI-COLORED
PASTEL PILE ON THE FLOOR IN THE FORM OF JIM & DOC
& SPOCK & C3PO & CHEWBACCA & FDR & TOM SAWYER &
NIXON & CARTER WITH THEIR PAINED SMILES, EVEN
A COUPLE STRAY SLUGS WHICH MADE IT THROUGH
THOSE HOLY & HOLLOW PEEPING TOM KEYHOLES,
HE GRANDFATHER CLOCK IN A WRECK IN RUBBLE
IN THE CORNER LIKE THE STUBBLE OF SOME BILLY
GOATS GRUFF, PRICELESS CHINA, THE PIANO IN PIECES
NOT SO MUCH A PRICELESS STEINWAY BUT A MOCK ONE
& HAPPENS TO BE A STEINBURG, THE CUCKOO WITH HIS
TONGUE LEFT HANGING OUT & FINALLY AT LAST
BUT NOT LEAST THE IMPOSSIBLE TO PLEASE BLANCHE
DUBOIS INNKEEPER OWNER WHO TELLS THOSE BRUTAL
LONG-WINDED NEVERENDING STORIES WHICH TORTURES
& TORMENTS THE GUESTS & TURNS THEM INTO INSTANT
GHOSTS & STATISTICS ABOUT HER BLESSED KIDS WHO

HAVE WON ALL THESE TROPHIES & AWARDS BUT INTEREST
INGLY ARE NOWHERE TO BE FOUND HAVING HIT THE
ROAD SOMEWHERE ON THE COAST: THE POLICE NOT SO
CURIOUSLY & CONVENIENTLY SHOW UP SEVERAL HOURS
LATER WITH VERY LITTLE FOLLOW-UP OR DAMAGE CON
TROL BUT JUST SIT DOWN AROUND THE LAST BREAKFAST
TABLE FOR THEIR ROUNDS OF 3 MINUTE EGGS WHICH HAS
GONE WAY PAST THE TIME LIMIT & ITS LACE TABLECLOTH
& CHOCOLATE CHIP SCONES & SPOT OF SPOTLESS TEA
& VERY CLEVER SMALL TALK ABOUT THE WEATHER &
DO VERY MUCH AGREE THAT THAT SCENT MOST LIKELY
JASMINE & NOT HEATHER & WHY IS IT ALWAYS THAT DAMN
VIVALDI & THE FOUR SEASONS & NEVER THE BOSS OR JON
BON JOVI; A LITTLE LATER ON COMES STROLLING THE
MAYOR REBORN FOR HIS RIBBON-CUTTING CERE MONY
WITH HIS GIANT SCISSOR & HARD HAT & KHACKIS
& BLUE BLAZER, PERFECT FACELESS MISERABLE WIFE WITH
HER PAINFUL SMILE LIKE THE PARTNER OF A PEDOPHILE;
HER ISSUES & ADDICTIONS & SELECTMEN
& USED CAR SALESMEN & PHOTOGRAPHER ALONG
WITH HIS CHEMICAL DEPENDENCY PROBLEM & ERRATIC
BEHAVIOR & THAT TOKEN GIRL TWIRLING HER BATON
& THE PARENT TEACHER ASSOCIATION & HUMAN
PYRAMID TO SUDDENLY DISCOVER HAVE PROBABLY
SHOWED UP TO THE WRONG AFFAIR & OCCASION
ALL LOST IN TRANSLATION THE FUNERAL PARLORS
& HISTORICAL DISTRICT WHILE PROBABLY NOT MUCH
DIFFERENT, PROBABLY NOT MAKING MUCH A DIFFERENCE

Faze 9:

True-Blue Stages Of Human Growth & Development

Adulthood.

best albums to have working the graveyard
at the pioneer hotel on bowery & little italy...

1. dookie (green day)
2. good gods urge (porno for pyros)
3. melancholy and the infinite sadness (smashing pumpkins)

Early Adulthood.

rap bands with funniest lines...

1. i got more hits than satyagraha o (beasties)
2. dropping more shit than white castle and ex-lax (naughty)
3. asked me did i like arsenio/about as much as the bicentennial (ice cube)
4. fat boy on a diet/don't try it/i'll drop your ass like a looter in a riot (cypress)
5. i'll bust through your wall like steven seagal (funkdoobiest)

Adolescence.

tapes made from vinyl hanging out with pals
at their country clubs during the summer...

1. after the gold rush (neil young)
2. comes a time (neil young)
3. the stranger (billy joel)
4. l.a. woman (the doors)

Childhood.

one-liners: juvenile delinquency horse-playing at the back of the y...

1. you remind me i live in a shell... (barry manilow)
2. ventura highway...in the moonlight... (america)
3. cuz we're living in a world of fools breaking us down... (bee-gees)
4. it's gonna take a lot of love... (nicolette larson)
5. in a land where they turn back time/in the year of the cat... (al stewart)

Faze 10:

The Form(less) Letter

This morning feeling rather depressed looking at the majestic mountains outside my kitchen window, desperately looking for something to grab onto hearing myself singing tupac's–"staring at the world through my rearview, praying to God he can hear you…" and casually came upon one of these truly lame generic flyers or letters my wife had posted right on the side of our refrigerator right when we had moved here and in a strange almost perverse and disassociative way felt myself comforted and placated by the fucken reality and absurdity of it all and even thought of calling her back, this so-called representative who we had never met at all, and asking her how everything was going, how things were shaping up with her new job and position and even probing her a little further in other areas and will tell you exactly why I was feeling (or not feeling) this like the straw that broke the camel or the cherry on top of whatever the hell you call and see why people turn to a life of crime, a matter of fact always admired those turned to a life of crime, most of them pretty sharp and bright guys like a shrewd and wise Lucky Luciano who I used to live right by in The Lower East Side and started the whole Cosa-Nostra organization and put the organization in organized crime and founded The Commission which brought together all five New York crime families but am straying so getting back to that letter and the whole bureaucracy and red tape of it all and am quoting verbatim or more so verbatim-quoting and mind you again had just moved to the neighborhood...

Dear Erica & Joseph:

I have been your Customer Service Representative
at the Sawyer and Ritchie Agency and have
enjoyed working with you for many years.

(uh-huh)

However, I am writing to share some exciting news!
Due to a recent retirement, I am in the process of making
the transition from Personal Lines to Commercial Lines. (uh-huh)

So it is with both excitement and sadness (uh-huh)
that I leave my job as your Personal Lines
Insurance Agent and transition into my new
job as a Commercial Lines Insurance Agent.
(uh-huh)

Be assured (uh-huh) that the staff at our office
will promptly respond to all of your Insurance
needs (uh-huh) and give you the same great
service. (uh-huh) We have hired Jocelyn
Dentworth to take over my position. (uh-huh)

Jocelyn worked for another agency before joining
the Noyle Johnson Family (uh-huh) and is
an experienced Personal Lines Agent.

Thank you for working with me (uh-huh) over the years
and for your loyalty to the Sawyer & Ritchie Agency!

But like I told you when you're feeling pretty low
and down in the dumps can mean the world…

(uh-huh)

Faze 11:

Core Of Criminalized

Dear J.,

Thank you for applying and being interested in working at AWK. Due to the nature of this position you would have to check on the girls during sleep time and this violates state regulations. I'm sorry we cannot offer you a family teaching position. We would have been happy to have you join our team and would like to keep your information on file for when we change things further and need a clinical position in the home. I hope you have a nice weekend…

Sincerely,
B.

Bee–

Yiiikes! Strange and never heard of anything like that and if in fact that was the case why did you come and have me interview in the first place? Seems a bit odd and strange. I've worked with children and adolescents for over twelve years and never have had one conflict or conflict of interests or complaint and to a certain extent this appears to be breaking some real specific gender rule in the code of ethics or fairness in hiring practice, never heard anything like that and do kind of resent the stereotype, but B., this is not aimed at you if it's a quote on quote state regulation, yet in my opinion, it unfairly assumes and precludes that someone of the opposite gender would do something harmful or inappropriate when wouldn't even think of god forbid crossing those boundaries or even for that matter crossing my consciousness (a matter of fact I could tell you literal cases and stories where I have saved children from molesting stepfathers who were cops and broke open DSS cases in Taunton, Massachusetts, as well as have multiple letters of recommendation from children's psychiatrists and colleagues) especially someone who is clinically responsibly trained and worked with multiple girls in group homes and shelters in Newport, as well as girls who have been sexually perpetrated and molested; so believe this lacks intelligent and fair-minded and professional and mature acumen and insight

as well as standards, and a bit hypocritical and backwards,
but suppose must respect those specific statutes and rules and
regulations of the state of Vermont (Just out of curiosity would
this apply too to pediatricians and gynecologists? Just curious
not being in any way smart or sarcastic but purely empirical
and didactic) if in fact this is the case; always been a very
responsible and diligent and consistent and supportive and
compassionate social worker working with all genders, and
sexual orientations, and histories of sexual and physical abuse,
emotional and physical neglect; this does in my opinion appear
to be something of a prejudicial decision, but have absolutely
no desire or interest to engage myself in it, as would not have
been able to take the shift anyway as mentioned to you earlier
due to that Wednesday; B. I'm disappointed to hear about
this as in my opinion lacks good judgment and professionalism
especially with someone who has been trained and clinically
supervised with children, youth and adolescents over the last
fifteen years, and only get constant praise and admiration
and even recommendations for my good work from colleagues
and parents alike i.e. other parents recommending me to other
parents, a fellow colleague asking me to mentor a female
BSW student who was having a bit of a rough time with
it, and that case I told you about of which a cop had been
accused of molesting his stepdaughter who was exhibiting
very sexualized behavior and brought me in to do family
therapy and eventually get a confession of which I did
and the poor girl instantly taken into DSS custody. I
think you need to rethink your choice and decision
and find you'd be far more guilty of those things
you are implying and subliminally accusing…

Take Care and Be Well,

J.

Faze 12:

On The Nature Of Alienation (that
feeling of feeling a lack of feeling)

1.sometimes i don't know think god
is not this all-knowing all-loving god
fearing being but maybe a dusty old
cold accountant malicious and mean
just there to check checks and balances
2. the ones who make it in america are the
ones who declare with a higher than holy heir
of confidence—"i have always been a leader!"
3.at the very chic cosmopolitan production
company all about attitude and presentation
they put all this money and time and effort
into simply making a 30 second commercial
for red lobster where all the burnouts (part of
the union and get paid to do nothing and gorge
themselves at the all-inclusive buffet) race vans
up and down the island of manhattan just to pick
up equipment to manipulate the public to construct
the perfect 30 second scenario of young aggressive
happy-go-lucky go-getters on the beach at the bonfire
and to show close-ups of toasted almonds being tossed
in slow-motion in the air just landing there safe
and secure on some sizzling seafood platter
4. camera pans-in on pan of ecstasy
5. in america they make the sports
and weather and cooking competition
didn't know need 4 people or some false
charming team to report such things
6. and when they finally show you
making it as some kind of mover
and shaker and career success
they show this woman dressed
in her very smart business outfit
on-the-go heading to some power
luncheon looking down at her cell phone
7. you find yourself cracking up behind
some flowing pie chart rested on some
easel the grand inside joke between

the king and court jester both proud
carrying union card members
8. everything can be broken
down to a yiddish expression

Faze 13:

Invention Is The Necessity Of Mother:
the advertising business

1.

how to sell an airline...

2.

how to sell the lie
how to sell the life

3.

how to redeem yourself
in 1 easy step and bring
about a rebirth with your
cute little down to earth
girlfriend by shopping
and getting it all done
at *the home depot*

4.

they got all these
different kinds of vehicles
while myself couldn't care less
just needing something to get me there
and back like a good ol' beat-up green truck

5.

in between players killing
each other they tell us
to drink responsibly

how dare they be so phony and patronizing
wasn't the whole point to drink irresponsibly
to try and forget it all and all your responsibilities?

6.

whistle blows from the tv
down the hall echoing
through your home

7.

people take off from church early
on sundays while planning
to make it home early
by at least 1:00 to
catch the game

8.

wonder if they go fast-forward
through "contrition" and all their sins
and confessions; how they most likely without
remorse go through their everyday life and existence

9.

as kids we used to sneak away
from bar-mitzvah services to try
and catch the rangers/islanders
series during the seventies i think
subconsciously trying to play the roles
of boys and athletes and maybe even
thinking this might attract girls playing
some absurd futile game of hard-to-get

10.

just once once want to see a head coach
get all pissed-off and send his player off
the ballfield straight to the showers for
excessive celebrating and dancing
in the end zone and then maybe
once more might find someone

(one of those heroes they're
always talking about)
to look up to

11.

holy apples
falling off the branches
in the orchard at the dump

12.

how to heal broken heart
on a crisp autumn day
in new york at *met life
stadium* over in
east rutherford

13.

how to order
kentucky fried chicken
through the drive-thru
whenever you come
out of criminal court
win over a girl's heart

Faze 14:

On The Very Unconvincing Nature Of The Influence
Of Media And The Opposite Effect It Has On You

1one wonders with all of our addictions and codependence and
brainwash of technology 2if simultaneously, likewise as such, we
haven't thus without even being aware of it, neglected other sorts
of very necessary inventions and fields of study 3as opposed to all
of these fit to (con)form perfect caucasian girl/woman/know-it-alls
4who have somehow become expert/spokespeople in the field 5(who
dress and play the role and are supposed to have so much respect for
6as representative literally and subconsciously 7(subliminally and in our
collectiveunconscious) 8of how we feel safe and secure and comfortable
with all of those suburban, seductive whore/madonna's 9who
'the majority' can relate to and we grew up with and now live
with in our psychosocial environment 10(archetypes and stereotypes
come to life) 11and may even dream and fantasize about on the 'safest
and most responsible' of levels) 12who conveniently have been imparted
and now willing to share with us 13(and make you feel included)
14with all this scientific and empirical knowledge, very insightful
and of course, highly-intelligent, about smart phones 15(and
all those gadgets and gizmos 'we must have' to make us feel
better about ourselves or boost up our baseline of self-esteem)
16along with of course not by coincidence our necessary dose
of psychotropic medication 17(all having their own made-up,
convenient, contrived and stilted, quasi-scientific 'exclusive'
language) 18as if we could not exist without it in these practical,
perfectly, lily-white, neat, set-up, faux moral and ethical commercials
19i know it may sound crazy though (and perhaps not reality-based)
but somehow think i may have even preferred it more back
in the seventies 20handsome and good-looking oj running
(for his life? for that pot of gold at the end of the rain/bow?)
through the obstacles of the airport (of course before we really
got to know him) 21or that gigantic pitcher of kool-aid which
suddenly sprang to life and went smashing through the wall
and made everyone euphoric and feel 'a part of' and belong
22the honeycomb kids cohabiting up in their treehouse
in their backyard 23having every tom, dick, and harry from
every 'walk of life' and socio-economic strata and background
and class and culture be involved with scenarios from mcdonald's

24as perversely even though a bit out there 25(as opposed to stagnant and preaching didactic and empirical material and data constantly spoon-fed to you and forced on you 26which does develop a bit of an 'absurd quality' and in my opinion, in the long-run either dilute and negate itself and lose meaning 27or make the individual feel far more lost and secluded and alienated) 28while back then, all appeared more so in a simple and innocent state of flux and movement and 'running towards' and left more room for the imagination, 29even more inspiring and motivating for those who suffer and must face the obstacles and challenges and conflicts and complications in their 'everyday life and existence' (whatever that entailed)

Faze 15:

Humans: the product version

people these days seem mighty proud (if that's what you want to call it) to turn themselves into products and don't even think about it and feel most comfortable around other products and if you don't resemble the traits and characteristics (if that's what you want to call this...) will actually go out of their way to alienate and look at you with such cruelty and hostility and hate and even absurdly get angry and then will go to the mall the most perfect grand hub-bub product of them all (matter of fact the whole town or township got designed or blue printed around it with all streets and avenues running into it as a sort of new world old world postmodern town square for those who settle down there) where they can purchase other products and whip out their cellphones without even looking at all in one fell swoop and with the same aloof and arrogant non-expression feel (if that's what you'd want to call) safe and secure all over being a part of the same product of productworld like some faux cartoon character super hero all having the exact same body language and not have to look at anyone or anything at all and then while strolling (keeping up that aerobic sex appeal they developed on the treadmill at the healthclub) can talk to other anonymous amorphous put together products who are in other
similar like areas talking back to these products so now you got products talking to products and this is the atmosphere and this is the environment but when you think about it how could you really call this (a social or cultural) environment at all then go into stores while still on those phones picking up products to keep the great literal and metaphorical product alive) and treat the humans the slaves who are there just to serve them like they don't even exist at all while still on those phones and looking away (because of course they are way below them in their delusional legend made-up hierarchal system) and throwing their charge card on the counter then signing and walking off (such a brilliant and keen coordinated acrobatic function) still on those phones these perfect little products and move towards the door muzak versions of brilliant sonatas continually going in the background to keep it all safe and sound then walk out the door still on those phones and while in the parking garage zap their car with a zapping sound to open their doors and deactivate their alarms in case some mass murderer or carjacker should happen to want to steal them or their cars (their greatest fear of all.all a part of the same mass produced product

and their privileged and entitled world and zoom around
at a brisk pace moving towards their targeted goal still in
sunglasses on those phones and while once again looking
away (with their pre-manufactured self-importance) throw
them their ticket (maintaining that look to look to ignore)
to lower level humans zoom off down the highway to the
greatest product of them all the synchronized safe and secure
suburb the perfect personified product of the heart and soul
home sweet home pot of gold at the end of the rainbow long
lost product that they have been so conveniently comfortably
(codependently clinging) collectively clamoring…

Faze 16:

The Phenomena Of Nausea

AP: You doze off in cold easy chair after a bout of insomnia.
spring training going down in jupiter, florida. this is how you
measure your mortality. seems like a pretty good way to go…
to go down slow. like when you used to hide your report card
and get into a heck of a lot of trouble and think there'd be no
tomorrow in the continuing drama and trauma and action
adventures of your backyard where your sainted mom
hung up your father's operating gowns on the fine line
mildly depressed even slightly devastated that there
was no one out there who could possibly save you.
who was it johnny rotten hollered–"i don't want
a holiday in the sun!" man that seemed to say
it all and say nothing at all as when it really
comes down to it really got nowhere to go

AP: I remember
glossy photos in
french textbooks
of like jean-paul
in some sort
of suburb just
outside paris
having a real
corny honky
dory party
with all his
buddies sharing
hors d'ouevres
and listening
to french
records
as this i
suppose

was like
what they
wanted to
show us of
everyday life
for the
youth
in paris
and back
then really
don't think
appreciated
those glossy
photos of
jean-paul
and his pals
appearing
to enjoy
the little
things
in life
actually
ironic ended
up stealing
the teacher's
edition to that
textbook right
from his podium
as always seemed
so proud and i felt
so proud that he
felt so proud that's
how far out i was
like o! la! la!
in how i
performed
and was
so natural
and fluent
in the oral
whole class
gathered over

my shoulder
but not particularly
good in the written
and looking back
kinda miss those
days of jean-paul
and his pals in
those glossy
photos in
the suburbs
just outside
paris appearing
to really appreciate
the little things in life

AP: Today had me another one of those *freudy
cat* slips of the tongue and out of nowhere
just started singing "in the ghetto you can't
remember your name 'cuz there aint no one
for to give you no shame" which seemed so
apropros and to fit in perfectly with the mood
and theme of my everyday being as of course
know it's really "in the desert you can't remember
your name" but when you get down to the nitty-
gritty both pretty much feel and mean the exact
same and may interchange the words 'ghetto'
and 'desert' and if you've ever lived in any
of these places both pretty damned accurate
and nihilistic as it's all just about the mood
that it puts you in breaking down the expres-
sion "freudian slip of the tongue" to how deep
down inside (on the most shallow level which
often is the most deepest) you truly feel about
that specific person or thing and the instinctive
primal mood of the concrete form of that being

AP: The schools out here all look like
prisons laying flush up against (ant) hills

with views of the mountains and drug deals
The motels of course all abandoned

The haunted houses all sit up
there as well giving the town
all its charm and character

Papers are still tossed in the afternoon
getting lost in mid-air in the middle of
the madness of a beautiful snow squall

AP: The swingers mow their lawn with their best bathrobes on
and ascots on, but have the reputations of being control freaks
and phony-baloney and know-it-alls, and it's more so just shit
like this in this small town that does damage to their reputation
than anything they happen to do for entertainment, a bunch of
smug and arrogant assholes who seem to thrive like most absurd
adults do in the grownup world off the size of their home (yet they
do have renters) maybe that they have a three-car garage, but are
simply just a bunch of real snake-in-the-grass real estate schmucks
who don't treat each other particularly well, ironically, interestingly
with their senses turned off, and know nothing about the real world.
not by coincidence, the opposite psychological phenomenon happens
with their children, who are fed lies and bullshit and the all-american
delusion, and give the impression of having very good manners and
etiquette (but with all that repression and rhetoric) turn out quite formal
overcompensating in the other direction soon to become little dictators

AP: One can apply the economic principles
of supply and demand to the philosophical
and psychological dynamics of self-interest
in mankind and realize none of it has anything
to do with any kind of kindness or compassion
something far more darwinian and machiavellian

AP: And so in the long-run and in the very end
may find those you thought to be the most
dangerous were in fact the most generous
and those the most generous actually
quite greedy and self-interested

AP: Based on the theory or saying 'people are bound
to make the same mistake' is that more so based
on something hardwired, chemical and character-
ological, or behavioral, or having something to do
with fate, and if that be the case is it not just a matter of
perhaps maybe holding out for a change in the weather?

AP: There are a lot of fish in the sea
but o it seems so damn polluted!

AP: Likewise and similarly i've always
liked the very beginnings of relationships
with women, as they're all like some sort
of very lovely and concrete confession
from some kind of trauma or damage
and felt honored that they would trust
me enough to confess all their feelings
and emotions, and for that matter fucked-
up shit to me, as always felt myself up for
the challenge (and able to connect and relate
to them) or more so just looking for me to save them
such words and phrases like—"don't ever make me
have to make a decision between you and my dogs"
"let's just keep it caj" "i have never had an orgasm"
a whole grocery list of do's and dont's, of places you
were allowed to travel and areas that were forbidden
where you were allowed to go and where you weren't
places you could touch and places you could not touch
what turned them on and what turned them off but interestingly
enough, and not coincidental when all of those goals had been

reached and accomplished, suddenly declared their undying
love for me (a very scary thought indeed) as suppose had
filled up all those empty holes and if didn't in kind instantly
respond or reciprocate their words of love were a dead duck

AP: So much of it might have just been i loved you
so just didn't know and couldn't get close so it just
happened that it happened that it happened that
it happened that i loved you so just didn't know
so just things like the sound of thunder coming
in like the sound of thunder coming in like the
sound of thunder coming in like thunder! thunder!
thunder! thunder coming in so it just happened
so it happened so it happened so it happened
so it just happened maybe it was i loved you
so loved you so just didn't know like the
sound of thunder coming in loved you so
much like the sound of thunder coming in

AP: I think what i really like about europa
are their protests always end up getting
so violent and passionate and taking it
to the streets and seem to really go
all out and mean something with crazy
bloody results as out here no disrespect
just seem like a bunch of old timers
or rich kids with way too much time
on their hands doing it as much for
themselves as anyone else holding
up very creative cardboard signs
in the town square thinking that's
gonna really ever do or change
anything in the government
like one of those soulless smug
asshole arrogant republicans
are gonna be strolling
to the state capital
with their morning

coffee and step back
and reflect and go you know
i never really thought about that?
how about a couple stones
to the ol' noggin? think that
might really shake things up
a little and do the trick (maybe
even make cognitive changes
to their thought pattern and
thinking) and alter their course
if you kinda know what i'm talking

AP: I can't begin to tell you
how fucked-up and a bunch
of slaves (what poor instincts
and common sense) are those
social workers gathered around
the treatment plan meeting table
at the mental health clinic like
the landlord sending out his
henchman superintendent
to represent him in his
best and worst interest

AP: Man these days it seems like who you freaken know
just to work on a fishing boat and funny i have worked with
a number of them as a social worker over at the methadone clinic

AP: Can't think of one good piece of worthy advice
to look back on and usually ended up backfiring
doing the exact opposite, acting-out, and needing
a far better piece of advice just to get me out of it

AP: Why do the wannabe aristocrat actors
act like they're not actors when you know
every one their cookie-cutter repetitive roles?

AP: People like to try to pretend you
don't exist to make themselves feel big

AP: Why do people alienate and act indifferent just to try and fit in?

AP: Exclusive, what a ridiculous club to be a part of
and when you are, almost like the mafia
impossible to get out of…

AP: Is the opposite of 'apathetic'
"are you that pathetic?"
say it fast and sure
that you'll get it…

AP: Clinical narcissists are freudian slips of the tongue

AP: Schmucks come a dime a dozen

AP: Always find it curious and interestingly
coincidental that those who uttered such
continuous clichés like man is capable of
doing such terrible things were the exact
ones with a constant pattern and history

(so disconnected, insensitive
and out there even the original
protagonists and provocateurs
not even knowing this nor
aware of their dynamic)

AP: Survival, fine line between self-annihilation
and wanting or the need and desire to move on…

Faze 17:

A Not So Formal List Of Grievances Written In
Aphoristic Style: A Shout-Out To H. Caulfield

For me I could never stand those passive-aggressive assholes
as to me were so much harder to tell than the actual aggressive ones
and if I could would kill them bury them and then kill them once more

All those very pleasant and formal church-goers
need to go to church again and then again
and again and again and again

People are always trying to save face
but if they only realized what a fucken
disgrace! all the absurd and ridiculous
and shameless effort and energy put
into the process and machinations
to try and save it would realize
not a heck of a lot of face really
left when you see expressions
and body language which all
seems pretty damn ugly

(How much more complete they
would be if ever once considered
being self-reflective and taking
some responsibility or considering
apologizing or asking forgiveness
but knowing the absurd and insecure
and brutish nature of man know
a "pure" impossibility and simply
sadly enough a rhetorical question)

What happens if you get to the top of the mountain
and they're still gossiping and griping (ironically
the ones who didn't follow through on any of their

words even went so far as to betray to be heard and
showed absolutely no remorse or contrition, or for
that matter, courage, and tried to manipulate after
that which only proves the repulsive nature of
their character and how much of a criminal act)
so I guess all you can do is to keep on moving so
says Bob Marley where I can't be found and all the
people you meet up with and come across along the way

Damn there are just way too many
triggers to all this rape and violation!
You wonder what the hell and if
there are any good triggers as well?
Guess there are the olfactory senses
happened to mention to bring back
pretty good and decent memories
so says Proust so says Sigmund

There's such an obvious disconnect
between those who see themselves
as "virtuous" and the actual ethic
and concept and practice of it

People use religion to their own advantage
manipulative like those pretty little sluts
in high school who just gave their attention
to the privileged few and tried to make everyone
else (the masses) feel like shit about themselves

Why does it seem it's never the pseudo-intellectuals
who get back to you so in fact in truth (being arrogant
and aloof) there is nothing intellectual about them and
something quite 'untrue' about them and thus the construction
(or deconstruction) of the term and statement pseudo-intellectual

Wow, there are some people who devote
their whole lives to reputation! What lost

and lonely and absurd existences
and slaves to perception...

Almost every tourist seems on-the-run from themselves
which appears like an awfully pathetic phenomena
drooling vampires with absolutely no passion or love

It is funny in a really not funny way
that every person or group who has
ever preached honesty to me turned
out to be the biggest (self-interested)
liars and phonies ever want to meet

What is that word or expression
where one thing can mean
two separate things?

I love that one—
"jumping off point"

Every assumption anyone has ever made about me
has been completely (premature and immature)
absurd, opposite, wrong and off-base in truth

and reality, and only sadly, unfortunately,
ironically, gotten me 'to know' *them* for
reasons I completely care not to instantly

What a pity how often they seem mixed-up
and confused (even delusional) in what
they think they know about you

Most of them seem pretty scared of themselves
trying to keep it all safe and secure for some
peculiar reason and seen nothing of living

When is the last time you can remember a subtle war?
One that started as well as ended for subtle causes?

I'd like to turn the tables and sue the conservatives
bring them up on charges of crimes against humanity
as in their ignorant denial of global warming may very
well lead to our final end, and know may sound like
a bit of an exaggeration but reminds me of this old
parable of this Jew who had escaped one of those
horrible labor camps and in complete horror and
dread went back (to the town) to warn them and
with a shrug of the shoulder said he was mad
and didn't believe him and within weeks
the whole village had been annihilated

I know this may reek of cliche and for that
please sincerely forgive me, but is there not
a fine line between the politician and pornographer
both pretty much interchangeable, the former quite often
busted for the latter, and both screw you over for a dollar

They should have assassinated the elder Kennedy...

Faze 18:

The Anatomical God Dummies

j. christ laid-out on phlebotomist's table…

a mickey mouse cup full of tears and betrayals…

goons laughing hysterical playing cards in the pill room…

a bullshit intervention set up for dummies and ventriloquists…

doing impersonations of their patients
(all have licenses) then faking compassion…

each window perfectly cracked to the *sane sigh lum*…

batman fumes…

they closed down the gym…

phase before they decided to bug-out
and pull on crime-fighting uniforms…

meticulously mowing lawns before
getting all worked up for the stoning…

geek twins walking higher than holy hybrids…

wives on hands and knees in the land of loveless marriage…

nymphomaniacs control the dead end
showing off growth & development
right around the bewitching hour…

fathers all embezzlers playing the roles of father-figures…

alcoholics going in for the kill trying to make the moves
on neighbors under the above-ground pool during the barbecue…

all's fair in love and war
all's unfair in real world)…

a recurring dream just can't get out of…

Faze 19:

Scenes From The Demented Wing

Patient Will Keep Pain Diary: from dream to reality
that will map out concretely the roots of his profound
and exacerbated suffering, and thus, consequently, is
presented the following treatment plan and soliloquies
…released to the streets after having been sedated and
screened by crackpot medical team (having successfully
removed "the scream") after murderous and mean have
turned heart and soul to swiss cheese; To try and reignite
and reinvent our dreams, as all of these new experiences
and encounters will become the key that will open the door
to our imagination, and in conclusion, consider the following

Psych. Eval. "High risk" (Fuck that shit! Pole-up-the-ass bitch
more like it!) *Not too far from *The Echo Room* down The
Psycho Ward corridor, *Zone Blue* one can hear the cat-call
massacre, like some distant nightmarish squall from a conch
shell—"Jer-ry! Jer-ry! Jer-ry!" (freakshow phenomena of
grotesques and clowns who carry on and scream aloud
to make fun of their fellow man) and the compressed
(medicated and muffled) groans of corpses, behind
coffin curtains repeat in parrot-like fashion—"Jer-ry!
Jer-ry…" *Down these hospital halls one can imagine,
one can recall, incalculable, palpable dusks, warm Sicilian
winds, willing women, trails of tobacco, halos, elfin faces,
fragrant towns, foghorns, tragic childhood of brilliant ball-
fields brimming over with raw potential uncovering colorful
and mythical fossils for the future, golden, blazing factories
of the evening bleeding and breathing all those impossible
wanderings and romantic, insane journeys simultaneously
illuminated through the filtered ambiguity of fantasy
*Sainted girls with pigtails sitting lotus-style on beds
waiting to be saved or simply held *Omniscient
doctors who have become "Big Brother" too big
for their britches (really bitches with Napoleonic
Complexes who play the role of "doctor") will
not even consult anymore their patients, just check
their records and change medications without performing

examinations, soon to become patients without patience
wanting to ventilate new concerns, issues and symptoms
and are left deserted (pathologized and ridiculed as
punchlines for the cute nurses) to hope and pray for
the triumphant return of these false Messiahs *While
a racquet is heard in the *Consultation Room* and interns
taken hostage against their will with hesitant grins forced
to listen to their *mesmerizing* childhood growing up in
Brooklyn *The nurses as well have their backs turned
from them busy speaking to their boyfriends over the phones
oblivious and couldn't care less what was going on–"Lock
down the icons! Tea with cake...Ha! Ha!" *Manic clown
adjusts her gown, fidgets with buttons and screws on her nose
in the elevator of *The Children's Hospital*; When she's off
her medication, she hurls vases from her window at random
men who resemble past boyfriends that shatter into a mosaic
of a million pieces in the courtyard when they return home
from nightclubs to try and bring a calm to the madness
and racing thoughts *Every so often, enter eccentric
tragic heroes who were killed off the night before
which include a formal pimp, casual hitman and flamboyant
preacher with girlish affectations, who cracks one-liners
at the expense of others *Maintenance is called in to polish
the tarnished pendulum that swings back and forth in the
newly renovated wing of *Cardiology* and while on hands
and knees with a filthy rag they dust off a map of the world
that balances below some beveled brass ball detecting shapely
figures of girls rushing in and out with x-rays to the *Exam
Rooms* *Knocked-out patients pushed on gurneys like sides
of beef about to be blessed by rabbis *Cradled in the crypt
of this cryptic kingdom they don't look you in the eye or
address you; they just focus with a pennypincher's (self)
hatred at your photo identification (their own personal
cross-examination with sickly scrutinizing scowls of
interrogation as you threaten their power for no longer
deemed redeemable in the bedroom) to determine
whether you are a nurse, social worker, intern, or
doctor; They'll even like some absurd satire from
"Animal Farm" go down the hierarchal chain
of command to determine if you are a surgeon
or pediatrician and then will decide whether to
'respect' or 'reject' you based on this "wealth"

of information *Down in the cafeteria, the
Inspector Clouseau short-order cook in his
crooked hat whips out his cleaver and whacks
at a wedge of chocolate layer cake, then shakes
the powdered sugar over steaming french toast
like savory snowflakes while the portly-packed
veteran with his portable belly without knowing
brushes up against the jelly donuts and pastries
*Lumps of rice pudding ladled graciously and
generously with cinnamon sprinkled over its
fleshy, lactating covering *Lemon meringue,
coconut cream and apple strudel oozing boy
hood memories and secret fantasies *Then
comes the sweeping Shostakovich soliloquies
from speakers hidden discreetly with squooshy
tuna sandwiches wrapped neatly in saran wrap
like young girls' asses pre-packaged in baby fat
deliciously designed for the *madmen, cops and
medical staff* *In the gift shop, sun-dried, semi-
retired Substitute Lady returns change methodically
to blushing babes equipped with flirtatious ways
draped in stethoscopes, sexy white capes, and
sneaking peeks from the cracks of their fantasies
*As cool Rasta pushes his gleaming, immaculate
radioactive machine down the hall to determine
where your life went wrong/where's it's gonna go

The Psychosocial reads as follows: 1 brain dead fellow
who goes by the name of Sal Manella dx with severe
head trauma and a support system of 1 haunted brother,
1 decapitated sister, 1 horse-fed mother, 1 fed-up father,
1 rosy-cheeked embryo with stolen stilts in the corner, 1
distant breaded relative rolling in dough, beaten and battered,
1 long-lost twin in the rockinghorse midnight wind, 2 *Crumb
snatchers*, 1 who lives in The Bronx and 1 who lives in duh
Brooklyn (suspected to be missing, 1 who most likely became
a saintly bum down in Nice blowing the elephant shofar for
poor blushing schoolgirls, sipping strong shots of sorrow on
the cobblestone corner contented, 1 clammy goosebumped
kid still waiting to be picked up at synagogue taking on
the role of suicidal glass animal tchotchke in the pawnshop
window) Every Sunday client attends hallucinations where

ladies in long black dresses usher him to the exit sign at
a casino. He grew up in the heart of the hollow foghorns
and hopes one day to return home when the moon rubs up
against the dawn in the rippling shadows of pachysandra
lawns where the trains storm in mixed in with the clip-clop
of distant hoofbeats, heartbeats, and heels of holy women.
Client claims to have spent his whole life searching for a
peace that was never found, violated by counterfeit clowns
and madness and chaos all around, and has been found
to simply repeat over and over in a slow Viennese drawl
—"2 slices of cheese and 1 cold roll…2 slices of cheese
and 1 cold roll…" In the background, a patient getting
hosed down, yells—"O my Lord! Wheeee!" 1 immaculate
gentleman missing, while cops feast on Chinese and half-
crazed ladies dream of Irish Stew in the vestibule with
wicked tempers and attitudes of reactive-formation
exclaiming—"Fine and dandy couldn't be better!"
while the mad, drunk priest sneaks in guiltily,
maliciously, mumbling, clutching a crucifix
stumbling to pay a visit to his demented
Auntie out of some obligation and spell cast by
his family, as the shrink arrives in the drip-dry
cold like c. de gaulle in a dapper blue overcoat
and beaming buttons of gold, dull-eyed general
just abandoned by his battalion, muttering mantras
with a macabre smile, knock-kneed, leery-eyed,
tippy-toed, believing they're all out to get him,
laying down the rules to try and piece together
where it all went wrong for him, and the doctor
in his spare time is a hit man who breaks legs
then feels guilty and sets them again, his bed
side manner, a sadistic riddle while male nurses
mutter in philipino—"You want to make out in
the medication room?" And the exterminator
sneaks cautiously through as the veteran who
everyone thought was a bum and social workers
sprayed aerosol on staggers over to the piano
to land a lick of Schubert and Shostakovich
leaving the speech therapists speechless
while here in the seasons of the haunted
and holy borough of The Bronx, NY
the days have turned blissfully violent

as flies show up and the boys assume
pugilistic poses planting punches on
sacrificial schoolyard sidewalks, and
when they break it up you can feel their
loss and pain and hurt with broken hearts
and expressions of shock, and the ex-con
who everyone wants out is the most soulful
of the bunch who sits in his wheelchair in
pools of redemptive sun, reflecting on lost
times and loved ones having lost his language
yet discovering wisdom and compassion in
the eternal miserable displacement of existence
visited by birds chirping, winds and seasons.
How women make breaking hearts a mindless
business leaving him shell-shocked with remnants
of promises and the hustlers from admissions
want him transferred for they can't get state
funding since he is legally rehabilitated, while
a slain accordion spills through the window
and proud, sturdy Russians whittle away in
The Power Room like twin Jepedoes breathing
life into their creations who used to be doctors
in Mother Russia and now can't get jobs any
better than custodians in America and lukewarm
lieutenants with animal crackers, lazy, lethargic
hanging from pockets sit face to face with staticy
soap operas and today for lunch they got *murder
burgers* that get dryer and dryer the more you
bite them and in the conference room, the state
stuffs their face plied and greased with sundries
and sweets, giggles and grapes, freshly-squeezed,
all you can eat, while in *The Demented Wing*, the
thief dx with anti-social personality cradles his
portable oxygen machine, like some imaginary
baby crooning lullabies before he was forced
into a life of crime and crime of living; time
on Mr. Coffee reads 11:51... Joe DiMaggio long-
gone still dropping a stone by the rose of Marilyn,
strange gospel spilling from the intercom with a
Polka version of "When the saints come marching
in." Claims to have been a widower but there is no
evidence at all to support this data and so it can only

be assumed that he is a sole survivor. Claims to have
contracted botulism from the disingenuous kisses
of a girl who didn't care for him. Claims that
women are wicked and have no(sense) of fairness
and this is what causes the division between the sexes.
Claims that as a child he so desperately sought approval
and attention that he'd spin days in the washing machine
tumble cycle to be more accurate and has a distinct
recollection of his mother opening his drawers and
discovering Barbie Doll heads that he'd snap off
of torsos. That life is a slow electric shock therapy
of the soul like flowers that were once wild and
now wilt and wallow and all that remains glows off
The Throgg's Neck Bridge. Claims to be housebroken
rather heartbroken (as evidenced by comments—
"Thinking out loud has driven me sane" and now
plays hardball with the best of them and derives
meaning from Cornflakes and bananas or rather
dogs and children. Discharge as of yet is uncertain
for it has as of yet to be determined the purpose
to his admission and will be monitored
closely for any cognitive changes…

Faze 20:

Starting From The Middle

on the first blind date they exchange diagnoses

he reads it and it reads—"warning! stay away
at all costs! very high maintenance! even a slight
bit crazy" but doesn't see it and relishes the challenge

she reads it and it reads—"way too much damage"
says—"no way!" in her perception of his inability
or possible lack of motivation to try and save her

on the second blind date they are both in denial
and compartmentalize and try to forget about it
as both die-hard romantics and thrive off histrionics

on the third blind date like the idea and concept
of what it all represents or the feeling or role
of being in a relationship or having 'found'
each other after being 'lost' for so long

on the fourth blind date they have their first one-night stand

on the fifth blind date their second and third

on the sixth blind date she cooks for him and he's a sucker
for this sentimental shit and always gets to him
and goes straight to win over his heart

on the seventh blind date in the madness of it all
turns impulsive and declares her love for him

on the eighth blind date he becomes more distant

on the ninth blind date she decides to tempt fate
even give it a kick in the ass and blurts out
once again asking him to marry her

on the tenth blind date discovering a bit of a traditionalist
even more of a romantic puts it off and says he wants to be
the one to ask and has even found he has lost a little respect

on the eleventh blind date they get into their first fight
due to the repetition of things and life creeping in

on the twelfth blind date like she's done so many times before
just shows up to his door and love becomes lust and lust
becomes love then vice-versa and back once more

on the thirteenth blind date they blindly look out the window
taxiing up on some runway in some jumbo jetliner, drained,
dazed and determined when denial, when life creeps back in
in a downpour of drizzle having purchased a split-level down
in the navel of the sunshine state where the palm trees constantly
sway in the miraculous self-soothing air-conditioning of jupiter

Faze 21:

Denouement Of A Very Lonely Man

*Who was that brilliant person
who put that proverb up around
the hotel door of *do not disturb*?

*I ain't kidding need one of those on a daily basis

*They should offer you the option of a holy bible
or superman comic just in case you get lonely

*When did the weather woman start doing her thing
waving and washing her hand over weather
maps for the very lonely man?

*Lonely like that song 'if you take the train
i'm on, you will know that i am gone…'

*Like a dozen salt bagels

*Like bruce lee not being able to land a leading role
and the biggest icon treated like an ex-con

*I liked it better back then when china was still
a distant and exotic land and tried to dig
holes all day just to get there

*I'm still trying to get there

*On the shivering shoulders of lou costello
being chased through those shadowy
spooky egyptian tunnels

*Washed down by the moon
on midnight kitchen table
cookies and cup of milk

*Left on the island over the drawer
where you store fish food and painkiller

 *Used to live off…
white-out, model glue, and visine
never getting those tv commercials

(think during anti-drug campaigns)

"when i grow up i want to be a junkie"
as seemed just as relevant and germane
as everything else that they were offering

*Pool-hopping with best friend delinquents taking miraculous cannon
ball bellyflops at midnight off diving boards in neighbors' backyards
really wishing it was naked and romantic with all those beautiful
untouchable mean and malicious bitches then piling into the car
like a bunch of overzealous clowns with our whole lives ahead
of us just over our shoulder cracking slapstick one-liners down
the bronx river parkway for bronx runs to pick up bags of ganja

*Returning home for those frozen pretzels in the freezer
and warming them up in the toaster-oven finishing off
mom's wine chilling in the refrigerator to some chilling
film-noir like *the third man* or *the stranger* then dozing off

Faze 22:

The Answering Machine (keeping confidences)

(beep!) whenever he feels really blue or
low and down on his luck he'll call up that
cognitive-behaviorist he left behind in new york

(beep!) good looking older english man
distinguished silver hair modest humble
subtle sense of humor and one of
those very sophisticated accents

(beep!) only one ever consistently been
there for him through thick and thin

(beep!) only adult could ever trust
or genuinely rely on who wasn't
making deals and had some sort
of agenda with sleazy manipulations
and emotional blackmail to take advantage

(beep!) even help him out beyond
the call of duty and beyond the job
description and for that he is always
thankful indebted and eternally grateful

(beep!) will just call up that answering machine
when he's being tough on himself or life and
existence or one of those ridiculous triggers

(beep!) better than any painkiller or liquor

(beep!) every so often hearing that nice and kind
calm refined british accent in that office in
the whispering trees right off central park

Faze 23:

Case # (dehumanization: from inhuman to human and back again)

Dear Mr. R: you are dead...we just wanted to inform you
of your status and state of your existence...we have you
on the record for being dead for some time now...please
do not call us...we will call you if we should need any
further information...thank you for taking the time
out of your busy schedule to meet with us...again as
mentioned above please feel free not to call us back...
we will keep your application on file for a year...in that
infamous proverbial time wheel and virtual quota stack
of ours that we tell candidates we will...but will never refer
back to...to prove you never have and never will exist at all...

Dear Case # am just writing you to inform you
in fact i am not dead and very much alive
and have been alive and kicking for some
time now...and am a survivor...whether you
like it or not...have had trials & tribulations
& revelations...have had setbacks & flashbacks
...arrested stages of development & even a #
of rebirths...have rolled with the punches and
if i see you in public they'll be two sounds...
me hitting you and you hitting the ground...

Dear Mr. R: we have you on the record
for being dead and will keep your
record on file again for a year...

Dear Case # for the actual record i did
your mom and wife last night...and not
particularly impressed by the experience...
for your information were frigid...tight and
uptight...and left me high and dry...so tried
them again on for size and ended up exhibiting
the exact same affect...please get back to me about
the nature of my status at your most earliest convenience...

Dear Mr. R: i just consulted our front office manager
about your status and wanted to inform you…you are
now permanently deleted from the record and back
in our system and may be considered as a viable
candidate for a future manager position…
please tell us if you are interested?

Dear Case #…wanted to thank you so much for your insight
and feedback and follow-up (for your wife and your mother)
and look forward in meeting with you in the near future…

Dear Mr. R: the feeling is mutual and look forward to
having you be a positive and productive contributing
member of our family and team…here at…we value

Dear Case # thank you for your patience and understanding…
(for your maddening reality having the inability to listen to a thing)

Dear Mr. R: if should happen to have any available free time…
would very much appreciate if could provide us some feedback
and insight about your experience…and if you could please get
back to us asap to fill out a quick customer satisfaction survey
so as we may know how we can better serve and assist you
in the future…if not please feed back into the loop-cycle
repeat process and protocol and routine and ritual over
& over & over & over again to prove or not to prove…

Dear Case # have you received any of my e-mails?

Denouement:

Mr. R: dozes off in easy chair cold as a motherfucker
to the spring cleaning expert on the weather channel…

Case # makes a name for itself…

Faze 24:

Scattered Rain

This morning out of nowhere
an owl just somehow suddenly
showed up to my front door after
having seemed to have spent a whole
lifetime through a life of storms having
tore off its wings ripped out his eyeballs
saying it was just so goddamn sick of
the world sick of living and humanity
and everything to be expected of him
sick of being so wise and humble
and self-effacing and having to lead
this god awful ungrateful lot of human
beings sick of being the butt of jokes
of punch lines and of being the moral
to all fables and simply sought shelter.
i too myself had given up just recently
quite a while ago almost like nietzsche
and his concept and belief and non-belief
or faith and non-faith in god playing hide
and go seek for no rhyme or reason
kafka being kafkaesque without even
knowing or even caring to know with
his string of bad luck and horror stories
and not believing in a thing for good reason
and simply found me fucking my tv more
specifically the weather channel not sure
what season it was anymore and if any
of that really mattered the start of summer
or start of fall and that nonstop chattering
weather girl always with that great big smile
and body to die for and awful taste in technicolor
clothing giving warnings about a soggy hong kong
the floods in colorado the high pressure coming
in from the kanadas and fog in chicago and that
time of year where the twisters and hurricanes
seem to just show up out of nowhere sweeping
and shuffling and pimpstrutting through the pan

handle of florida. when he saw he wasn't gonna
get a whole hell of a lot out of me and i was in
just as bad shape as him he lowered his head and hit
the road without those wings without those eyeballs
like some down in the dump lounge singer down on
his luck having lost all his passion and interest for
mankind like knowing there was no money to be
made out here, myself knowing as well and had
a couple bucks in my back pocket eavesdropping
and hearing some insane advice from that weather
girl something like "rain is rain, pouring is pouring"
and decided to visit and finish off all those states
i had never been to like the dakotas and nebraska
and *texas radio and the big beat* and now find
myself deep in the deep shallow south of my
being lost somewhere brooding in the bible
belt to try and find and make something of
myself nipping from pints of mad dog 20/20
and writing love letters in the form of haiku
on the back of postcards to my girl up north

Faze 25:

Last-Ditch Love Letters

I see myself brooding in the lobby of my prison
I see myself brooding in the lobby of my jail cell
I see myself brooding in the lobby of my sentence
I see myself brooding in the lobby of my confinement
I see myself brooding in the lobby of my state of mind
of guilt and grief and doubt and conflict constantly
on-the-run with nowhere to go and no place to run
I see myself brooding in the lobby of my escape tunnel
somewhere between one of those gigantic softee cones
on top the ice cream stand and the cross on the cathedral
I see myself brooding in the lobby of the cathedral
in the lobby of the lake in the lobby of the mountain
I see myself brooding in the lobby of the terrarium
through the pine tree windows of the courtyard
I see myself brooding in the lobby of the seasons
locked-out desperately trying to get back in
I see myself brooding in the lobby of the dusk
going down and breathing life into the night
where they keep the courthouses and central
lock-up in the lost land of bailbondsmen of
new orleans peddling my bike like a madman
with mad passion back & forth (as if fleeing
from being a criminal now being a number)
still absurdly seeking approval from my trial
after being falsely charged for resisting arrest
after big pasty white trash cops beat the fuck
out of me for being a yankee in a true-blue case
of abuse of power and mistaken identity
I see myself brooding in the lobby of my
ptsd gradually becoming more fragile
and keen like a pile of leftover kindling
the final fate of the long-lost dying romantic
I see myself brooding in the lobby of every *waffle
house, popeye's, howard johnson's,* and old time donut shop
in the glazed neon streets of the chewed-up wishbone
of america somewhere between the rain and stars
I see myself brooding in the lobby of the graveyard

I see myself brooding in the lobby of the foghorn
in the lobby of the train horn whose muffled
mourning soothes me to a savage calm
I see myself brooding in the lobby of the church bell
whose echo at sundown through the shadowy town
triggers and reminds me and proves i finally belong
I see myself brooding in the lobby of every wasteland
and homeless and abandoned park knowing
every broken man and lost soul and bum
and wino on a first nickname basis
junior and judah and snowball
and hotdog and hollywood
I see myself brooding in the lobby
of the blessed urban movie theater
for a blind date who will never show up
I see myself brooding in the lobby between
the midnight and dawn, between the dreaming
peaceful brownstones, between the stray cats
and dogs, literally laid-back in my easy chair
in the weeds of the lower east side rising above
I see myself brooding in the lobby of every
slavic diner in the slant of the solemn
twilight knowing practically every
stranger and hustler and drug dealer
who passes in front of contemplative window
I see myself brooding in the lobby of the lighthouse
the lobby of the greenhouse somewhere between
the sand and sea finally at last with nowhere to go
I see myself brooding in the lobby of my nightmares
knowing the true holy dream is hidden deep
down inside there beneath the sacred core

Faze 26:

On The Origins Of Political Satire And Idiocy Of Authority

So decide to take the day off. wife and kid and mother-in-law
at the farmer's market in vermont and think to go up north.
never been up there past burlington into canada. all excited.
got your new enhanced license in the mail which allows you
not to have to get a passport like a kid his first day of school
with his pencils and rulers and the border patrol some young
smug little humorless punk playing god in his booth tells me i have
to go up to see the police. doesn't give you a reason why like being
sent to the principal and already immune and used to it and you wait
for about five minutes and no one shows up so wonder if i'm parked
in the right area and decide to pull up about 5 miles per hour to a sign
which reads *p*. you think for the police but apparently not and for parking
then two big fat goons of the opposite gender (but very much the same
creature) with their hands on their pistols and sirens and alarms going
off tell me very mechanically very demonstratively as if trying to
put the scare and fear of god into me to get out of my car and to
sit on a bench on the sidewalk so they can inspect and rip it apart.
apparently had been stopped because there had been a couple boxes
in the back which i forgot that my wife and i had taken out of storage
nostalgia she wanted to sell for a yard sale all very suspicious and her
all excited about moving up to vermont then while they were all bent
over in tight right-of-way uniforms searching with a fine tooth comb
suspiciously scavenging for drugs or some other sort of contraband
or to make some big score or names for themselves and find the pot
of gold at the end of the rainbow simultaneously upon them probing
me supplied them with the answer at least 3 or 4 times why i was
in canada and she kept on asking me over and over again the same
goddamn exhausting thing as if she was never listening to a thing
i was saying and just wanted her own little neat (far more sloppy)
narrow-minded version like some ignorant thug-bully without a sense
of humor and told her i was just taking a nice day trip and apparently
that wasn't a good enough explanation. you have to have a very specific
destination or agenda and seemed like the perfect metaphor for adults
and tourists and grownups and the grownup world and the way you're
supposed to be and how they try to keep you down and just long-term
damage they inflict on your brain with their incessant overbearing
brow-beating ways even tried to supply the analogy so you can't

just get in your car and take a day trip and drive around
to like clear your head. had even told them the clear and
concise true-blue honest answer and was just interested
in checking it out for when my wife and i and child finally
came up there then she tried to get smart and out-smart
me with semantics. told me that was not 'complete.'
by that point i had had it and didn't give a shit
for my nice day trip into canada had already been
ruined with this absurd and humorless abbot & costello skit
of literalism and forced to play her out with her own words
(and tricks) and break down the proclamation 'that was not
complete' and told her that was about as complete as i can be
and what did she mean that that wasn't complete and told her
i can't be anymore complete than that. think she was somehow
trying to prove i wasn't complete or that she wasn't complete
or never had been complete and with her abuse of power was
somehow trying to find a way of being more complete. i even
as a last straw started paraphrasing andy warhol and said 'why
don't you just give me the question and also the answer and
then i can answer it the way you want me to' of which she
started to of course get more proportionately pissed as i
had turned the tables on her and was starting to beat her
at her own ridiculous and rigid game. finally i could see
where her abuse of power was going with this theater
of the absurd power-struggle and answered–"well
i was thinking of maybe perhaps heading to montreal"
and she appeared to instantly change her tune and replied
like some damned if you do, damned if you don't parent
that that was what i mean by complete so apparently i had
to feed and supply her with a 'complete' lie or falsehood
to make everything seem more logical and plausible to
make my way and entrance into canada. even mentioned
if she wanted or interested could look up my name
over the internet and could see i had several books
out in poetry which really seemed to ruffle her feathers
and get her offended and got defensive and said she would
not supply any sort of favoritism. interesting as i had never
even thought of it and had never crossed my mind and was just
being very matter-of-fact as by that point was probably feeling
totally criminalized while the other swine who had been ripping
apart my car and unloading all the clothes from my kid growing up
for my beautiful wife's yard sale she was so much looking forward

to decided to randomly ask what's your education as didn't
understand his line of questioning either but by that point
was looking forward to the confrontation and challenge and
told him i had a masters degree in social work of which i
had already told them multiple times before that i was in
the profession which instantly appeared to shut him
the fuck up or show him up and was hoping he was
gonna pursue it just a little bit further and was looking
forward to break him down and deconstruct him on
a clinical and characterological level and decided not
to continue with his inane idiot line of questioning
then they told me i had to go in to see the customs
officer which i of course asked for more clarification
while by that point think had already been practicing
the art of self-defense or gandhi's "civil disobedience"
which had them both frustrated hating me even further
because i was far more articulate and never had shown
any doubt or fear as that concept and phenomena had
worn off a long time ago until he finally or i finally
explained that perhaps that that was their criteria
of which i at last made a complaint to this beautiful
young girl with freckles who was all very kind and
cute and compassionate like some long lost doe-eyed
first love you had lost your virginity to and lost so long
ago. well canada did turn out to be quite lovely almost
felt like it had windmills and it was all in french exactly
how i had pictured it like ripped straight out some text
book and seemed like a whole other world and was
in europa all over again and when i got home was
forced to call their supervisor who appeared totally
sympathetic and understanding and validating almost
as if saying and agreeing o! la! la! what a shame with this
wonderful french accent like some old french independent
and will have to fill out an incident report with their names
on the computer after my worn-out day begins to wear off

Faze 27:

On-The-Run Through The Ruins
To Make A Name For Yourself

I drink cupfuls and cupfuls of motel water
i take in my fair share of mournful daughters
i want to know when they finally bury me under

i'll take great pleasure in knowing
i made absolutely "nothing" of myself
i made no effort to make a "change or difference"

took absolutely
no interest
in interest rates

how they fluctuate
how they affect my fate

a beautiful blushing sad and sulking teenager
stands like a rare pearl unaware of her sex appeal making
her all that much more appealing in her bikini way above it all

some alabaster angel who obscurely appears seductive & scared
some self-conscious & solitary soul stranded in the high holy hills
above her above-ground pool in many ways looking to be rescued

a spectacle for us spellbound spectators on these rough & rugged
roads like ghosts constantly wandering alone winding through
the deep dark mountains in lumbering log trucks making our
trips through the forest.

when you get into the tourist village
signs remind us—"business district
historical district" which always
makes you anxious & nervous

some sort of fear of intimacy
& avoidance & once more

are forced to play the role
of soul escape artist.

dreamy
& distant

you become
horny & intimate

(maybe sense something of a fake oasis)
the cathedrals & ice cream stands
& diners & shoe repair &
sports on tv tells us about

multiple absences from summer school
and won't be able to rejoin the football team

at the university
in september.

you are comforted within the cradle
of chattering sheltering mountains

keyholes looking
out to clouds
& cornfields.

that girl becomes a fantasy of flesh & bones when we lie naked
vacant numb dumbfounded dripping anonymous lost & alone
in our aluminum siding cottage with "million-dollar views"
when the thunder suddenly booms in the gloom of your
room waking you up startled by this strange & unfamiliar
sound thinking that it's some wood pile tumbling down
thinking that it's the old junkies and criminals coming
through your air-conditioner when really it's just the
pitter-patter of the rain finally falling down to know
how she pouts on her throne way up on top the world

where they keep the radio stations
tv towers and beginning of fall.

you leave your room
healed & redeemed
crispy & clean

restored

with absolutely no need
for guilt or anger
for any kind of
explanation
nor leave any
sort of note

Faze 28:

On The Function Of Dysfunction

1

Mist spilling down morning mountain
(like silky lingerie slipping to ground)

2

Tinkering in the fog
always a fine line
between dreams
and delusions
where all
great thoughts
and ideas stem
from the grape
and wine and
civilizations

3

Hot ice trucks coming
into town for carnival

the freaks and sideshow
acts from the union with their
chemical dependency problems

4

They're putting up a brand
new wing at the haunted motel

5

Excavators oblivious to dug-up bones
Sainted milfs doing their rounds...

6

While everything really goes down
up in the sputtering, lit-up, mysterious
erotic imagination of silhouetted victorians
and a drizzly, closed-down, late-night town

7

The deer on your midnight lawn
are your wake-up call and when

your eyes meet theirs that moment
means more than any rapport

you have ever had with
any one of these neighbors

8

You are an extinct creature
and know your freedom

like they don't know
their prisons

9

(Escapism,
buddhism,
balloonism,
blueism…)

10

At my funeral when they're doing the elegy
gonna say you gotta be fucken kidding!
you're as phony as when i was living!
get up on the wrong side of the bed
and turn over a new leaf...

11

May they bury my mug
shot at the bottom of the sea
right by my mug of tea
stained angel wings

12

There's such a fine line
between the scent of cigarette smoke
and smoky swathe of autumnal leaves

autumnal mountains going
down in the sun of evening

13

At the end of civilization
it will be the end of evolution
some old man in his gray beard
on all fours like some pensive
lion bleary-eyed looking out
from the cave with one eye
open squinting taking in
the last twinkle of light
something that language
cannot ascribe and what it
means (or does not) to be alive

14

One must stop to smell the moses...

Faze 29:

Traits & Characteristics

He'll just sit back in leather chair
at dusk could sit there all night long
right in front of that ripped screen door
waiting for the mist from the mountains
to come seeping in and there's something
damn relaxing about it and wonders why
he never thought about doing it more often
he'll just sit back there staring at the stairs
wishing and hoping and imagining they'll just
open up like the opening to that sitcom what'ya
call *the muensters* and who was that? cousin it?
lerch? uncle fester? no matter any one of them
would be a presence and keep him company
and be a savior in the condition and state of
mind he finds himself in and now really able
to get and comprehend family dysfunction
and what it means to truly have a support
system no matter how fucked-up and
damaged no matter how much a freak
or madman just a matter of when it truly
comes down to it no matter how clichéd
it sounds who's really around (who's
there and hasn't vanished into thin air)
during thick and thin
during periods of crisis
during low-lying levels
of depression and then
can find out who your true
friends are or for that matter
who's human (or what separates
the sincere from the disingenuous
that one honest man from the stranger)
just sits back waiting for the headlights
and dragonflies and wisps of radio from
his wife to come barreling in whether just
a distant reflection or decides to come crashing
right through making her grand entrance a good

looking girl from the bronx and whatever decides
to do to him looking forward to it and will take
it like a man and suck it up whatever half-crazed
or high-expressed emotional lesson she wants to
teach him as never really had much of a problem
with rock bottom as when really got to the bottom
of it was when he was at his most clear-minded
senses most lucid and able to make the most
sense out of it and actually perversely most
sympathetic and able to truly get and
comprehend and understand it

Faze 30:

Call It Redemption

The waterfalls
are once again
turned on and
rapidly falling
like crazy
having melted
miraculously
along the side
of the mossy
green granite
highway holy!
hallelujah! amen!
alas all the tourists
are leaving, the horses
put back out in the mud
the paper mills churning
the buried may now
finally rest in peace
the dairy creams opening
been a long bruising winter
and finally mud season again
and the boys with the beards
hang out on the windy mill
front porches of chimes
with their dirt bikes
and delinquents
and gigolos
and wise ass
geniuses still
dreaming in
the barnhouses
with hangovers
right where they
put up a golden
chinese restaurant
under the mountains
which will become

a haunt and destination
for long-lost losers
and lovers; they've
decided not to go
to the bonfire
cause hear
there's gonna
be something better
and twisters tearing
up the state carnival
the court is literally
back in session
and so is industry
and those perfectly
uptight pasty caucasian
senators the legislature
returning back to town
with their very sincere
smirks and frowns and
don't even live around
here while prisoners
transferred in paddy
wagons back to their
home in their jail cells
to the prison (their sons
they always brag about
a chip off the old block
become enterprising
drug dealers literal
sons of a gun
with actual guns
and rap sheets
and long lists
of rich kids
who owe
them dough
and don't give
a crap and act-out
cause know daddy's
gonna always be
able to bail them
out and meet their

future betrothed
able to relate
to them and been
through the same
type of guilt and
shame and manipulation
and emotional blackmail
at their mandated
anger management)
waitress in the diner
who's a good girl
and hard worker
and still making
minimum wage
and the shy
blushing
angel
pushing
her vacuum
in the lobby
in the resort
in the mountains.
you and your son
get home and he
puts the country
radio station on
in his bedroom
and works on
a new experiment.
stolen 3-d glasses
his sainted thief mother
keeps proudly on the mantle.

V. A Tourist Guide To Nodding-Out

Rapport

This morning Dylan woke up with a tremendous tummy ache
decided to assign it a nickname and call him Big Bad Bubba
and give him a big bath with bubbles and Dylan and Big Bad
Bubba crept into the big bath of bubbles. We decided to call
his frog Zuckerman and the pirate Danny the Pirate, and
apparently scuba diver, Scuba Diba! and all the amphibians
played together, did dives and had races in waterworld, which
was a part of waterland, or vice versa, while Panda and Sharky
kept a watch out over all of them on the rim of his kingdom, and
the sudden silhouettes of rabbits crept in and came in over the snow
right through the morning window, and first band of sunlight broke
around the trunk of a cedar in the form of a purple and then pink
and forest-green, and when this was all done that tremendous
tummy ache we had called Big Bad Bubba and his amphibian
friends who we called Zuckerman, Danny the Pirate, Scuba Diba!
Panda and Sharky, picked Dylan up and that terrible tremendous
thing which had invaded his belly in the morning was all gone.
Now what to do with the rest of the weekend?

Tom Daugherty lost a PBA tournament.
But he didn't just lose, he had the worst
score in any televised PBA event ever.
And even his son mocked him for it…

Report

—Did you go in the ball pit today?

—No, someone pee-peed in it
so they had to close it down
but the room was left open

You open up a package of fishsticks
which reads—"Real Minced Fish..."

Tom Daugherty lost a PBA tournament.
But he didn't just lose, he had the worst
score in any televised PBA event ever.
And even his son mocked him for it...

Melancholia

When I was a kid and my mom making supper
I used to love to hang around the kitchen counter
and try to eat the raw meat as she'd instantly slap
my wrist and read off a whole list of possible diseases
I could get I guess your normal mother son relationship

Now I hear myself hollering at my kid–"What's that crap
you're watching? It's driving me crazy!" "It's the sharing
show daddy" "Hmmm..." and continue to shape my meatballs
and casually hear myself singing the song–"I wish I was in the land
of cotton...Look away, look away, look away, look away, I wish I was..."

Spring is just around the corner
as pitchers and catchers report
down to Spring Training in Florida
and the much awaited swimsuit
issue out for Sports Illustrated

Tom Daugherty lost a PBA tournament.
But he didn't just lose, he had the worst
score in any televised PBA event ever.
And even his son mocked him for it...

Drained With Your Eyes Bloodshot Hungry As Hell

Doesn't it just feel a hell of a lot these days
like people constantly trying to kick in your door
and know there hasn't been anyone home for so long?

Tom Daugherty lost a PBA tournament.
But he didn't just lose, he had the worst
score in any televised PBA event ever.
And even his son mocked him for it…

Bonnie & Clyde

The remains of a punch line
remains of snake eyes
in the back of a dusty
pair of ripped Levis
the remains of Ray
Bradbury's dandelion
wine, remains of
mock apple pie.
When did those
lotteries come into
play in those Edward Hopper
gas stations up and down Route 66
trying to pick up chicks, first love
who worked there right above the sign
which simply read "Bait, Night Crawlers"
Didn't know to be a poet had to submit
a check or money order like one of those
1970's disco albums from Zenith television?
86th 'em like the fucken Roadrunner then
took Polaroid shots with their Polident smiles

Tom Daugherty lost a PBA tournament.
But he didn't just lose, he had the worst
score in any televised PBA event ever.
And even his son mocked him for it…

Somewhere Between A Shriner's Convention
And Leisurely Stroll Through Bethlehem

They got this whole thing I swear
every year and aint exaggerating
like some half-crazed very sane
silly sadistic reunion like some
running of the bulls through
the streets of Pamplona
reenactment of Jesus
and schmucks literally
tying themselves up
to a cross and taking
that infamous final
walk of humiliation
and judgment
through the poor
Jesus parade route
of Bethlehem and
tie themselves up
neat and convenient
to some newly-bought
made-to-look fit-to-form
mock cross (comes in
all different shapes and
sizes something like a
small, medium, large)
and you got all these
cookie-cutter tourists
on cookie cutter-crosses
(interestingly not at
all too coincidentally
a bunch of cut-throats)
posing sincere and earnest
like monks on cell phones
heading with their sandals
and robes up the slopes
of the Himalayas supposedly
originally to contemplate to

become centered and their
pals or friends and acquaintances
sticking their very smart smart phones
up in the air and taking shots of them
what's next? They all huddle together
trapped to their souvenir crucifixes
with grins from ear to ear for the group
photo? The famous pyramid? Gather for
a cup of cappuccino with their crosses
at the table? A bottle of Gatorade or
Vitamin Water cause dehydrated?
When they get home do they
have a specific photo album
devoted to the whole affair
so they can reminisce
and boast and bore
the hell out of friends
and keep on repeating
the same old tired tale
over and over and over again?
The greatest story ever told
literally told over and over
and over and over like a
broken record turning
it into some remake
or sitcom for your
viewing pleasure?
Some boring cowboy
sob story which ironically
torments and tortures?
Have it instantly transferred
and superimposed onto
holiday cards or a plate
for the wall or a special
slide show presentation
where they invite friends
and family for wine and
cheese? Thank the lord
they can't do selfies…

Tom Daugherty lost a PBA tournament. But he didn't just lose, he had the worst score in any televised PBA event ever. And even his son mocked him for it...

All In All All In The Eye Of The Beholder

Travelers Opinions: Room not so great. I was saving up
last piece of matzoh and ended up turning into a gigantic
insect which crept across my floor and ate my Speedos.

When I brought this to the attention of the clerks
working at the front desk they just started to guffaw—
"Ugly American" or at least that's what I think they said?

Bring Mad Libs
and word puzzles

Pez?
Edgar Allen Poe

All the postcard carousels ran out of postcards of The Dead Sea
and couldn't believe charged me extra for the halvah and honey

Good Piece Of Advice: Bring crucifix, a chai
and shrine, bring pot and peace pipe
potato kugle and matzo bri

Bring bible and bagels, Miracle Bubbles...
snake bite kit, suntan lotion, and moon pies

Salt pills and a guide who gives
you a reason to get on in this life

To get through lies
to live and die

Reasons why and why
not to climb Masada

Get us out the mess
we're in Messiah

Sincerely
yours?

Tom Daugherty lost a PBA tournament. But he didn't just lose, he had the worst score in any televised PBA event ever. And even his son mocked him for it...

Leverage

I.

Leaves fall off the trees
   like chips flying
at a Las Vegas casino.
   He falls asleep drunk
at the *Pink Flamingo* motel
   to language tapes slurring
always trying to improve him-
    self, make a name...
thinking back to his 1st love
   2nd, 3rd, 4th
& crawls to the bathroom
    on all fours

II.

They crash commemorative plates
          over each others heads
those dashing portraits
          with splashes of color
you name it...
          Elvis, Slim Whitman,
that country dude
          who supposedly sold more
records than The Beatles
          the men who walked on the moon
JFK, Reagan, Barack Obama
          then in a bizarre twist of fate
with everything shattered
          (all of American civilization;
lost, foreign & dumb/mess/tic lives)
          bloody & broken & battered
start to make-out (that makeup sex they're always
          talking about
all those phases, all that damage) & has the opposite effect
          & starts to all
all of a sudden make sense

        & come together
(like being on the outside while also
        the inside of a prayer)
redemptive, like the return of disco
        & all instantly
put back in perspective

III.

Hollow, after having been
    torn apart
in more ways than not
    popover
to the refrigerator to share
    the leftover
perogies & blintzes
    the best
way to share leftovers
    & stare
faceless out the window
    into the face
of the sun while the late noon
    neon bulbs
from the casinos start to take
    shape & form

IV.

Folklore made up
    of the sum & loss
multiplied & divided
    in unequal parts
a mosaic & mural through
    the great big
vast empty keyhole
    of some lost
& nihilistic culture
    fallen, shattered
& put back together again
    from a forgotten

   & remembered period
       from so long ago

V.

The mu/dead weather
     telling him all about those
western wildfires
     hurricanes hurtling up & down
the coast like toast
     the rolling bones of storms
which always make him
     feel so much less alone
& closer to the skin
     & bones of the soul
those big beautiful bluegray twisters
     swallowing up the horizon
tumbling over the beatdown brick mills
     & factories & hotels of some
bleak, abandoned, done-in, old coalmining
     town shut down
in down & out Kentucky
     taking off
to The Heartland & Southern Plains

VI.

He splashes water on his face
     (as if this could make
anything better) in that sink & mirror
     in the corner
ducks out the door of The Pink Flamingo
     to the smell of dusk
which eternally smells of swathes
     of cheeseburgers
& fries & mayo from barroom windows
     open doors of pharmacies
& porn from downstairs basement
     bath houses with rivers
coming in from used-car mountains

  heads past the pawnshops
& pool halls & bailbondsmen & coroners
  in many ways
in almost all ways never to return again

VII.

A new
  & improved man...

Tom Daugherty lost a PBA tournament.
But he didn't just lose, he had the worst
score in any televised PBA event ever.
And even his son mocked him for it...

A View From On-The-Run

I remember even back then
when I used to runaway
on ferries to Sicily
observing all the
sophisticated classy
hard-working young
couples and pristine
and persnickety
wannabe aristocrats
in front of great big
looming Mafioso
mountains of the evening
with flashing glistening
carousels silhouetted
on the lido beneath
the burning mysterious
stars with woeful forgotten
widows hung out to dry on cactuses
on the promenade and those handsome
modest sharp-dressed mothers and fathers
brooding, removed in deep thought, keeping
an eye out on their gorgeous brood of tumbl-
ing children and thinking this was what it was
the whole life cycle frontwards and backwards
and how strange and absurd and difficult it all
seemed to be and being old enough to stay
in the exact Zen-Buddhist moment of being
brilliant nowhere nothingness of anonymity
keeping my cheap clean room on the sea
with the young, budding, flirtatious sisters
housekeeping always seeming to naturally
reek of talcum and powders and perfumes
and peek-a-boo portholes in my tiny tiled
thimble room cradled somewhere at the end
of the world on The Mediterannean sweeping
in all the sea and wandering rambling history

The luscious seductive goddesses to die for
like bronzed olive-skin voluptuous lionesses
on the boardwalk sneaking sweet secret smiles
and the young stud homosexuals also trying to
pick you up along shore knowing you were a
foreigner and solitary and alone and that you
had just as much to live for and not to live for
falling asleep
to strange saints
and crucified souls
limon liqueur in
tall svelte bottles
picked straight
out the polished
window from
the cathedral
from the gallows
from the opera hall
from the orchard
a deck of cards
and postcards
leftover pencils
from public libraries
in a land thankfully
where no one knows
or even cares to know
you cause it was always
those types of people who
could never ever begin to
know a thing about you…

Tom Daugherty lost a PBA tournament.
But he didn't just lose, he had the worst
score in any televised PBA event ever.
And even his son mocked him for it…

Life In A Picture Puzzle Frame On The Wall

I want to live
in the old dead
woman's home
fully furnished
dead woman
included
with all
that drab
opaque
furniture
going
through
the same
daily activities
and routines
and rituals
those little
portholes
in which
to catch
every
season
watching
the build
up of clouds
and downpour
of rain and drizzle
observing every
last leaf fall
one by one
by one
by one
helping
myself
to tea
and scones
and at day's end
turn off that lamp
holed-up in the corner
which will be that old

antique tourist souvenir
fisherman looking
like he's eternally
winking giving him
only a slight tug
at the noggen
as your dreams
will be all those
old time reel to reel
home movies before
they had sound
to them which
made them
and all its
characters
proportionately
that much more
animated with
everything
in the world
to look forward
to without all
the bullshit
and betrayal
and drama
and damage
all those fake
and phony
bastards
constantly
feed you...

*Tom Daugherty lost a PBA tournament.
But he didn't just lose, he had the worst
score in any televised PBA event ever.
And even his son mocked him for it...*

*Sometimes You Just Get So Unbearably Lonely
Melancholy You Can't Even Begin To Imagine*

And keep on sending me updates for my Facebook
and haven't been on for ages; Do you know him?
Do you know her? As if putting together these
different affected sounds and syllables will be
the cure to all of my problems (only ironically
making me feel more faraway and fictional)
and find I can really relate to Kong scaling
the heights of The Empire State Building
through the mist and smog just to try
and escape the monstrous masses

You look back to when you were a teenager
and you and your pals drunk and intoxicated
would suddenly decide to climb the inside
midnight girders of The Manhattan Bridge
which looking back now feels so liberating
connecting The East Side and Brooklyn

No telling…

*Tom Daugherty lost a PBA tournament.
But he didn't just lose, he had the worst
score in any televised PBA event ever.
And even his son mocked him for it...*

Margarine

I was watching these very cute girls
for college bowling on television
think it was something like
Sam Houston St. vs. Nebraska
and this very narrow girl with bifocals
pale, fragile, was just standing there
still as can be, determined, driven,
staring down this pin for the spare
and at the last second the ball just
curved off to the left and missed it
and rolled off into the empty blank
darkness of oblivion and vanished
into thin air and the rest of the night
just stood there stone-cold, shivering,
frightened, frozen, like that solitary
pin whimpering away in the shower
until her mom had to lift her out
and guide her and throw that towel
around her wet waif weeping body
and lay her down in the bed, like
some fallen pin on her side, sobbing
all the way into the night, her pride
instantly wounded and damaged
feeling sucker-punched and shot
by life, watching the sun go down
like margarine melting and dripping
over one of those *Thomas' English
Muffins* with those nooks & crannies
Would she ever be able to show her
face again, that was the question?
They never ever seem to show this
in the commercials for college athletics
How life really is just a game of inches

*Tom Daugherty lost a PBA tournament.
But he didn't just lose, he had the worst
score in any televised PBA event ever.
And even his son mocked him for it...*

Blues: A Different Sort Of Lullaby

I was singing to Dylan his round of every day goodnight lullabies
which included The Beatles and Buddy Holly and suddenly saw
Charlie Brown staring straight at me and it was strange 'cause
for one split second thought it was me I mean he looked exactly
like me only it didn't freak me out and was a comforting feeling
and just made me feel far less lonely and almost felt at that
exact moment like I wish I went right down in the plane
with him and continued singing that romantic harmony–
"Just you know why, why you and I, will by and by, no
true love way..." somewhere down there in the wisps
and tumbleweed of Lubbock, Texas right before the
whole rock & roll thing was about to break open
restless, frustrated, trust me I fucken get it
with passion and spirit at its core nucleus

Tom Daugherty lost a PBA tournament.
But he didn't just lose, he had the worst
score in any televised PBA event ever.
And even his son mocked him for it…

A Requiem

I don't care if I was the 1st, 2nd, 3rd, 4th, 5th,
6th dude who walked the face of the moon
think I would have brought a lunch bucket
whole bunch of fruit jars perhaps a teacup
and spoon and shovel in some moondust
and bring it back to the planet earth so
a couple years later when I was feeling
a bit under the weather much older and
lonelier when I was suffering from a really
bad bout of insomnia I'd just bury my hands
deep beneath that moondust and feel all that
stuff rushing over the rough surface of my
hands my palms my knuckles my fingers
and fall right back into slumber with
that moon streaming through my
window hearing the echo of
acorns starting to fall onto
the roof of my home

Tom Daugherty lost a PBA tournament.
But he didn't just lose, he had the worst
score in any televised PBA event ever.
And even his son mocked him for it…

Ibuprofen

I'm not quite sure what it is that makes
me feel so sympathetic to my wife
when she gets sick? Is it the gray
tube socks of mine she puts on
to make herself feel warm? Is
it bathing her beautiful nude
and lovely body and form
you haven't seen in so
long? Is it that uneaten
cream cheese bagel
still in a sandwich
bag girls love to
prepare for their
job slaving for
that awful fucken
ungrateful boss of
theirs? Is it that big
purple bag with a monkey
on it I bought for her at *Walmart*
stuffed with every possible thing
under the sun looking eternally
on the run? Is it her gratitude
in getting me a warm cup
of coffee Antiguan blend
waiting for her in the
Cumberland Farm
parking lot? Or is it
just keeping an eye
out on her while she
conks out in her pink
bathrobe with pockets
full of pills and aspirins
in front of the cooking
channel breathing
like Cleopatra
Queen Isabella
in Moses' basket
in the bay window
with gigantic icicles
hanging down

like daggers
watching some
spider form its long
escape route tendril
spinning around
from the ceiling
keenly amazed
at its being
finding them
both to be
just as fragile
helpless
vulnerable
and stunning

After she wakes up
she casually tells me
her mom just told her
someone jumped off
the rooftop across
from the school
where she works
at in The Bronx

(a kind of reverse solstice
or wake-up call to usher
in the new season…)

You sneak a peak
through the pocket door
glad to see her finally reaching
for the *Tempt-ee* cream cheese

Tom Daugherty lost a PBA tournament.
But he didn't just lose, he had the worst
score in any televised PBA event ever.
And even his son mocked him for it…

Somewhere 'Round Early Evening On Avenue B

My wife gives me PTSD
I mean my PTSD kicks
in I mean it jumps out
its skin and ask her
every so often if
she can just reduce or
turn down her volume
want to return back
to the womb for all
the wrong reasons
bartender can 'ya...
the weather is the sum
of the expression of all
the madmen passing in
front of the window

Tom Daugherty lost a PBA tournament.
But he didn't just lose, he had the worst
score in any televised PBA event ever.
And even his son mocked him for it...

May It All Taste Like Gin

Always admired
the alcoholic for
his undying devotion
to alcohol just always
seemed so damned down
to earth and determined
full of passion and half
crazed conviction
like some scene
from a play
where all
madness
began and
never quite
ended where
everything got
stolen and went
missing in action
and like some
bleary-eyed
innocent ghost
desperately
grasping
absurdly
tragically
trying to
recreate
that drama
staggering
stumbling
doing figure
eights anything
humanly possible
to get back to the
source of the trauma
his 15 minutes of fame
eternal lifetime in prison

Tom Daugherty lost a PBA tournament. But he didn't just lose, he had the worst score in any televised PBA event ever. And even his son mocked him for it…

Killing Time

Me and a good friend of mine (at least at the time) when we used to work there at the bookstore and just to kill time and were really killing time or time killing us would ask all the random customers and strangers who didn't seem to have much of a life and killing time as well but in much more vulgar obvious ways questions I suppose to get a reaction or shake things up or strike up some sort of conversation if they could be any animal what would they be and they used to either get really flustered and angry or simply ignore us and knew right there and then exactly what animals they were as they stomped and flew out the door

Tom Daugherty lost a PBA tournament.
But he didn't just lose, he had the worst
score in any televised PBA event ever.
And even his son mocked him for it...

Etc. In Other Words Ed Fix Wrecks

When language is no longer effective and just doesn't make
sense anymore and all that matters is a reflection of the crow
sailing way up above in the sky blue sky over pines to the sun

I always fantasized about my mom's friends taking me in,
the children's psychiatrist, who I believe has always had
a little bit of a crush on me leaving me rambling messages
some real intellectual going down on me not knowing
what she is doing and still doing all that explaining

Tom Daugherty lost a PBA tournament.
But he didn't just lose, he had the worst
score in any televised PBA event ever.
And even his son mocked him for it…

*Multiple Choice: on the nature of
culture and civilization in america*

Temporary insanity, permanent sanity
Temporary insanity, permanent sanity
Temporary insanity, permanent sanity
Temporary insanity, permanent sanity

Circle the one which seems most appealing

*Tom Daugherty lost a PBA tournament.
But he didn't just lose, he had the worst
score in any televised PBA event ever.
And even his son mocked him for it...*

Semantics

I remember working in 'the luxury hotel business'
as a reservationist on the graveyard shift and literally doing
extra reading in my station like Otto Rank's "The Trauma of Birth"
while I had to recite straight off the script shit like…"Good evening
The International Hotel & Tower…How may I assist you?" and
knew they were snickering in the background or whispering to pals
sarcastic shit like…"How may I assist…" and again if you didn't read
straight off the script they'd write you up…or if you ad-libbed at all
would walk you down some long impossible hall and into this brightly-
lit room…swear to god…like you were being interrogated and had to sign
some sheet of paper…like some lowdown criminal to admit your guilt
for committing some crime like improvising…and remember this one
time making this nice connection with some housewife from like Ohio
and telling me this hilarious story where one time she had stayed at this
luxury hotel and woke up in the morning and on the doorknob it read
something absurd and silly like…"taken over by so and so management
team" …and started cracking up and I naturally responded by saying
something like…"O my god that's wild" just trying to be validating
while apparently they were monitoring my whole exchange and
once again had to be walked down that long hall and wrote me
up this time for taking the lord's name in vain…swear to god…
did you say?…Imagine that…being escorted down some long
impossible hall into a brightly-lit room and them asking you
…pressing you…if you said 'O my god' and have to sign some
sheet of paper to tell them in fact you did…the main guy who
stands in the lobby…always forgot what they call him…probably
blocking…was this real smug German dude…I suppose because
he somehow thought he was better or more cultured than you
because perhaps you took reservations or something absurd
and crude or superficial and satirical like that…and on one
of those long miserable nights or graveyard where you were
sure your shift was never gonna end…sitting there with head
in hand with headphones on…he came in for some corny shit
I guess for purposes of team morale or to try and prove he was
one of us or on our level or a man of the people…acted shocked
and surprised when he suddenly saw I was reading Otto Rank's
"The Trauma of Birth"…and made some real asshole patronizing
condensing remark or comment or another like…'Wow! You're
reading that? Very admirable'…like I should feel honored to be
flattered by this smug motherfucker when probably seen more

of the world and women and had a better more well-rounded
education...well apparently I never quite made it...as suppose
I got walked down the hall one too many times...and wasn't
capable in keeping to my script and lines...(of cooperating)
...being a team player or a positive and productive member
of the family and cowering and feeling honored to be flattered
by some higher than holy phony schmuck or another...or those
very significant and profound exciting competitive intra-department
struggles to test how committed and loyal you were...usually having
something to do with some form of double-talk or backstabbing and
gossip and rumors...and so eventually they got me like they got Capone...
on something completely irrelevant and dumb...when I was just trying
to make someone feel comfortable and modest and humble...simply
be human and natural with some housewife from Ohio...must have
slipped my mind with Otto Rank's "Trauma of Birth" by my side

Tom Daugherty lost a PBA tournament.
But he didn't just lose, he had the worst
score in any televised PBA event ever.
And even his son mocked him for it...

Scenes From The Convention

Seems out here they seem to work their asses off
to become actual an acronyms to turn themselves
into an acronym to have a whole resume of an acronyms
to go to meetings to exchange an acronyms not ever sure
anymore what they represent or what they're for but feel
big and strong in throwing them around deferring
passing the buck and paying respects and praising
the almighty an acronym and then leaving feeling
all warm and toasty all over real confident in their
conviction in having reached this very significant
self-important position of top secret exclusive meetings
in their hierarchal and self-entitled ladder of an acronyms

Tom Daugherty lost a PBA tournament.
But he didn't just lose, he had the worst
score in any televised PBA event ever.
And even his son mocked him for it…

On The Nature Of The Memo

This is a memo which refers to last week's memo which confirms (or disconfirms) if received the memo from the week before and if so or did not so please respond to that memo which confirms the memo which preceded that and the one which came before

Look forward to seeing you and yours and hope will be attending the annual New Year's luncheon at our CEO's country club. This year the theme will be square dancing so please dress...

Tom Daugherty lost a PBA tournament.
But he didn't just lose, he had the worst
score in any televised PBA event ever.
And even his son mocked him for it...

Double Major

I want to be a registered nurse and a certified nut
what'ya gotta do to become a certified nut
as think i've probably done most of it
and would pass with flying colors
and probably earned most of
my credits simply from life
experience from broken
romances and vulgar betrayals
and then with my license would
just heal myself right there on the spot
yet most of them that i've met and known
in real life were a bunch of real-life fuck-ups
and drama queens and so much more about
self and not close to being anything resembling
that ethic of compassion as ironically always
felt could relate so much more and felt more
comfortable around those diagnosed with
that rare disease of being a certified nut

Tom Daugherty lost a PBA tournament.
But he didn't just lose, he had the worst
score in any televised PBA event ever.
And even his son mocked him for it…

Demographics

I wish there was some sort of statistic
for all those who did themselves in
cause they just got sick of the rain
and wind some nondescript stick
figure simply discovered
coiled-up collapsible
bones expressions
even body language
in the hush of dusk
in some spare room
in someone else's home
in some township
on the outskirts
of some even more
nondescript metropolis
which ironically just made him
feel more down in the dumps
and anonymous thus should
be a statistic simply just for
all these tedious significant
kind of just got sick of
everyday grind of life
absurd and ridiculous
meaningless existence
sort of demographics

memo just shows up in everyone's
box Bill M. died over the weekend…

Tom Daugherty lost a PBA tournament.
But he didn't just lose, he had the worst
score in any televised PBA event ever.
And even his son mocked him for it…

The Perfect & Practical Happily Ever After

Pretty soon you're gonna be able to get one of those payment plans
which will even provide half-off coupons for your funeral ceremony
sponsored by Walmart and they're gonna call it a Walmart funeral
and able to get the most competitive and economical pastor and
plasticware and professional mourners and even funeral psalms
done by those reality show Caucasians with pre-manufactured
feelings and emotions somehow singing downhome blues and
gospel and after you are lowered under in a Walmart casket
next to the other past products now sponsored by Walmart
the pre-packaged procession will take off from the cemetery
to the Walmart buffet which will provide a vast array of Walmart
discount delicacies and displays with one of those very sentimental
feel-good compilation Walmart c.d.'s allowing you to practically and
very safely and securely sit back and reflect and believe and maybe if
you get lucky feel at last finally even pleasantly refreshed and redeemed

Tom Daugherty lost a PBA tournament.
But he didn't just lose, he had the worst
score in any televised PBA event ever.
And even his son mocked him for it…

Nothing Gonna Take My Pride…

You hope one day America will be led by something of a porn star
with that porn star expression like "give it to me big boy deep and
hard" some Bodhisattva with bipolar disorder engaged in one of
his grandiose episodes and bawling hysterical like some sort of
madman some sort of drug dealer always watching his back
looking over his shoulder not just someone who chopped
wood like Lincoln T. Roosevelt and Reagan but someone
who actually drove trucks for a living or made bagels and
comes out to the podium dusting the flour from his apron
some loosey-goosey vaudevillian Jimmy Cagney
Fred Astaire Mickey Rooney character tap
dancing slide shuffle slide to the stand going
"Meet ya 'round the corner in a half an hour!
Meet ya 'round the corner in a half an hour!"
then finally I know I found me someone I can
truly relate to and rely on look up to and believe in

Tom Daugherty lost a PBA tournament.
But he didn't just lose, he had the worst
score in any televised PBA event ever.
And even his son mocked him for it…

Junkie's Munchies

If blocking, denials all that shit
that's just way too difficult to deal
with I got enough blocks to fill a city...
No wonder why always craved the anonymity
to be a stranger coming up the subway steps
in Brooklyn creeping through midnight
Cleveland Pear and going to that little
diner on the corner to order a medium
rare cheeseburger with raw onions
and a side order of leftover freaks
and hustlers who never grew up
who had nowhere to go or for
that matter (the 'where with all')
to ever leave the neighborhood
I always felt most comfortable...

Tom Daugherty lost a PBA tournament.
But he didn't just lose, he had the worst
score in any televised PBA event ever.
And even his son mocked him for it...

You Can Ring My Bell

You know looking back at the disco era
those divas really did have good and
soulful and bluesy voices and think
just forgot that all or maybe just
took it all for granted and never
ever really realized it. I lived
just outside the disco era
and was just a little too
young to haunt those
nightclubs but what
became big and
a new phenomena
and much the rage
was the divorce rate
and all those parents
who suddenly took on
whole other identities
and split-up
and went single
and fled the suburbs
for their fancy-schmanzy
condos in The Upper
East Side having
no idea the true-blue
and collateral damage
it might do to their kids
and remember having
sleepovers with my pals
when they weren't around
and always discovering
their stash somewhere
like in the night table
rolling them up with
the seeds and twigs
still in 'em flicking
on the electric fire.
People forget how
good those divas
actually were...

Tom Daugherty lost a PBA tournament. But he didn't just lose, he had the worst score in any televised PBA event ever. And even his son mocked him for it...

A Portrait For Some Peculiar Reason Never Painted

How to paint: a nude Puerto Rican woman
and not get a hard-on and getting hard-up
developing a crush feeling down on your luck

The Puerto Rican parochial school girls who used to giggle
in those short skirts and just wait at the bus stop right
below your window at Cloisters right around dusk

Tom Daugherty lost a PBA tournament.
But he didn't just lose, he had the worst
score in any televised PBA event ever.
And even his son mocked him for it…

Statistics

Surely one of the greatest crimes against man
is a woman who refuses to give him affection
and leaves him literally and spiritually helpless
homeless, abandoned, out there, with nowhere
to go, by his lonesome (left at the alter) even with
nowhere to run in this cruel and cold unfair absurd world
brooding and ruminating and introspective, disconnected
feeling estranged, alienated, done wrong, and then whether
he likes it or not, even with coping and survival mechanisms
just feeds into that self-fulfilling prophecy vicious cycle of self-
destruction, cold and distant, turning into the symbolic and literal
stranger, "the criminal," wanting to commit whatever crime there is

Tom Daugherty lost a PBA tournament.
But he didn't just lose, he had the worst
score in any televised PBA event ever.
And even his son mocked him for it…

The Magical Whirled Of...

She used to I swear
like to take it doggy-style
while addicted to all those
what'ya call 'em Disney films
call it what you will what you
want Madonna/Whore Complex
arrested stage of development
a freak it's all irrelevant
would just bend over
arch her ass perfect
right up there as she'd
gasp and grunt and I'd
thrust it in and out then
both fall down dead tired
euphoric hysterical and
after lay out like some
Tinkerbell literally blushing
from top to bottom head to toe
while we'd fall asleep to like some
theme song from Snow White or Pinocchio
Snow White and Pinocchio finally laying there
liberated left alone blissfully hollow glowing
in a heap of flesh and bones (with no strings
or wings attached) at last free to be relaxed
with nowhere to go just two lost souls
dreaming in their dreamworlds

*Tom Daugherty lost a PBA tournament.
But he didn't just lose, he had the worst
score in any televised PBA event ever.
And even his son mocked him for it...*

Hard To Get: a counterargument

I always preferred promiscuous girls
as just felt like creative extensions
more intuitive and independent
and willing to take chances and
learned so much more about the real
world like diamonds coming from
coal and pearls coming from
shells almost a part of the natural
language all that fluid chit-chatter
pillow talk which came after
as the prudes obviously just
left so much to be desired…
and simply tired you out and
always needed to be flattered
almost as if more fond of and
enamored by seeing their image
or reflection in the mirror and
thus in the long-run not really
that interested or caring so much
to engage in the challenge and battle
as you picked up these futile patterns
actually just neurotic and guarded
(and felt selfish and not generous)
without a whole hell of a lot to offer
more accurately made me feel more
uncomfortable and real pissed
off and hostile and in a sort of
fucked-up and damaged way
found could not trust as much
if that makes any sense at all?

Tom Daugherty lost a PBA tournament.
But he didn't just lose, he had the worst
score in any televised PBA event ever.
And even his son mocked him for it…

Borderline Disorder And That Great Secret Hideaway
Hidden From Everyone And Everything In Sleepy Hollow

Those couple of months were like the best ever
as they worked on so many levels; She had just
gotten off a really bad marriage and looking for some
mad action adventure and redemption and had never
had an orgasm and looking to explore sexual areas
she had never explored before and treated me like
I was just the man for the job and was up for any
thing and didn't know what I was in for and
looking to rope me in and declare her love
for me like three weeks into the relationship.
I was into it as had seemed like some pretty
crazy shit and had lived such a solitary existence
and had felt completely neglected by the ignorant
by those who pigeon-holed and pathologized me and
underestimated me up to that moment and my feeling
was like fuck 'em all as now it's my time to shine and
you got and never had any idea and the chances she took
and looking and willing to go all out for for two underdogs
who had felt and lived way too long in the shadows stigmatized
and having to fulfill self-fulfilling prophecies and play rebellious
roles against half people who would and could never ever fucken
know; Those were some of the best times ever and everyday felt
like a whole existence which had never once been experienced
and knew spiritually and romantically always had it in you

Tom Daugherty lost a PBA tournament.
But he didn't just lose, he had the worst
score in any televised PBA event ever.
And even his son mocked him for it...

Little Spring Memory...

We had already picked out a boy's and girl's name
before we got married. Had become romantically
involved, fiancées in our second year of internship
and had met at the mental health clinic in The Bronx
over at Yeshiva University. Really feeling as free as
can be, taking the fleeting trains uptown in the evening
to Harlem like on the wings of a firefly high on opium,
wild orchids, The Heather Gardens, taking midnight strolls
through Cloisters, returning to slow dancing in Washington
Heights apartment to you name it, think then it was K.D. Lang,
Dido, and Mary J. Blige feeling blessed, cursed, frightened
and alive, proposed to her that very night not even knowing
I was gonna to Prokofiev's *Romeo & Juliet* on Valentine's

Tom Daugherty lost a PBA tournament.
But he didn't just lose, he had the worst
score in any televised PBA event ever.
And even his son mocked him for it...

Are You Going...

My whole life has been a recurring dream
from that last scene in *The Graduate* where
Benjamin Braddock played by Dustin Hoffman
is constantly running away running towards trying
to find Elaine to dodge all those awful grownups
and obstacles to find her and stop her from
getting married then classically rebelling
ripping off the cross from the cathedral
jamming it in the handles and locking
up all those cruel and mean snarling
horrible devils in their hypocritical place
of worship then taking off after that smoking
chugging bus in late-Sixties Berkeley California
in our wedding uniforms finally catching up to it
and sitting back in the way back sweaty spontaneously
victoriously with a confused but contented smile reflective
and thoughtful while all those old timers just turn around
staring at us bewildered blankly blindly mutely like we
are the madmen when with youth and spirit all in that
moment know so much more they are the madmen
heading towards our long lost and nowhere
destination and not really giving a damn

Tom Daugherty lost a PBA tournament.
But he didn't just lose, he had the worst
score in any televised PBA event ever.
And even his son mocked him for it...

VI. Bally's: scenes from the overground

I. The Male

The old timers are even more
caddy than the women

sounding like a clever
coup of crackheads

talking a mile
a minute

trying to stir
up trouble

almost as though
staving off the inevitable

In the background you
can hear over the radio–

I ain't got nobody...

In the locker room
they break balls

"You're good at getting
down the scooter pies!"

while you mutter
mantras in the mirror

something
like a cross

between Stuart Smalley
and Travis Bickle

I ain't got nobody...

It appears customary in the case of the male
of the species to frequently gather around
each other and more often than not
around just one chosen individual
while casually taking a nice stroll
on the treadmill; around those
they feel most comfortable
or fond of or familiar
then crack one-liners
like some sort of cardio-
vascular roast which appears
to represent some kind of male
right of passage, as they present
with the exact same configuration
when fixing a car out in the borough
of Brooklyn, or hardhats from the union
on the side of the highway, all gabbing
away like a mess of mimes over the one
poor guy grinding away at his jackhammer

I ain't got nobody...

"Hey Lou! You did a good
job in getting it down!"
as they all start
to crack up
with him
stuck
under
the bar
grunting
gasping
guffawing
trying desperately
from a bet to push
his body weight
up off his chest

I ain't got nobody...

They say such simple
things like–"Another day"

and maybe, just maybe, that's
what it's all about, another day

I ain't got nobody...

II. Culture

On the treadmill, you feel like Jesus walking on water...
(keeping your head above water) most of the time bipolar

in this mad dash for freedom
in this mad wild flesh & bone asylum

where people try to attract each other
by some sleazy, scared truth or dare

stuck somewhere in no man's land between
self-conscious and impulsive more often

than not manifesting itself
in obsessive-compulsive

I ain't got nobody...

You like to imagine yourself simply taking some long lost stroll
to The Netherworld, for all you who don't know, that mysterious

& mystical, ethereal place Ancient Egyptians talked of somewhere
between the material world and afterworld, and when they ask—

"Where did he go?" they'll say—
"I don't know, He was here a minute ago"

I ain't got nobody...

So we try to make ourselves into indestructible, mythological heroes
into very desirable sirens, seducing and bringing down whole cultures.

On the muted television they show slow-motion
commercials of succulent lobster dripping in butter.

Often I like to look out these windows and sometimes
conceptualize and try to imagine Evolution from the first

single-cell organism to the fish to amphibian to when that
first creature with tiny microscopic legs decided to finally

ditch the ocean and crawl and explore the shores
from the dinosaur to our Lord to World Wars

to the US to the USSR and everything else
that came in between; The Beats and Times Square

I ain't got nobody...

From skulls to Polio to Acquired Immune Deficiency Syndrome
very similar to the reverse phenomenon of Evolution dealing

with the decay and disintegration and
degeneration of the human organism

I ain't got nobody...

Interestingly too, if one were to trace our race back to the origins
of primate, it all came back around, about face, full-circle, that being

AIDS to the ape
and orangutan

I ain't got nobody...

When you look out into that parking lot you think a lot
of all those great games of stickball that lasted till dusk

trying to hit the ball a mile long, dreaming of those long
pink Cadillacs which would escort you towards the future

with no looking back, a little
like the machinations of Evolution

I ain't got nobody...

You wonder where is that great gold Rolls that will pick you up
and deliver you through the screaming gulls, screaming girls

(in the fragile folds, lost & found somewhere
between coincidence and fate, burnt at the stake)

to the hamlet of Fall River for the secret spread
solstice, platter, last supper of lox & bagels

I ain't got nobody...

When you look out that window you sometimes feel so damn alone
in the world forced to become mean & tough, kind & compassionate

no one could even begin to fathom or know
as you see cops in their cop cars doing their

rounds and imagine yourself back there like so many times before
this time in handcuffs showing them card tricks cracking them up

I ain't got nobody...

Up here, you have no fears, as all moments, transitions,
interludes, phases, stages in your life start to become clear

All truths, half-truths, successes, failures, betrayals, desertions,
deceptions, hypocrisies, conflicts, crises, characterological

and behavioral patterns of those
you once believed in and never will again

I ain't got nobody...

Yet know too after one of these liberating workouts when you cross
the puddly parking lot up on the mountain top; when people's useless

rhetoric and language designed to hurt you no longer affects you
when their ridiculous games and ways they try to displace their weak

and fragile identities and pain onto you becomes
see-thru and can simply shrug them off and continue

you know you are clearly
on your radiant way

I ain't got nobody...

So they tell you you must try to find a way to control and contain
all that rage, yet it is written all over, not written at all on *their* face

then go out into the real world and make a name...
that it is all simply just one big leap of faith

but turns out when you get to this new & improved place
ironically, they're all just as, if not more, phony and fake

I ain't got nobody...

You start to think that maybe all of modern culture
and society historically lies somewhere smack-dab

in the middle of the cotton and heroin trade
How we base our overall functioning

somewhere between "Consumer Confidence"
and "Presidential Approval Ratings"

to diligently determine our commercialized & collective
belief and faith as a thriving & productive democratic society

I ain't got nobody...

How all of these suburbs simply got laid out; where's that Levittown?
What was the big phenomenon? That they were able to knock-out

the exact same house of mass-production in just a couple hours
in record time as if in some bizarre and benign race against time

for all those returning gi's as though insuring
and guaranteeing that the overall collective

psyche would realize one big warm
fuzzy feeling of security and stability?

I ain't got nobody...

As you really know deep down inside
under all the skin & flesh & bones

all it ever had to do with was the heart & soul having absolutely
nothing to do with shallow & acquired language & roles

Bones of the penguin
Bones of the comedian

State reservation, state of Montana
Horseneck, Holy Ghost Road

I ain't got nobody...

What do you do when none
of them believe in you?

When all you can do is extract truth and faith
from the smell of the sea, the smell of the farm

Smell of the fish, smell of crops
to know it's all simply fish heads

and coal & clotheslines
that made this whole

masterpiece, catastrophe pop.
How it all rolls up, the origins

of civilization to the freak shows & metropolis'
transported on the back of flatbeds as specimens

to the laboratories to be
investigated and invested in

I ain't got nobody...

From the blackberries, from chimneys
which will lead you back to the bones

of the factory
of your sanctuary

I ain't got nobody...

To something you wish you could believe
to some place you wish you could call home

when you got no other where to go
but spend the rest of your days

with bulls in the mist
rather than con-artists

full of shit, bullshit, arrogant & ignorant
who take your heart & soul for granted

America's concept of forgive & forget
send them off to prison and let them...

I ain't got nobody...

Send them off to the group home, boarding school,
house of detention...new used & abused ultimatum

anger management,
psychotropic medication

They say some of the highest
taxes are out there in Texas

I ain't got nobody...

Newspaper blows across your lawn on a balmy morning the day
garbage men come and weather-worn headlines read "Cop Killer"

"Cape Killer," really not sure, as it suddenly dawns on you
none of it really matters, none of this makes any difference

I ain't got nobody...

How now they even have whole villages, townships
which breed and mass-produce clowns having pawned

& stolen all their affectations
& expressions & body language

straight from "The Real World" and MTV Television.
One might even be able to make the mild conclusion

that the young male Caucasian has become something of a cookie-cutter
rather unconvincing caricature with his manufactured anger and reactions

in the big bad brutal suburbs of mean
strip malls & split-levels & ranches

I ain't got nobody...

'Tis the season for when the lawnmowing
people start to rev up their engines to take

out rakes to overcompensate and
feed the perfectly manicured illusion

(paint-by-number scenarios searching for missing pieces to the puzzle
to try and make ridiculous and routinized lives appear more livable)

I ain't got nobody...

Fiery red *Home Depot* mulch the color of The Apocalypse
accentuating The Virgin Mary, mailbox, and satellite dish.

Homes sit on cul-de-sacs like half-crazed cathedrals as you
know every filthy & sleazy hypocrite behind these peepholes

Every alcoholic & adulterer, every backstabber
every perpetrator of parasitic gossip and rumors

Every soulless husband, heartless housewife, and brainwashed child.
Yes, I can confirm from experience, denial is not just a river in Egypt!

It's alive and well right here in America!
(The weather gets us closer to God...)

I ain't got nobody...

Out here, they measure mortality, emotional-state
by how well you landscape and can gauge whose man

whose woman walked out on them, deserted, abandoned
by how they let their lawn go, developing the do or die

Fuck the world, I don't
give a damn if it grows!

I ain't got nobody...

And don't you know it is clearly only in
the creeping shadows that will save your soul!

The ice cream man's dead and gravedigger
busy gabbing away on his cell phone

The sign on the side of the road reads—
"God Bless America" and right below

"Heineken
Amstel

Lap Dancing
Rated #1 Strip Club"

I ain't got nobody...

Next door to miraculous mountains
of majestic, multi-colored mulch

I ain't got nobody...

Right next to some pre-fabricated mansion literally made
to resemble a gingerbread home next door to another one

I ain't got nobody...

Appearing to be influenced by Louie the 16th
or for that matter even, Frankie the Thief

I ain't got nobody...

Next door to convenient little aluminum siding shacks
which stash leftover logs & fishing traps & portosans

I ain't got nobody...

Why just the car? Why not put an alarm on the shed?
On the step kids! On the shrubs! On the mulch!

I ain't got nobody...

On the mailbox! On the two-car garage! On the trees!
On the lawnmower! On your prize-winning garden!

I ain't got nobody...

On your prize-winning catch! On the candelabra!
On the plastic-wrapped furniture! On the wax fruit!

I ain't got nobody...

On the violin! On the vibrator! On the family pet!
On the family portrait! On the family secret!

I ain't got nobody...

So we have all become o so single-minded & successful
yet if we have failed to do it without dignity or respect

or soul or class where does that really leave us?
What does that really make us?

I ain't got nobody...

The captions remind us–"Developing News...
Unfolding News...Breaking News…

There has been Another Shooting in
Colorado...A Triple Murder in Texas

A Stampede of Sunbathers down in Miami
Beach, Florida...A Killing in Las Vegas..."

I ain't got nobody...

Out there in cineplexes, where they serve fake dripping cheese over warm
nachos, it's all about special effects, a cross between sadistic & satanic

God forbid in this fragmented and fucked-up culture we should
ever get too close to any sort of intimate character development

I ain't got nobody...

Plato's forms have turned towards a literalism
of the perfect form on Spring Break flaunting

the exact same cookie-cutter muscles, aerobically
sculpted, shaking tits and asses like a bunch

of pimps & hookers
in front of the TV camera

I ain't got nobody...

I don't know, call me old-fashioned,
but think I so much more preferred

the 40s & 50s when there was still
mystery and room for the imagination–

"Missing College Co-Ed
In Carolinas...In Aruba..."

As the only options to turn to, slow-motion
instant replays of The Hail Mary where you

actually put all your faith,
dreams, fantasies, and memories

I ain't got nobody...

Your whole past, future,
all the way up to eternity

Watching those unbelievable muted greats in the backfield
Jim Brown, Gale Sayers, Walter "Sweet Feet" Payton...

and know it's never about complaining, but just simply
staying on your feet (keeping the adrenalin flowing)

while they try to take your legs out
from beneath you and got so much

passion & gusto (mad heart…)
might even drag the whole tumbling

team to the end
zone with you

dodging, scrambling, barreling over the enemy
like some raging radiant river rambling to the sea

I ain't got nobody...

They'll show you close-ups of the assembly line in the factory
of pharmaceutical pills, computer chips, and wooden golf tees

as if these are the exact things that will keep us grounded, well-rounded,
reality-based, and make us more whole and complete human beings

I ain't got nobody...

The corny cartoonish captions made to attract your attention–
"The Fight For Iraq" (making it sound so noble & glamorous)

then hit you with–
"Faces Of The Future"

and wonder if it is just a simple coincidence
or much more complicated and convenient

how all those flashbulbs that went off "Last
Weekend In Los Angeles" on the red carpet

gave off the exact same apocalyptic image as great
big guns of battleships blasting off their ammunition

forcing you to draw similar selfsame conclusions…
How America has become something of a caricature

between some cheap blonde and brutishly bringing calm
(to a war-torn…) by threatening to drop as many bombs…

I ain't got nobody…

while you look out pigeon-shit windows
dull-eyed and distant to trees of Winter

over the stripmall parking lot to people's
bare boob-tube, monkey bar backyards

I ain't got nobody…

You even go so far as to think when you were a kid
in school and the schoolyard is this how you saw…

Is this what you pictured about the wonderful "grownup" world?
La Rochefoucauld, the late-great philosopher, who inspired Nietzsche

to write all those brilliant and bold bleak aphorisms
pretty much broke down man to a transparent species

of simplistic "self-interest" who thrived and functioned
off role-playing and rhetoric; how lonesome the single

solitary soul of integrity
and character must get!

I ain't got nobody…

So says I the long-lost understudy to Plato and Socrates.
Even looking back, retrospectively, this denial and deceit

disassociation if you will, can start as early as the developmental
stage of puberty and run throughout the whole entire length

of poor and pathetic
delusional being

I ain't got nobody...

What a pity when you think back on all these horrible
transcendent patterns of history from Socrates to the birth

of civilization to the great
societies & cities & suburbs

it has always been those of the keenest & most imaginative creativity
who got excommunicated ironically and pathetically by a herd-mentality

who did not have a clue or care or come close to
having the ability on how to engage in the most

simplest and civil forum of
discourse or communication

I ain't got nobody...

From abusive parent passed down to a whole other
hollow generation of brainwashed and brutish kids

whose eyes, whose light, whose spirit
look switched off and hidden

(sexless soulless sister of the self-destructive suburbs
giving birth to a whole new breed of spoiled creatures)

I ain't got nobody...

It is not by coincidence that this has always been
manifested by the malicious and mediocre masses

desperate yet interestingly
always at a safe distance

I ain't got nobody...

One can easily make a clear-cut comparison
on the history of society & culture & civilization

to the bully in the schoolyard
whose soul has gone numb

and all his buffoon and bastard
punks & pals of real-life scum

gathered around in their callous
close-nit circle thirsting for blood

I ain't got nobody...

All of America laid-out in perfect little neat and tidy subdivision plots...
this is the plot, each man may now have his own particular plot, his own

special safe and secure territory in which he no longer
has to necessarily relate or interact with anybody

I ain't got nobody...

Kind of interesting, how they get placed in the category of plot
a little like some convenient crackpot cemetery, as the suburbs

seem for all intents and purposes a slow-death "Land of the Lost"
land of make-believe, which appears to bring about as much

psychological & spiritual damage & hostility as anything
satirically entitled such perverse things as "Peaceful Valley,"

"Congeniality Way," "Comanche Circle," "Gabriel's
Loop," "Trail's End," "Subdivision Crosswind..."

I ain't got nobody...

Just off the stripmall where they keep the physicians
and name each office after some Native-American

as what was the plan? To slaughter and conquer and divide
practically a whole nation then grace the periodontist

and pediatrician with the rare distinction?
Flags fly high over the turrets of Taco Bell

I ain't got nobody...

They do this too for malls & golf courses & bowling alleys & schools
for when you cross over the border to some brand new town or village

then present a plaque of some Indian draped in loin cloth
to help represent when it was founded and discovered

I ain't got nobody...

Mother who's lost all pigment & expression returning home down
the dead end in her climate-controlled luxury tank to pick up and

deliver her privileged & entitled
brainwashed litter of little saints

I ain't got nobody...

It does become an 'absurd' & perplexing phenomenon how 'the tourist,'
'the general public,' so-called 'upstanding citizen' in Caucasian America

will ultimately become a stranger to his cultural environment,
to himself, and his loved ones, as he always takes with him

his arrogance & ignorance, self-importance & self-interest,
privilege & entitlement, false omniscience (confidence?)

literally going out of his way, whether he is aware of it
or not, due to delusions of grandeur & narcissistic features

to dishonor and disrespect (even humiliate & alienate)
'the native' with his attitude of "you are here to serve me"

or "it's some honor to be in my presence"
yet when he discovers that all his fellow followers

(the lost & pathetic tourist, obvious wheeler & dealer)
are engaged in the exact same function & activities

routines & rituals (false acts of "action & adventure")
still have the exact same issues, as their wives have

lost all romantic interest, having turned impulsive or indifferent
still have a litter of ungrateful & spoiled & self-centered creatures

when all gimmicks & contraptions & exclusive equipment
cannot & will never save him (his predictable & transparent

roles & defense-mechanisms) he cannot help but to turn
or pitifully remain miserable & malcontented having sucked

all the life, the last ounce of soul from his culture & 'all-knowing'
environment from the native, eventually, inextricably from his own

unrecognizable family-unit like his dull-eyed wife does at ice cream
stands or like she once did several years back to attempt to win

his favor or win her man, then will leave these tourist towns
with the selfsame personality & mentality and thrive & function

and engage in the exact same 'classless' body language (passive-
aggressive sort of confrontation, yet never having the courage

of his conviction, or as the black man put it–
"They started it so we're simply ending it")

in foreign lands as you always
know exactly where they're from

I ain't got nobody...

You start to think once more (taking your cardio-vascular stroll)
how peers may have always resented or even scapegoated you

due to you being content with simply minding your own
business and marching to the beat of your own drummer

Heart rate...Weight...
Calories...Breaking...

And even eventually developed a bit
of a "Fear of Intimacy" or simply later

on not wanting to let people get
too close to me due too to a whole

hell of a lot of controlling and manipulating
from a rather domineering figure of authority

I ain't got nobody...

then ridiculously having the nerve
to try and place a pathology on me

I ain't got nobody...

(Imagine that? How maddening! How could you
not help but to fulfill the self-fulfilling prophecy?)

only to come to the conclusion just a little bit
later how overrated is personality and identity

I ain't got nobody...

You start to wonder if you look up
to the sky from one of these things

if that might
count for praying?

I ain't got nobody...

The shadows of seagulls swoop down
the sun-splashed sides of *JC Penny's*

Sometimes you wish you were one of these beings
and simply never seen from or heard from again

I ain't got nobody...

Man, seems to spend more time out here than on the ocean
mankind seems to spend more time here than out on the sea

Seagulls climbing and scaling the sky
until they're completely out of sight

away from the eye, away from the lie
away from all that can possibly be denied

I ain't got nobody...

Speed, Time, Incline...
Wow! you remember back

to those beautiful terrible times with real-life speed dealers
from The Lower East Side when you didn't have a dime

climbing up the bus escaping The East
to find something else deep-down inside

I ain't got nobody...

The breast of The West; as a restless teen having no idea your destiny
already looking to be redeemed, meeting junkies jaded from Jersey

racing cross-country, sipping away at last-ditch doses
of methadone and in their own wild and desperate ways

in defeat, trying to find
a way to make ends meet

I ain't got nobody...

Climbing those steep, sweeping streets (inclines) of Frisco
hustling all day stealing steaks and then selling them

back to the Russian hotels in Tenderloin
for half price; learned more about real life

from these guys, these thieves, those tourists...
the real slime and crime of mankind, nevermind

I ain't got nobody...

Never complaining, always just climbing
the steep, sweeping incline (believing

you had to pay your dues for the true fruits of later life)
wondering when and where alas will be that sweet decline

standing on top great Chinese hillside
and looking out over the whole brilliant

radiant shimmering Pacific seaside satisfied
at the end of the day with a great big burrito

and brisk bottle of Mad Dog 40/40
your laundry literally hanging

in dusty, dingy sun-splashed hotel room
with pawnshop radio which kept you abreast

of all events in the world, sporting events, baseball still being played
still hearing the crack of the bat through static somewhere out there

in breezy Candlestick,
Wrigley, St. Louis...

I ain't got nobody...

Awwwh! Mother of Frisco
what do you have left to offer?

I ain't got nobody...

What do you have left to spare?
What do you have left to bear?

I ain't got nobody...

I am left empty, vacant, hollow
in despair (alone, acutely aware)

I ain't got nobody...

and if you really do care
you shall find me there

I ain't got nobody...

lost somewhere between truth and dare
beneath the stars, beneath your stairs

I ain't got nobody...

careless
without a care

I ain't got nobody..
.

as perhaps all I ever really simply
did was give a damn and care

I ain't got nobody...

& have lived & died so many times
& experienced so many times

I ain't got nobody...

the blatant & brutal hypocrisies
of mankind, absurd coward crimes!

I ain't got nobody...

I am so past anything that might
possibly be offered or described

I ain't got nobody...

(denied,
defied)

I ain't got nobody...

The final fate of the hustler, to eventually,
existentially, end up excruciatingly lonesome

I ain't got nobody...

while through expressions, dialogue, and body
language he's able to peep everything they're

I ain't got nobody...

about to pull on him
a couple steps ahead of them

I ain't got nobody...

(Can't help but to feel abandoned
and them constantly threatened

I ain't got nobody...

as they know he knows
everything about them)

I ain't got nobody...

Hell, it's gotten to the point
my ghosts know my phantoms!

I ain't got nobody...

Gazing through my lonely lattice of Eddy Street and witnessing
all of half-crazed extraordinary humanity suffering and surviving

moving blissfully, blindly, to the literal great divide of life
and death separating the shadows of the solitary song bird

and his environment, whose long stray guttural and ghost-
like echo encompasses and engulfs the whole west coast

with wings spread out in silhouette protecting all
lost souls who for good reason have lost their mind

I ain't got nobody...

You realize your arrested stage of development
really began and of course ended some time

somewhere around the "Skate Key Roller Rink" where
you excelled in disco at bar-mitzvahs and sweet-sixteens

returning home proud and sweaty
with trophies and romantic dreams

I ain't got nobody...

yet heard something like it had burnt down
or closed down due to some kind of shooting

ironically forced to have to pass
this deserted abandoned building

every day later on in my life while
traveling up and down the highway

I ain't got nobody..
.

III. The Female

The women on the treadmills
appear just a little bit different

more damaged and desperate, distant
obsessively flipping their chick mags

I ain't got nobody...

as it seems like each page
they snap is some man

who has done them wrong
or has caused them scorn

I ain't got nobody...

then will get off and bend over
for your viewing pleasure which

becomes the literal and proverbial
baggage they're still willing to offer

I ain't got nobody...

and give you long stares in the mirror
in which you never know (never knew)

how to react caught between their act of
seduction or just becoming another victim

I ain't got nobody...

And decide to play it safe and acknowledge
them then go back to the muted commercials

dreaming of having one of those luxury cars
with a sun roof on top while hearing a long

slow Miles Davis jazz horn with paratroopers
coming down from up above to save your soul

I ain't got nobody...

Then of course there's the very pretty girls
like some rare pristine and precious pearl

with their Betty & Veronica primped-up
ponytails and perfect pair of protuberances

like freshly ripened pears
ready to be picked

I ain't got nobody...

Nipples like some terrific and tender gift looking to be pricked
to be licked by some swashbuckling idealized fantasized prince

by some kid who will eventually suckle
and save it and bring about a whole other

different point
and purpose

of arousal and stimulation
of development and maturation

I ain't got nobody...

Ironic, how originally it's used for purposes of seduction
and later on, to flourish and function, both psychological

and phenomenological
forms of validation

I ain't got nobody...

When they come back to wipe down their equipment in a very neat
and orderly fashion it is as if they are cleaning erections, baby's spit

as from a simple and crude male point-of-view
it is not only the womb you want to return to

but also the lips & hips & tits too
to hope to heal a bit of the blues

just a simple and sweet
raw naked interlude

to try and rescue
you from you

key in the keyhole
refreshed and renewed

I ain't got nobody...

It is true they will often try to tempt me
and just plant their precious bodies

on the machines right in front of me
leaving me to imagine what is going on

down there, deep in between juicy, sweaty, secret
honey pot sweet nectar, ripe avocado, moist kiwi

then when they leave, once more give a sneak peek
and grin with flushed, blushing, red-apple cheeks

I ain't got nobody...

Interestingly, they turn out to frequently be very nice and bright
girls, yet who also as well looking and willing to do certain things

to try you on for size, to experiment, to fulfill
all those repressed and wild and filthy fantasies

I ain't got nobody...

And always appear in their culturally and socially acceptable groupings
of three just right for seducing and scrutinizing and selectively choosing

the male of
the species

I ain't got nobody...

VII. When Flash Gordon Called Groucho
To Tell Him The Market Had Crashed:
    how to make ends meet

Drop the wife off to her babysitting gig to 3 nymphomaniac girls
with short-shorts and long milky legs at their *Pepto-Bismol* home
with great big fake paper-mache pillars and twirly-whirly shrubs
also need a tutor but decided against it as do a hell of a lot
of flirting and be a conflict of interests (I don't see it but...)
all you hear out here are dogs barking in the distance which
is a really nice sound when the sun goes down and a bunch
of wiggers in their little purring souped-up race cars zooming
through a fairyland of artificial lawns and bizarre pyramids
of token picket fences and lantern men and Virgin Marys
and aluminum siding and all-weather shutters and
decorative trees; daddy died about ten years ago
and sad and trying to sell the home and been just
trying to hold on for so long; you've been looking for
freedom your whole life long and out here it seems
like it but know deep down inside it really isn't
the sun going down like eggs over easy

When they are gone we feed the cats
and actually a real good feeling at that
and climb up their long flight of steps
to the side porch with this beautiful
and bizarre expansive view of other
people's perfectly plush backyards
set up like some artificial hierarchal
feudal system and feed them and never
see them with just a cup left in a big bag
and they are *outside cats* and think there's
something really nice at that and every time
we go there the bowls are just licked clean
left completely empty not a one to be seen
maybe after just returning from some very
curious and necessary day of exploring

So we never ever quite seem
to see them but know something...

I am neither an evolutionist nor creationist but believe all existence
emanates from a white girl's pussy and boy's dreams and fantasies
(maybe even one of those wet dreams) in the nineteen-seventies
when the sun goes down and barbecues go on in the back
of some deep and green plush suburban backyard right
around the above-ground pool with a pair of binoculars

Leftover shishkebob in a piece of tinfoil in the refrigerator

Man I'd rather out here them think me crazy
it's just so much more convenient and easy.
When we first moved out here they used
to all look up to me and used to think
what could they possibly see and want
from me as I have absolutely nothing
in common or a thing to say to them
and actually ended up feeling far more
empty and lonely and incomplete and also
knew by the 'common' character trait and
human nature and herd-mentality theme
of man these exact selfsame people
who were looking up to me would
be the exact same people who would
eventually look down on me; That's
just the way it always seems to end up
and pan-out and work out here even if I
swear you're minding your own business

The greatest Americans were the slapstick
comedians and those who got assassinated

Kill or be killed on the highest and lowest levels
all for the sake of progress awe forsaken progress

One-up the neighbor
One-up the paradise

"Hey boss what's his fantasy?"
(ibid. Tattoo and Mr. Rourke)

The suburbs seems like a constant struggle with the illusion
of the(ir) hysteria and neuroses as well as fable and folklore

Are you struggling with depression?
No depression's struggling with me

The very sane have always driven me crazy

Do not disturb as already deeply disturbed

I suffer and feel pain
on a daily basis therefore I am
not so sure about all that thinking…

Where is my splintered rickshaw
coming down from the gods?
Ready or not here I come

Getting so sick of all this cute little fancy wannabe
HDTV competitive cooking cartoon dance scene
those aggressive Yuppie from Hell go-getters on
what'ya call it *The Apprentice* I mean who thinks
up doesn't think up this shit and want to vomit
all over the judges and contestants, like a bunch
of slaves trying to make themselves worthy of
some see-threw sleazy Nazi tribunal, rather stake
up a graveyard for the non-exclusive, for those who

would otherwise not be known and ignored and taken
for granted and forgotten, the wino and the bum and
that dude you see wandering everyday up and down by
the side of the road, stray dog at the end of the boardwalk
and cat just trying to make it with eyes behind his head
dodging in and out the shadows forced to be a survivor
in the big bad city, as they will all get admitted
no questions asked and no freaking ceremonies

The discos always seem in very dangerous
crime-ridden areas just on the industrial
outskirts of town where the streets end
and cobblestone begins like some insane
half-crazed paradise (every man every
woman for themselves, how they get home
purely up to them) like suicide like romance
exactly the way they always wanted it to be

The country clubs are always in the opposite direction
where they murder you slowly at the end of the gondolas

Bank teller with Tourette's
who has episodes, and curses and
says vulgar things to his customers
who keep on coming back for more
a small town and word gets around

Think if I was to do a character study of myself
think I'd be very much like The Blues Brothers
who think had a heart of gold but a little
misguided and sadistic and oppositional
defiant and couldn't keep themselves out
of trouble; when I first saw that film believe
I was drunk somewhere back in The Eighties

with a bunch of friends I didn't want to be around
and felt like it lasted way too long and could have
used a hell of a lot of editing which I suppose
I guess resembles something of myself

Most rebels were not rebels
until they were forced to rebel
put in the corner way too many times
with backs backed up against the wall

I'm that suspicious package left on the doorstep
of the parade and when they go to open me up
I'll explode with kvetching, more so leftover
Chinese, bouquet of dried-up black-eye susies,
my old scratchy blues records, razorblades,
rulers, protractors, loose change, coffee beans,
nude Polaroids of past girlfriends, and those
Buddhist birthday candles I used to spark
up all by my lonesome in the murderous
portholes of *The Times Square Hotel*

A longish title about meltdowns and murder and mayhem
in no particular order over a cup of spilt milk or visa-versa
which I suppose is virtue shattered when the whole damn
map goes flashing scarlet based on t-storm tornado warnings
in the middle of babbling Bible Belt America which instantly
triggers drinking bottles of *Cool Breeze Mad Dog 40/40*
beneath the higher than holy lonely stars not knowing
one living breathing soul in the backwoods of Alabama
miss Biloxi Mississippi after getting off the Greyhound
still smelling and feeling every last blessed cursed part of it
like pungent dew trickling off the sweet sticky stamen and petals
of the splendid magnolia flower with new-found partner criminal
actors you felt like you knew forever which in most ways
did with similar experiences damaged hearts and souls

you met on the bus from Port Authority who lived right
across the river running away for the exact same half-
crazed (half-sane) dirty filthy deserted abandoned reasons
of being misjudged and misinterpreted and underestimated
hoping for some sort of freedom which is constant chaos
divided by a sudden flash of clarity and contentment
hoping for some miracle or redemption out in the exotic
land of steeples and smokestacks in the holy firmament
of Alcatraz San Francisco all ending up like Jesus nodding
out on the corner of Tenderloin District or laid-out on the table
of the phlebotomist and hospital and methadone clinic and prison

He thinks all his pain and wisdom still stocked away
in that pawnshop transistor radio kept on that little
night table next to the lonely solitary queen-sized
bed at *The Jack London* in Portland, Oregon
a scenic view of the alley when they
still had junkies and drag queens
who added a slight touch of class
and ambiance to the community

They're stoning all the little people living in the snowglobe
who are just trying to mind their own business on the dusty
shelves of the pawnshop at dusk. A little later on out will come
the older men and freaks from the peepholes of the steam baths
right next door to those goblet flasks of midnight-blue and forget-
me-not purple potions in the twinkling sundown pharmacy windows

So much to forgive and forget in rippling trail of echoing foghorns
There's a love letter he's been meaning to write for so damn long

People always like to put down rock-bottom
to criticize and glamorize and make too much
of rock bottom; for me I've always preferred it
and liked it better and everything it had to offer

the views and scene and senses so much more acute and
felt more comfortable and so much more detail-oriented

Tonight hope the tree frogs will drag me into their garden

Shaggy laid-out on kitchen counter, contorted, broken-hearted
eyes bulging, with hand up to God, Jewish/Sicilian style from
the old neighborhood like god come on can you just give me
a break? Can you give me something? Can I get a witness?

In the madness of it all all you can do is drop to your knees
and bend your head over your kid's bath and with his big blue
sparkling magical eyes and mop of dirty-blonde hair pours his
watering can of water over your head and with bubbles all over
me starts cracking-up hysterically. This is the only real cure for
a mad scientist and the only thing that can heal him. There are
little salmon candles in the midnight-blue candle holders on
the sill and you look up to the turquoise sky and a fog coming
in from the farm. Shaggy now leans like he's semi-retired against
the shells with a candle lit in the dark kitchen and a dryer which spins

She tells me—

"Last night a Chinese kid just showed up in the backyard.
He popped his head over the fence and asked if he could
play; his name was Vincent and his dad was a scalloper.

He refereed the two other boys wrestling…

I retort—

"Tonight Word Girl was in the land of Boogie Oogie-Oogie.
I left my bed and walked down the hall like Frankenstein"

To the land of no worries
relying on painkillers
and martinis—

"Baby, I'll leave the lights on, please wake me…"

VIII. The Railroad Flowers

1

My wife
picking
wild
flowers
alongside
the railroad
said they're
all about
to go so
wouldn't
be a problem
and placed them
in a summer vase
whose portrait
and profile
reminds
us to
not to
remember
to forget
and to forget
to remember
both just
as equally
important

1 ½

To know just before it's all about to come down
in small town it all smells like a gigantic hotdog
that fried chinese wonton with thunder crashing
around the steeple of the cathedral and you sit
in your car like some bizarre undercover staking
out bonnie and clyde and dillinger still not sure
of the signals knowing deep down inside none
of that really matters waiting for wife and child
outside the movie theater and some great big

bulging edward hopper pale-yellow sea captain's
mansion with gigantic bay windows for phantoms
at the end of the alley and young pretty high school
teenage ticket taker poking her head out every so often
from the crack of the crackerjack alley door to take a smoke
and when the lightning cracks sneaks her way out the creaking
front door to take some serious curious look up there like tesla
the first real original discoverer of electricity who never got his
just due and paid his dues and faded into oblivion like all the
pleasant contented bums do with absolutely nowhere to go
and now roam through this depressed new england town

fathers come to pick up their clean-cropped sons from the matinee
drop-dead daughters with pure hope in their eyes drive through in pickup
trucks heading home with still something to look forward to in this world

2

Buckets of rain pouring
past the blue spruces
of the library window
it's times it's afternoons
like these where you feel
at your most comfortable
your most at ease
with those holy haunted
victorians embedded
in the mountains
winding staircases
& attics climbing
up to the foggy
tumbling heavens
& ground-round
of muffled trains
in the background
carrying granite
from town to town
& the bums & freaks
& madmen at their
computers claiming

contracted work
for the secret service
& young girls trying
their seductions on
for size (like home
work assignments
seeing what guys...)
then lifting long legs
climbing back on bikes
& vanishing in the rain
deliberately never to be
heard from or seen from
again again who was it
who said freud think it
was in his *civilization*
& its discontents
having to do all
this repressing
& role-playing
just in order
to function
in a dysfunctional
society or do i may
be/have that backwards
probably where all neuroses
and defense-mechanisms
and obsessive-compulsive
come from yet all kind of
(ir)relevant as fucked-up
and comes out the exact
same way and eventually
find yourself daydreaming
your life away of viewing
your ashes on your kitchen
window sill with nowhere
to go and nothing to do
still later on you'll
put tchotchkes
& cactuses
out on the
wraparound
to give them

a good wash
down in the
downpour
with a view
of the forest
entranced
at last under
the influence
& dominated
by the echoes
& tremors
of thunder

2 ½

Wrestling son
inside outdoor
thunderstorm

after mom sees us
wandering through
town in her pickup

with his spider
man galoshes
off splashing

through only
the really deep
puddles climbing

the steep hills
with pencil like
steeples looming

over the hills
of his school
a sign stuck

to the fence
reads all the
sleigh rules

3

Wild blonde-haired cherubs
with library books opened up
over their heads like roofs to
a pagoda run through the rain
after mother with an umbrella
not too dissimilar than a duck
and her bright-eyed ducklings

3 ½

After watching
sunday morning
tv with the kid
you think you
hear "rain to fall on
the wolf in vermont
expected t-storms
rest of the week, vegas"
and just sit down there
on the little black sofa
in the kitchen transfixed
looking out to the backyard
forest and wonder where
does the owl go when
it starts to come down?

4

In the dusk
with a couple

of extra bucks
will get *house of tang*
& watch all the pretty
& young classy blonde
ladies of vermont (pure
vibrant down-to-earth
almost old-fashioned
filled with hope
also a little lust
which in more
ways than not
makes them
complete and
of course to die for)
returning home from work
over narrow industrial bridges
and you try to find the train station
for reasons completely opposite
but for reasons more times
than not actually quite similar

4 ½

You imagine fantasize reality-based
those pretty young ladies who plant
themselves outside the *price chopper*
with cardboard signs below mountain
asking for support and think later on
what would be so wrong to return
and like offer them ten, fifteen,
twenty bucks if they just allow me
to give them one long-lasting kiss
no making out no touching body
parts just some last desperate
fantastic kiss after ten years
of marriage and then return
them back to their spot
and head back home
along the river

5

I'm still
hungover
defenses
down
soul numb
heart open
from running
away so many
times so long ago
staying at little motel
at the end of the tracks
at the end of the world
with the only sound
the spare (the bare)
sound of splendid
blaring trainwhistle
in the background
those long empty halls
and not a soul around
like the final bastion
for runaways and bums
and the closest you will
ever come to the concept
of blessed solitude what
it feels like to love
to have lost love
as if stoned alive
and made it though
the living dead
ruminating
reflective
rundown
seeing
through
all the lies
the only
soul
survivor
only living
kid alive

out there
in there
self-aware
on the outskirts
of reno, nevada

5 ½

Half-crazed
half-sane families
with their steamy
navy-blue windows
stuffed into whitewashed
alleys who just plop down
there trying to sneak peeks
with cockeyed views
waiting for the parade
to come on through
& not sure if it
really ever does
& suddenly hear a
whole hell of a lot
of mad hollering
& not sure where
it's coming from
the floats or
the madmen
& not sure
if in truth
if in falsehood
any that really matters
you think also besides
just having those all too
familiar & formal floats
from like the police benevolent
society or the historical society
or society of pipers or society
of masons which all have felt
sincerely more so like forms
of social & cultural alienation

& brainwash & manipulation
should have one for husbands
who cheat on their wives
mean-spirited & malicious
alienating wasp women
whose husbands pay
no attention to them
recovering alcoholic
& dope addicts
with relapses
every so often
& then feel like
really got some
thing to root for

6

Convict convicted of being a convict
no different than any seductive
manipulative bitch in her ball
room gown on the bail
bondsmen corner

her hourglass figure
which measures the minutes
of your mortality and helps time
to go by quicker (which is the great
thing about love & lust & women) as if
it naturally thankfully never even existed.

they bury them late out here
on the weekend at dusk
and the farmers
look far better
in their suits
(not in a sexual
way far classier).

after some long hot day
your wife picks up two
big bottles of seltzer
with some sale on
german bologna

as the convicts head back
to their dusty downtown
ramshackle apartments
past the procession

of miserable high maintenance
wannabe aristocrats in their
evening gown processions.

the red hair girls are to die for
and a girl just in her softball uniform
blushing cheeks and cleats as if after
some war wanders down main street
aimless and lost with absolutely nowhere
to go but in a strange sense a sense of
belonging right around that age of
being self-conscious and demure

you waiting for some father figure
finally to simply put his palm
on your shoulder and go–

"it gets no easier"
as you fade away
in your midnight basement
glancing through screen
door down to the forest

6 ½

I love how my wife
crosses the tracks
to the good side
and steals very

formally planted
flowers orchids
hibiscus around
historical plaques
and monuments
being a good-natured
girl from the bronx
and tells the kid
keep the car running
and how she just
naturally rationalizes
(her rational lies...)
saying such spirited
things like they were
wilting and you telling
her those weren't
the ones you were
supposed to take
but her pleasantly
denying not listening
to a word you're saying
and blowing you off
(she loves me
she loves me not?)
and arranges them
very precisely
and thoughtful
in the vase
of our back
yard porch
looking out
to the forest
before the storm

7

-we ran into gabriel at the playground and they threw crabapples

-had a pocketful of waterballoons

-and showed us the long slide and said it was bad in the winter

-and gave us a whole list of the meanteachers

-i'm gonna go tomorrow to talk to the principal

-he said sometimes his mother lets him ride his bike before supper

7 ½

Do crows grow in the rain?
their silhouettes?
their brains?

8

Mountains stretching out panoramic
endless and engulf and encompass
you like some ethereal clothesline
permeating the deep blue heavens
as nothing else matters and don't
care where you end up here or there
as you dip through the fomenting clouds
and don't care if you ever come out again

8 ½

I prefer rodin
when he put
down his
hammer
& chisel
& was
eating his
oscar
meyer

bologna
& cheese
sandwich
in the hot
scorching
sun of
rome
ruined
some
where
around
the ruins
of roam

9

Alcatraz
these days
seems like
the pot of gold
at the end of the rainbow

9 ½

Where are
the saints
(are coming)
the saints
(are coming)
they promised
taking off with
ears popping
and vanishing
off into the obscure
just cause you hurt
does not not make
you strong matter
of fact in fact

just all a bunch
of little punks
playing roles
people these
days just seem
way too sure of
themselves and
resemble to me
more so idiots
and assholes
remember
the scene
of the crime
came before
and not after

10

Je ne sais pas
should be translated
into every language
(all fucken cell phones
should be gotten rid of!)
and put on flash cards
like bob dylan and his
subterranean homesick
blues with allen ginsberg
in the alley gonna rent
one of those mobile
homes on the river
for the weekend
and zoom off
with my wife
to quebec city

10 ½

Dawstoievsky with your wicked & wonderful & o.c.d. intense
sense of humor! jean genet king & queen of the saints & thieves!
rimbaud madboy genius runaway of the parisian suburbs & country!
baudelaire who rebelled & turned away from the cheap superficiality
of aristocracy & into the filthy beautiful spleen of the city! jean-paul
sartre with your constant bouts & episodes of anxiety & nausea of
which of course i am completely sympathetic & trust me there's no one
more who gets it! proust i envy you who wrote all of *remembrances* from
the plush mattress of your queen-sized bed with news & views of the
vagabonds & seductresses in the dusty carnivals of paris & your maid
primping your pillows & bringing you tea & crumpets & helping you
literally re-copy & paste the edits! albert camus peek-a-boo! where the
hell are you! i'm feeling just as lost & down in the dumps & blue as you
& look up through my bleak dusty skylight every once in awhile not just
to spy a sign of the weather & falling rain & snow & pinecones & lowly
elevated influences of lightning & thunder or to instinctively know that
i exist not just because i think therefore i am but also feel just as alive
if not more from the visceral & peripheral senses which brings it all
together & helps me to instantly identify forget all the lies & nihilism
& dread & hope even more for you to show up like some awkward
slapstick comedian crawling like some super hero cat burglar cary grant
inspector clouseau maybe even young adolphe menjou old humphrey
bogart character across my slanted window just one lost & forgotten
missing action evening like that derelict/delinquent cat-calling thief
huckleberry for buddy t. sawyer in the whee hours of one of those
deep southern fried sweltering mysterious mischievous magnolia
midnights just to make life & existence seem alright & just to
get by & more relevant & bearable & worth living

11

You also keep it
open for the blaring
lightning & thunder
for the rain pouring down
through the pine & maple
& hope to go out that way
when deep in slumber

as no one would know
like you used to go
to movie theaters
as a poor young soul
feeling comforted
by the tremors
of trembling
thunder rumbling
around the doors
& like back then
be exactly both
the hero & villain
in one of those
insane creaking
westerns when
the weather
came in

11 ½

Wild tomatoes
woven in & out the fences
which divide the river & railroad
& humid holy wild apples whose
boughs hang over like an alcove
& will soon fall from the heat
into the shadows like little
treasure troves there for
solitary contemplation
the beginning & end
of arrested stages
of development
like the wild boys
on skateboards
literally picking
up all the pretty
tomboys of the
town turned-out
turned down
turned away

from their homes
wild as hell looking
to settle down
like the once
wild out of
control
bad boy now
all dressed-up
like a soldier
not exactly
reformed
leaning
up against
the brick wall
of afternoon alley
& trying to sweet talk
all the naturally radiant
edward hopper girls to die for
as if growing from all the dust
& folklore of the town & mountains
apparently falling for their uniforms

12

Boys in their bloody aprons
just hanging out, drained
exhausted, silent, solemn
self-effacing with nothing
left to say, looking as
if they have all strayed
pensive and ruminating
taking cigarette breaks
taking long drags
on the windswept
splintered steps
of a fading day
right by great big
rolled-up piled-up
stacks of wood
& barrels of beer

stored in the back
of true-blue broken
back yard brick
warehouse porches
located directly across
the huff & puff muffled
now you see 'em now 'ya
don't wailing train tracks
which secretly delivers
granite from town
to town which
secretly stretches
to endless destinations
through the miraculous
gorges & valleys & rivers
& mountains through the corn
& apple orchards where they give
warnings of bear & moose & ice & wind
& rocks falling & give a peek out of the side
of your eye every so often to the desolate parts
all the way out there in north country up into kanada

12 ½

Strange elfin-faced delinquents
far more sacred than any of those tourists
or evil mean-spirited (who try to steal spirit)
parasitic witches cool casual cruise their pickups
looking always messed-up on-the-run from the slums
through the hush-a-bye lawns no one really knows everyone
knows them down that long stretch of mad verdant wilderness
and rumbling road which divides the foothills of the mountains
and rundown river rambling through the mysterious magical town

13

I have become infatuated
with herculean clapboard
weather-worn haunted houses
(nothing haunted about them)
with their massive rundown
heaving skeletons stuck out
leering down on all of the town
and mountains (a moon pleasantly
beaming blotted balanced on its
broad shoulders behind the clouds)
from way atop impossibly steep lawns
impossible to mow (saw a guy the other
day dragging his lawnmower methodically
back and forth from on top the hill like some
mechanical fisherman with a rope attached
to the throttle like some insane brilliant
ingenious routine & ritual up & down
up & down up & down up & down)
radiant young dreaming college girls flirting
with me from a distance searching for love
(where was i so many decades ago and seem
to like me a little more being something of
a decent good looking dad) drifting in cars
on top of plateaus like the pale heads of
sprinkler systems and myself ducking
under the bent boughs of crab apple
trees as really what else can one do
but take it all in and be flattered
and simply live for the moment

13 ½

Live for that
whole mess of
dappled apples
having tumbled
off the branches
into the gutter

into puddles
sailing free
and wild like
a runaway child
down the holy hill
after the downpour
to the blissful
insane oblivion
of delicate heaven

14

D. and i debating on the tracks
about the 7 continents myself
convinced greenland is one
of them; he says daddy it
isn't and we go back and
forth and he retorts
well what about cuba?
with the deductive
logic that it's an
island as well
and i go hmmm...
dylan that's a very
good point and turns
out my eight year old
son is right and i am
wrong which does
the body good
and we head
home up
the steep
slope
through
the short
cut at dusk

14 ½

Buddhist blues absolutely nothing left to do
but lay out strewn in my steaming room
watching *green mountain cable* and some
of the most gorgeous dropdead girls
voicing their college taught issues
debating taser guns giving ins
& outs on farmer's markets
& how to act & function
& what & what not to purchase
& how to speak to a farmer
& barter vegetables
while the rest
of the leftover
choir slouching
around the table
seem strangely
sad & silent
& uptight
& frustrated
like sexless
sexually-
repressed
porn stars
looking for
the next punchline
& promised land
& for the cause
of global warming
climb up long
sky-blue ribbons
backwards
like one of those
strip club poles
to sky-blue sky
in lovely leotards
doing very erotic
& seductive
& symbolic
moves that only
college girls can do

& the whole audience
giving a(rousing)
round of applause
really dreaming of
them in far more
compromising
& controversial
positions
in the middle
of the lawn
on the stately
state capitol

15

Construction workers hard-working humble just minding
their own in the scorching summer digging up bones right
outside the golden dome & the barber inside the hotel
& clan of curious boys & of course that one token girl
magically moving from bench to bench as the day grows
old & that same old eccentric man with pipe & paunch
smoking on the corner of the library & cathedral

15 ½

Construction girl
in her hard hat
with chiseled
cheekbones
real hard
worked
brooding blue eyes
and blonde hair
and bronzed
and tanned
and sun-burned
from the scorching sun
it seems like no one seems

to care or give a damn so damned
solemn and damaged and reflective
radiantly silent out of class and culture
and customs kept down keeping it all in
taking a long sincere drag while holding
that sign all day which simply reads *slow*
sad, somnolent, going with the flow with
mad heart and soul feeling eternally ignored
you happen to run into her every other day
in this small town of a city of pity and take
secret sneak peeks from the side of your eye
knowing you shouldn't be and her knowing
you are which is the whole holy fantasy
folklore of it all like the perfect portrait
always just a little out of reach
mournful and seductive
always a bit of a thief

16

Those gorgeous glowing
edward hopper girls
delightful, demure
in their store-bought
window display
pretty print
dresses stroll
beautiful blushing
blow diner pharmacy
corner on the corner
of the covered bridge
and redemptive raging river
oblivious to the miraculous
sunshower coming down
on them like mermaids
seductively stretching
on the corner
of course
without a doubt
knowing exactly

what they're doing
with logging trucks
tankers filled with fresh
cow's milk straight from
the horse's mouth bowing
down on heavenly dairy
farms rumbling past pink
houses and madmen and
hitch hikers and old ancient
new england libraries where
you can still see clear through
to the looming secret velvet
portholes of gold copper
shingled haunted and holy
victorians sitting flush up against
the lush make-believe mountains
so they stroll over those narrow
rundown sundown bridges
over rivers which run through
town bulging burgeoning from
days and days of rain hugging
rising up right against the red
brick walls of factory buildings
barrooms and old time movie
theaters and beauty parlors
and barbers literally in short
shorts with smooth creamy
milky-white legs lanky
crazy sucking on their
lollies (lord knows
where the parents
are but who in
the hell really cares
and why would any
of that really matter?)
the monster still cringing
crouching clutching right
onto the dusty charcoal
bell of the belfry looking
down on it knowing it all

16 ½

There is nothing more
(self) soothing and healing
than the nature and beauty
and configuration of a woman's body
to a man who has lived a life of crime
more accurately stated crime of living

17

Every
time
i ever
disrobed
unclothed
some girl
i always
felt this awful
strange mixed-up
feeling of guilt and pleasure
but didn't seem so much
them as always appeared
to go straight for the gusto
right into their fantasy world
wild absolutely no conflict at all

17 ½

How wildflowers
along the railroad
grow like the shapes
of a seductive woman
posing and taking off
her clothes unlatching
lowering and dropping
her towel and bathrobe
coming out of the shower

petals blowing off flowers
getting ready for ceremonies
in the wild dusk of summer

18

Just a place
to be left alone
to cum and die
and bleed like jesus
on fresh clean sheets
and not be discovered
until like a day later
distant disheveled
finally at last found
the long-lost stranger
when they wipe away
the stars & constellations
from your faraway expression
from the crevices & cornices
of the wraparound porches
of victorians & haunted
houses of the bums
& madwomen
who reside
on the border
of the wilderness
& lost civilization
with steep sleepy hills
which creep & tumble
& wind & stumble
through the schools
& steeples through
the cathedral bells
going off exactly
on the hour 1,2,3,
bong! bong! bong!
& the leftover
dew & drizzle
of lost & lazy

lullabies finally
at last dividing
the dream from
the nightmare
the mean stare
from those truly
sincere & self-aware
the guilt from mythology
the rape from drapes of reality

18 ½

So isn't it strange in the very end
all you care about is the muffled
wail of freight trains through

your ruffled curtains
that sway and swoon
with the spirit & beat

& rhthym of the wind
with the secret streaming
scent of sweet forest smoke

creeping in
through sun
down crack

in your window
in the transition
from seasons

from the stray see ya'
lata' summer to the settling
savior cooling-off of autumn

a beautiful
and bountiful
you're surrounded

screaming of distant freight
trains like some long-lost
soulmate & companion

always around you
you thankfully can't
and wouldn't wanna

get rid of
even if your
life depended…

IX. The Bones Of Buddha

Beatific geek freak pushes his long train of supermarket carts
in & out from the parking lot and into the super stop & shop
as this rhythmic routine & ritual all day long makes him feel
like he belongs makes him feel content whether he knows
it or not (which is what it's all really about & to want not)

So is the old timer with his paunch & suspenders pushing
his lawnmower down the sidewalk focused & disoriented

So are the visions of past radiant girlfriends from the deep whispering
hissing country mostly those redheads of delicate & different shapes
& sizes just showing up as mirages alongside the railroad making
him ephemerally contented just like the seasons which penetrate
all the bullshit & pettiness & brutality & cruelty of human nature

So is the railroad which runs through heaven as well
& only makes the local stops & slows to a crawl
through pastures & rivers & villages & forests
& winds through hills balanced up on top the pinnacle
& vanishes like magic to the holy unknown final forgotten

So is the brilliant leper-like towering sycamores
spotted & historic with surrounding ruffled lace
curtain pachysandra which makes it all beautiful
& bearable & gusts of wild whipping wind
which tugs back & forth through the trees
muffled rumble of distant trains of the suburban
evening while not sure if it's the local or breeze

So are the blasts of seasons & seasons & seasons & seasons!
& all those details & elements which come along with them
the only thing in the whole wide world which can save him

So is the distant creaking forest which sounds exactly like
a creaking door & creaking porch & creaking floorboards

So is the old man who strolls with teacup & saucer
through rusted bedsprings discarded in his garden
some ghostly soldier sleepwalking through carnage

So is the town drunk who is content & content (not to feel)

So is the hustler & junkie & seductress & gigolo

So is the angel-slut from the disco

So is the madwoman in the booth of the drive-in

So is the hitman with nothing to do and nowhere to go

So are the hitch hikers and man who is desperate
and lonely and just needs some fleeting companions
to exchange stories and make his life worth living

So are fragrant flowers & smoking forests
which stream past his window & makes it
pop all that much more & much more surreal
& brings back his whole anguished attention-
seeking, blissful, cotton-pickin' childhood

So is ex-convict and ex lover
meeting up at the boxcar diner
somewhere between the midnight
& constellations below stapled
silhouette of the mountain

So is the phantom in the window of windswept
old brick new england bed & breakfast
restless, reflective & silhouetted

So is the rushing river gurgling alongside the depressed
missing-in-action mill town, ravaged, rundown, raging,
radiant, always has been, always will & surges & spills
all things spiritual & for that reason (if that's what you
call it) & that reason alone never need be questioned

So is the pristine whitewashed library which sits
like a cathedral and the cathedral like a library

So is the whole town whitewashed in rain
after the insane storms come washing all
the shit away storming from the heavens
cleansing redemptive and getting rid of
all the filth & devils turning everything
perfect & pristine haunted & holy again

So are the madmen & the hikers & the burnouts
who hang out with hangovers hung out
to dry on their porch all day

So are the mountain men secretly meeting up
on the mountain with nothing much nor a hell
of a lot to tell as their eyes tell you all and so much
more than all those you never ever wanted to know before

So are the very wealthy blonde girls
who stroll along the perfectly manicured
grounds & fields of their boarding school
seducing & already searching for husbands
on the lacrosse & rugby fields (who
will never have a fighting chance)

So are the widows in their garden
& firemen in gleaming red trucks

So are the strange women with straightened hair
done just a little too staunch with a hot comb or one
of those eggs you sit under in the town beauty salon

So is the simple general store which sits nestled
on the lake in the woods always a saint always a savior

So are the groomed yaks just roaming back & forth
without a thought on gentlemen farm farmland
from the mountains to the white picket fences

So are the cows
who sit solemn & alone
without a worry in the world
not just for storms but also dense fog

So is the beating palpitating heart
of the ladybug taking in the sun

So are the warm splintered paddles
whose reflections have been hypnotically
drip-dropping eternal water since time began

So are the fables of the madmen & their moms & dads
which never seem to change (nor anything back then
& everything straight ahead) 'cause that's all we
got to hold onto which is the straight-up blues

So is that mute motel in the shape of a horseshoe
at the foot of the foothills & beat down & blessed
chinese & bowling alley & cemetery beneath the stars

So is that old time movie theatre always
with those crooked cockamamie letters
looking like they're constantly about to
fall off & tumble giving it its character

So is all the spirit & memories of moments & time
& moment in time experienced in all things in life

So is that pretty spirited tomboy girl
blowing up her big red balloon right below
true-blue world war II cannon on a sunday afternoon

So are the cherubs playing by the lake all day
putting their stake in minnows & tadpoles

So is the lone egret patient reflective
standing all alone on the marshy shore
looking out in wonder at the lone swan
minding his own and paddling the pond

So are the new-born mini butterflies just come to life
bright orange & be speckled who sail like feathers
flitting along the trails without a care in the world

So is the country dog pleasantly and passionately proud
head down sniffing dewy dandelions keeping on the trail

So are blue-gray rabbits with snowy-white tails
just come out of their holes after a long winter's
season playfully dodging and chasing each other
like delinquent brothers in and out of the brambles

So is the sudden crash of rambling thunder, radiant, resplendent
meandering in & out the mountains reminding the lone swimmer
to come in but doesn't quite convince him & does the opposite
& inspires him & makes him only swim out that much further
like a prisoner just let out of prison getting reacquainted with all
those elements he had been missing & had missed out on for so
long *craaaaaaash! (waz that?) muuuuuuudha! brudduddda! booo—udha!*
like some spiritual song from the gods & looks forward to the
cursed blessed fate that it might possibly bring on then some
sudden secret breeze sweeping through the gloom & doom of
darkening sundown snaking swamp lagoon then down it comes

So are the peepers who always surround your home
after the rains come down right before the night falls
without even knowing keeping you from feeling so alone

So is the call of nightbirds right around dusk
who you will never ever really get to know
but whose transcendent spirit and warble
you know better than any living soul

and menagerie of echoes
appear to protect & bandage
like a mummy getting ready
for the afterworld the only words
which mean a single thing to him

So are those old grumpy bullfrogs creaking their choruses
from rusty rocking chairs somewhere between the lake
house and lagoon beneath the bust of a beat-up moon
like some slow suspended game of ping pong
between a dope addict and his muse

So is the spirit of the sunken old dutch colonials
right along the same border between the prairie
and shore which used to hold sons and their first
love budding daughters in their polka-dotted bikinis
frolicking free as can be beneath eternal shadowy
valleys of indian bone evergreen mountains

So is the last old timer simply dreaming
in the ashes & cinders of a burntdown
revolutionary war inn & tavern

So is the silhouette of those *whoops johnny*
whoops johnny midnight-blue mountains

So is the remains of poor road kill
who just didn't quite make it
whose spirit is still stirring
more sacred & vibrant
than any supposed
human being

So are those glowing nocturnal creatures
of the deep-dark forest like amphibians
creeping from the ocean to the swamp

somewhere between that stage of evolution
& existence to how we now know it
how we never wanted to know it

& want to regress back
to the wilderness

X. A Reenactment Of Waking Life:
stanzas of the season and notes of a misanthrope

1

what if jesus had made it?

2

i want to be buried in a casket
in the shape of the fetal position

3

i want to go
down as one
of the greatest
mad scientists
of all time having
found and discovered
when they open me up
really got the soul of an
angel suffering from mounds
of self-destruction and back-
up of brainwash mixed-up
from a very subtle more like
awfully obscene and obvious
emotional spiritual neglect
not a put-down perhaps
the reality and criteria
and having to had to
constantly act-out
just to assert and
figure out my identity
and ego without even
knowing it on-the-run
from lord knows what
looking over my shoulder
for that pot of gold
at the end of
the rainbow

4

what it feels like your whole life
to be manipulated and cheated
how can you not help but to be
come something of a thief
romantic criminal
hustler comedian?

5

when will
amerika be run
by a bodhisattva
by some good
ol' gigantic
holy-moly
grand poobah
sacred mock buddha
nodding out on heroin
up on top the mountain
with terrible tourists
going up to worship
and going down as
shaman no shame
man *nocturnes*
by chopin
and when
the sun
goes down
finally at last
now in shadow
silhouetted
no longer
awful horrible
instant judges
of alienation
while all you
hear are the wind
chimes at dusk

in the hush of
amen alley
haunted
chinese
restaurant

6

everything you fought against
everything you railed against
all that resistance and
acting-out and active-
rebellion shit from
juvenile delinquent
childhood were all
the true-blue truths
(used against you)

7

on the nature
of culture
& civilization
i look inside
my refrigerator
and it simply
reads "cold
colder…"

8

i look into cup
board at all
the shot
glasses and
cocktail glasses

wife has ripped
off from barrooms
and cocktail lounges
and casually mention
"don't you agree things
stolen have the most
meaning" she simply
ignores me and blows
me off and is the
exact answer i am
looking for as i do
have a past history
and well she is from
the boogie down bronx
and looking back
at those times it
really does hold
the deepest
meaning
greatest
sense of
belonging

9

a man must be a man
must be a madman
who wears many
hats to keep up
with his wife's
moods 'blue mood,
you saw me standing
alone, without a dream
in my heart, without a love
of my own...' i always loved
those films and real-life situations
where the main character was faced
with multiple challenges and had to dig
and build and burrow his way to freedom
through some escape tunnel, the twilight

zone, escape from alcatraz, vegas, valley
of the kings, egypt, the holy land of israel

10

tv projects an 'archetypal image'
but what happens when that image
is simplistically repetitive and cookie-
cutter about violence and war and
the end of the world and not sure
if it's a video game, movie (a film
gone straight to dvd, blue-ray or
hd) a commercial or the news
made to instantly shock you
'pull you in' as if any of that
would really matter anymore?

11

infamous infomercial man found dead
from an apparent drug overdose known
(never quite known, better seen and not
heard, or vice-versa) as the marilyn monroe
of stain remover & pressure cookers survived
by his fellow spokesmen & telemarketers
for erectile dysfunction, hip-hop aerobics
& late-night cubic zirconia while projected
archetypal image has been flown back to
beverly hills mansion through the static of
not fully-satisfied, guaranteed money back
broadcast towers, blinking & blaring at half-
mast to that fictional, existential, never-never
land, never quite glanced by a woman, child
or man in king of prussia, pennsylvania where
all great ideas & inventions hail from some
where between the sweet smell of success
& stench of failure reeking of that persistent
stray, pungent swathe of cocaine, baking

powder & household detergent, cut, sliced
& diced, broken-down & built-up by those
grandiose up & coming cut-throat entrepreneurs
not too far from the heart of the historical district
of distant hidden meth labs (you do the math)
where residents dare not speak up or speak
out out of fear of retribution or payback some
where between the cracked bell & belltower
in the higher than holy hysteria of these here
united states of america where paul revere
is isolating (perhaps even feigning) suffering
from a situational depression & social phobia
being quarantined from the status-quo, having
contracted a very secretive serious case of ebola

12

when roosevelt gave those news footage speeches
in a can of peaches in the back of aircraft carriers
used to think what gigantic kid could have put
that together and must have had a hell of a lot
of rubber cement:: f.d.r. always with that long
svelte cigarette reminding you of the penguin
from batman with his sidekick churchill who
resembled the eternal and irrepressible
w.c. fields and how could anyone possibly
beat them tough luck for the other side
as hitler played by chaplin that sad
sack poor little tramp never had
a fighting chance while not by
coincidence sent back black-
listed to his homeland england
by McCarthy and his paranoid
clan of henchmen after everything
he had done for them:: when roosevelt
gave that final rousing speech for his
4th inauguration they said it was as brief
and as brilliant as the forefather of our
country george washington and in my
opinion sounded exactly in rhythm

and timber and eloquence like
the good ol' t.s. eliot:: you mutter
your man-made mantras code of
survival mechanisms which has
gotten you through the toughest
of times at your midnight edward
hopper window with the moon
beaming off the geometric lines
of the roof of the barn in your back
yard:: jesus trembles and with all their
lies and betrayals have made a spiritual
connection to know all's quiet on the
western homefront all been crucified

13

memo: think about it almost every
great modern tragedy happened
(and could have been avoided)
from a certain type of ignorance
and complacency (absurd
and asinine state of non-
urgency) global warming,
the world trade center,
training those madmen
down in the lone star
state, airport security,
school shootings, the
titanic, hindenburg,
all those rum &
coke cruises from
the costa-concordia
to the staten island ferry,
the holocaust, the purges,
korea, vietnam, to our
most recent venture into
the theater of the absurd
out in iraq & aghanistan
like some where's waldo
search for weapons

of mass-destruction
believing we could
turn a military
dictatorship
into a feasible
& functional
jeffersonian
democracy,
every genocide,
every atrocity,
presidencies,
assassinations
from a to z...

14

i'm not sure what's worse?
        (horse dragging a hearse)

delivering them like spam
        & sardines in a can

                in *pan-am's*
                   & *amtracks*

        cross-country
     after they whacked
lincoln & kennedy

        or long-term
terminal character
assassination
of obama?

    who was that other president they took out?
was it mckinley?

        what did he do wrong
& what did he do for a living?

                    did they name one of those
            long brick schools
        in the late-sixties

in the split-level
        edifice wrecks suburbs
                            after him?

15

where i live up on
top of the mountain
top is a *walmart*
and what it means
to reach the top
of the mountain
top is going
to that spot
and does be
come some
ting of a
pavlov's
dog every
time i got
to head
up there
they also got
a new psych
iatric hospital
and emergency
room and *howard
johnson* and *t.g.i.f.*
so whatever mood
i'm in or whatever
shape i find myself
in seems like
the perfect place
to take myself
out to that
walmart

on top of
the mountain
top and those
other parts
depending
on my base
line of moods
and behaviors
and whatever
kind shape
i find my
self in

16

the hardest thing is rolling out of bed
in the morning without hitting the floor
trying to figure out ways of rolling back in
(suffering from bouts of melancholia how
come they don't use expressions like that
anymore? seems so much more apropros)

17

know the only thing which ever gets me up
is that big blinding ball of sun which beams
straight through my blinds and goes right
to my soul like some kid who's
been picked on way too much
and turns into one of those
super heroes smack
dab in the middle
of bleak burnt-out
nowhere postmodern
blasee stripmall america

radar coming in from the tv towers
& ancient mythological heroes of old

18

what happened to those good
ole elizabethan days when
people threw themselves
onto their swords
like shish-ka-bob?

"well i used to love her
but it's all over now..."

19

who invented the bugzapper?
the deviled egg platter?
the pie-eating contest?
the pig races?
jellybeans stuffed
in jelly jars displayed
in pharmacy windows
for contests & lotteries?
the flush-faced alkie
running the carousel
down by the beach?
the life insurance salesman?
the bible & vacuum cleaner
salesman showing up
from door to door?

20

that expression "extra-marital affair?"
instant divorces lickety-split in vegas?
tassels & sequins of topless dancers
& desperate & pathetic businessmen
both just as lost & faceless
looking to make their
final stand?

21

that phrase "all-inclusive"
suddenly turning peasants
into aristocrats no matter
the class or background?

22

wonder if man on the moon
ever looked down through
the blinds of my window
searching for faith too
(or more accurately
blues, blessings,
prayers, mantras)
and something
to hold onto?

23

that kid who ran away to the circus
how come nothing's been written
about his return trip or where
he is and his status or was it
just pure david copperfield
and bartelby the scrivener?

#24

perhaps billy the kid
rummaging through
old love letters, then
stuffing them back in
that kid safe you got
for chanukah (sp?)

with that sandwich
bag of bb's and
unused rubber
guess the relics
from boyhood you
cherish and treasure

25

there's this really weird and fucked-up
paradox and contradiction in america
(used to never be this way) but these
days all those so-called cool and hip
areas are only the people who can
afford to be there; multi-millionaires
and if you dare enter there give you a stare
like who are you and you don't belong there

starving artists who don't seem particularly hungry
(who me? you god-duh be kidding! i've done and seen
it all and can assure you *you* are the mistaken identity!)

26

don't know never ever got into the whole poetry performance
thing, not exactly sure why, as maybe just appeared a little too
much of a shtick or who you know, or more so all in the phony
and flamboyant delivery and emotion of it all as opposed to the
substance and true-blue suffering and experience you had to
endure to get it all down on paper or having to be part of some
kind of conformist culture or group of writers and exclusive
self-entitled collective who give awards and trophies to each
other 'cause they know each other (of course never having
had to do with any sort of real angst or alienating or pain
or suffering nor having to go it alone in more ways than
not hitting the road) and everyone and their mother and
little clique and group cheering them on so it really was

not so much a conspiratorial thing or having anything
to do with a social phobia just could never get into it
so much, and only imagined doing so like a good ole
young miles back in the day with his back turned from
the audience or something real half-crazed and dramatic
like some old rival or girlfriend suddenly showing up
from my past, screaming something rather absurd and
radical, demonstrative and significant and trying to make
an assassination attempt and me dodging it as have always
had good street instincts, but really appreciating their efforts
and conviction and having earned a whole new round of respect
for them going out for a beer with them after the whole affair ended

27

we used to hang out and lean up
against the nuclear plant in winter
smelling the warm bread from red

brick chimneys of the bread factory
silhouetted in the evening lying flush
against the mountains through the alley

buzzed in the hush
of the halo of breath
of the holy desolation

of muffled lamplight
and intimate friendships
and close-nit conversation

the whole town wheezing
and sneaking back home
along the wriggling river

28

global warming
"i didn't mean
anything i said"
think that should
be the gravestone
on the planet earth
after everyone's
been put to bed

29

you know with what seems
like these days what we see
over the news with things
& towns constantly breaking down
& an abundance of global warming
& hurricanes & twisters & tornadoes
striking & leveling & knocking-out
the deep & shallow south & bible
belt & heartland & wasteland
along the atlantic ocean
all that neglect & bullshit
& bi-artisan corruption
after the storm hits
i think back to those good ol'
time ancient traveling circuses
with all those misfits & monkeys
& elephants & freaks & runaways
& mad scientists & barkers & soothsayers
& apothecarians as i don't know just felt
so much more innocent & functioned
& got along so much better on so
many different levels as something
really to be said about the simple
things in life while leaving room
open for the imagination

i mean how running away to the circus
felt like a damn fine way to make a living…

30

as such when global warming finally does show
up in all its rare splendor and form i'm gonna
get me one of those *nathan's frankfurters*
…funny i spent a good amount of time and
period of my life out in coney island, brooklyn
isolated, secluded, with my simple, stray, solitary
window on the pounding surf right off surf avenue
after the madness of it all, working the graveyard
hustling a yellow in manhattan (ironic, did survive
that all) but all gotten so damn vulgar and expensive.
they do have another one right in yonkers right next
to *yonkers raceway* where i used to just see those lights
beaming during the sweltering summer evening right
off central avenue like some insane demented coliseum
and all those little alkie jockeys casually leaned back
in their goggles, like rickshaws to the promised land
so yeah think i'm gonna get me my nathan's frankfurter
from there when global warming finally shows up in all
its rare splendor and forms, as used to spend a hell of
a lot of downtime down there in my young adulthood
haunting those *barnes & nobles* when they first came
out, picking out my helping of that madman dostoevsky
and then maybe if i was well-behaved, taking myself out
to *movieland* to see "the goonies;" those were some of my
most meaningful and profound, sentimental and romantic
of times, and wouldn't trade it for all the tea in china
and crime and punishment i found myself getting into

31

i want to suddenly get held up by the pharmacy
with their token stockings over their heads
yet will know exactly who they are as not

particularly swift or streetwise and too
cerebral, as left on their starch-white
smocks with their names on it–"hey
bob is that you? joceyln? angelica?
you're such cards!" and for figuring
out who they are get a month's supply
of percocet and xanax and dice and
jacks and *hershey* bars with almonds

who was it said takes
a wise man to play dumb?

32

why
people
develop
a hankering
for heroin
lox & bagels
loose women
with similar
backgrounds
(trauma/damage)
and experience(s)

33

the queen leaves
her face at the
puppeteer's
difference
between
familiarity
& distance

34

wife heads out to bring in
the halloween decorations
the brussel sprouts and kale
from the november garden
kindling from the barn
the fire and false alarms
going through the motions
as all just comes down to
going through the motions

35

almost every job i apply for
am in so much more need of
like some sorta life skills assistant
you gotta be kidding need myself
one massage local anesthesia
and bong hit and can assure
you every single last one of them
is some all-knowing pompous idiot
good deed-doer straight out of school
don't know their ass from their elbow
enter you in inputted in their computer
with your treatment plan and baseline
and checklist as the targeted client or consumer
already with some pre-packaged language and
short-term and long-term goals which is required
to be met as audited and accountable to the state

"life skills assistant"
need me one of those
yeah, forget about it!

36

as a kid with the whole dim-witted dynamic
and phenomenon of rock bottom how could
you even know it was rock bottom because
you *were* at rock bottom and still had not
yet developed the intellectual prowess or power
to know you were down there so did everything
humanly possible to get out of there and acted-
out and were mad and wild out of a certain sense
of trepidation and fear and dipped down to even
deeper levels to try and make a name for yourself

37

i know this is gonna sound a bit odd
and something of a bizarre metaphor
(but don't think you will once you find
out where i am coming from) but every time
i ever got a girl after all the sacrifice and struggle
strangely enough with all those natural feelings
and emotions of guilt and remorse (far more
i am sure than any sort of matador) and eventual
sort of empty bravado and 'the getting of' and 'the
conquering of' and sacrifice (even a bit of slaughter)
felt just a little less than more 'the killing of the bull'
(wondering if that mad, coy battle was even worth it;
that inane, futile and fun 'going back & forth' testing
of each other's defenses and identity and ego, seeing
how far each one was willing to go) and instead of
that supposed (and symbolic) red cape, her panties
and her bra and all those other accoutrements
and seductive clothes (meant to attract and
'distract' and play possum and hard to get)
found (lost & found) lingering on the floor

38

gargle all the gargoyles
all of fate & existence
& the madness of
the world with a
quart of malt
liquor fatal
charm &
pretty girl

cracking yourself up
couldn't keep your
self out of trouble

becoming a regular
in detention hall

should have gotten my
letter of recommendation

from the monitor who
probably knew me
better than anyone

"awww shucks..".
so says jimi hendrix

#39

my first love the girl i fell in love with was this
beautiful blonde with blue eyes from the rhineland
named andrea she was really smart and rolled cigarettes
and we fell in love with each other and spent evenings
in deep dark taverns drinking beers myself looking pretty
damn decent in my fisherman's sweater and her to die
for then sleeping all night in her basement with snow
drifts coming up around the window. she literally picked
me up while i was taking these long contemplative strolls
through the gorgeous winter wonderland of the suburbs

and was with a french girl and told me they made a bet
whoever i called first i would be their boyfriend i remember
calling her up because i thought she was nicer and kinder
and more attractive from the train station when the mad
snow was coming down before i headed to grand central
all i remember during that time was listening over and over
again to bob dylan's (of course johnny cash) "nashville skyline"
and brooding all day about her and how every day and night
felt what it was like what it was like to live and to die…

40

are we all just surviving living and dying
blocking compartmentalizing from some
breakup for no apparent reason just poor
circumstances and timing from a first
love so long go unholy aware of it?

it's all one big long pathetic
tragic sigh by gabe kaplan
from *welcome back kot-ter*
nihilistic version ("i'm putting
dishes away don't bother me!")

41

see marriage as something sort of delusional
draculian, dr jekyll & mr hyde-like; husbands
and fathers like some leftover wheelbarrow
water-logged in the rain weighed down
with wet soaking leaves by the barn

42

think that famous psychologist eric b. erickson
may have gotten it all wrong or too much of a

good thing and left out a stage from his stages
of growth & development when friends of mine
a little post pre-pubescent started to just naturally
with no apparent precipitant event become bullshit
artists and very driven and single-minded, opportun-
istic and goal-oriented, pretend like you and your
relationship never even existed at all preparing
themselves perfectly for the grownup world

43

"cry uncle! cry uncle!" never understood the origins
and derivation of that statement and why cry uncle
as most uncles i grew up with i liked a lot. was it
that uncle who drove a truck for *the new york times*
out of canarsie, brooklyn who we were always fond of
and always just sat silently alone, modest and humble
in the corner at family get-togethers? was it that uncle
we never knew what he did for a living, probably a bookie
and whenever we saw him, had a transistor to each ear
listening to the mets *and* the yankees? was it that uncle
from oceanside, long island who made a killing and ended
up becoming the district manager for lazyboy down in hot'lanta?
was it that uncle who started out by sweeping flour off the floors
of the bialy factories and ended up becoming a multi-millionaire
and owning a string of pants factories up and down the east coast?
i never understood that statement "cry uncle" and whenever some
overly-physical imbecile or schmuck on wheels or family member
had you in a headlock, twisting your arm behind your back, was
sitting right on top of you, kicking the shit out of you, practically
killing you, bullying, demanding cry uncle and finally flush-
faced completely out of breath just decided to give in and
go uncle and for some strange reason like some miracle
when they heard that catch-trigger phrase just got right
off you. who's that uncle they were always speaking of
and suppose like almost everything in life never really
find out but discover what it is that will get you through
and simply allow you to survive and function and move on

44

families (immediate/extended) are political
often of a dysfunctional configuration

with their unfair, token scapegoat
and set-up alliances and broken

or established lines of
communication; why

i have always been apolitical
and run as an independent

45

manhattan's always been something
of a long-lost brother to me, long-lost
family member or myself unbeknownst
lost & alone & longing spending days
embraced in the grace of the gritty
ancient 1950s green plate glass
harcourt-brace building; its
different levels like some
contemporary castle
of antiquity losing
& finding myself
in the anonymity
of the madness
of the hustle & bustle
of the garment & diamond district
when it all becomes clear & keen
working a second job swingshift
on the weekends as an assistant
manager at the art movie theater
on 57th st. masturbating in the balcony
to foreign movies to give myself a little
relief, release from reality all by my lone
some deliberately giving myself vertigo
disequilibrium looking out for kong

on the tippy-top of the empire state
building spending all day hanging
out in that park not too far from
the chelsea making small talk
with the starlings & secretaries
at lunch hour outside the flat-iron
building spending a whole day months
years in alphabet city chilling in tompkins
square park with brilliant black scholars
who used to be artists & had their hearts
broken by white girls having had given
exhibitions at the guggenheim & whitney
spending all day studying at the new york
public library waiting for my scroll to show
up lit-up like numbers on the big board at
aqueduct raceway & then taking it back
to those long mahogany waxed tables
under the opaque cathedral windows
with the seasons squinting through
becoming smarter & wiser with
bums & winos, young girls to

die
for
mad
woe
man
aban
done

46

somewhere over the rainbow
now a long empty railroad
apartment with nowhere
to go & sudden explosions
& episodes in the lower east
side on ludlow & orchard
after their boyfriends
just up & left them

& now do time & bids
(biding their time)
with respites
at bellevue

47

back then i remember i used to sleep
with a switchblade under my pillow
as i guess it just used to make me
feel more safe & secure living on
the ground floor of long railroad
apartment right off the courtyard
in the lower east side right below
the swallowed-up stars & sagging
clotheslines, good & decent puerto
rican pals of mine who i used to
play ball with kept hidden 9's
in their *converse* sneaker boxes
in their closets in the projects
simply just for protection
so yes i guess it all worked
to our advantage cuz don't
remember ever having night
mares surviving off thomas
wolfe & t.s. eliot & cold
miller genuine draft beer

48

"you had to be there..."

man i always hated that expression
cause i can assure you if i was there they'd be
saying the exact same tired old thing about being there

49

i want to be taken hostage
by one of those anonymous
handkerchiefs with knockout
potion in it and wake up in
a land i always dreamed of

50

sometimes it just feels like we're
being taken hostage by the hostages
(or maybe just were taken
hostage a long time ago
as they're miserable)

51

martyrs going at it
playing mind games
with each other

accusing each other
of murder of being
more of a martyr

52

in my melancholia, i keep on forgetting i'm a happy man
stuck in the interrogation room with all those mandated
judges and buffoons, and for the first time in so long
feeling settled and at one, while they grill me and try
to throw their weight around, getting more angry and
frustrated that i take it all in stride and not intimidated
and turn the tables on them and beat them at their own
game hearing through the gated windows of the prison–

"come out with your hands up! we got you surrounded!"
i tell my interrogators—"tell me something i don't know"

look forward to fish sticks & sloppy joe
slow trains through chicago
high on liquid methadone

53

sorry, for me the world
was first created from
those silent home
movies to when
they took out
kennedy to
the beatles
on ed sullivan
to when michael
jackson was first seen
on stage much the rage
doing that spine-tingling
moonwalk something
he picked-up straight-
up from james brown
to a wild awestruck
half-crazed audience
stages of man
stages of growth
and development
stages of mortality
which all lie somewhere
between forgiving & forgetting

54

an idea to invent one of those body cleansers
just called "whore bath" for those with pasts
romp around my kitchen in birthday suit

in childhood holster with toy pistol
and a ten-gallon cowboy hat

55

boy
  hood
    be that

margarine
&
marmalade

masturbation
    real window
to the soul

mar
 i
gold

56

that pyramid
table of elements
of 8 essential vitamins
on the back of a box of cereal

57

the medication
on the kitchen counter
simply reads "monster"

58

we lived in a better world
when we had *the munsters*
and *the addams family* never sure
who was who and what was what?
who had who? was it wednesday?
it? lerch? that pretty promiscuous
milf lady with the long spanish pet
name (reminded me of best friends
mother from argentina as if any of that
would really matter?) and seemed like
everybody just resided under the stairs

59

how life was just like some long
eternal surreal game of truth or dare
some strange affair between virtue and vice
that fight or flight syndrome unable to decide

60

spending whole summers reading the buddhist
bible, irving stone's, 'passions of the mind'
and sherwood anderson's, "winesburg, ohio"

dostoevsky, jean genet...
kerouac's "desolation angels"

61

tracing the figure, texture
of your first lover

midnight revelations
in pre-dawn basement

62

returning home (in love)
stoned, buzzed, bleary-eyed,
bronzed, handsome to a place
you couldn't anymore
really exactly quite
call home, feeling
done wrong
deserted
by friends

63

not knowing what you did
and a family you would
never ever quite know

who could never possibly
know a thing about
you and suddenly

turned
silent
old

64

blue turning the color of red
and then scarlet and indigo

65

seeing feeling
all the senses
of the seasons

through a crisp chilly
contemplative keyhole
how it all smelt like

delicious burning woods
whispering prayers mantras

66

chants of
the desperate
passionate restless
silent and stirring soul

67

exactly like those
windy whispering trees
feathering your window

68

that exact moment
in time when obsessive-
compulsive behavior sets
in as a substitution for all
the madness & conflict
between instincts
& passion & that
nagging super-id

that split from
reality to fantasy
to archetypal being
invention of mythology
& superstition & taboo
& routines & rituals
all the way back to greek
& roman (greco/roman
wrestling) & egyptian times
to freud to hitchcock to sub-
lime brilliant & self-destructive
howard hughes to jean-paul
sartre & his counterpart
camus franz kafka

69

being shot in that schmaltzy
romantic champagne cup
capsule from the canals
of venice to the straits
of the nile seeing
baby moses
drifting by
on a piece
of matzoh

70

don't get back to you 'cause they think you're
dangerous. me dangerous? that's some of the
most hilarious absurd shit i've ever heard!
have always been one of the most innocent
romantics on the face of the earth. believe
the same way they treated tupac, and so off and
mistaken. as a kid me and a good buddy of mine
bought one of those wine making kits at a yard
sale and thought if it actually worked would be

able to use it to ask out all the pretty girls we
had crushes on in town, and put it under his
sink in his kitchen secretly rapped in towels
but heard it ended up exploding from all the
pressure...david birnbaum in his basement
rolling sushi waiting for the second coming

71

my son became friends with the boy
who my wife bought the coat from
and said–"that used to be my coat"
and now hang out with each other
lifelong chums and his name is ryan
and today she and dylan saw ryan
in town with a big horse's head on
and gave a great big wave and said
"hey dylan!" he's also not recently
been wearing socks with holes
in them to bed as claims
they give him nightmares

72

the first time you tried marijuana
the first time you touched the soft
skin miraculous flesh of her bosom
the first strand of pubic hair down there
beneath the silk panties to her vagina
the first time you got laid walking on
cloud 9 like jesus walking on water

73

ibid: where is the milky way
        factory?
                three musketeers?

the first time
    you got laid
        & made a name

74

sacrificing a virgin, what the hell was up with that?
i mean where did they come up with shit like that?
like what? were just hanging around the campfire
or around the pueblo, and were thinking, life's
pretty fucked-up out here and we want our crops
to grow so out of respect to the gods we're just
gonna snatch up the prettiest girl in town, that
doe-eyed girl with the rosy glow and strip her
down to the bone (had to be something little
sexual as well) and then will all be good
to go, no questions asked, better to be seen
and not heard, wonder how she felt about all
this? her parents? her extended family? that
boy who had a mad crush on her? third cousin?

75

the puerto rican girls
to die for precious
as pearls sitting out
on summer stoops
their proud mothers
putting hangers
around their
bellies to
see how

much they
have grown

#76

sheets swinging beneath
tenement windows
welcoming home

older brothers
from prison

having robbed
a string of *friendlys*

mama having kept
her humor about her

77

gangsters from the neighbor
hood strutting with tokens
in their ears towards
the pool on pitt st.

78

that pool when
ever it emptied
during the season
filling up with leaves
would read haiku
all by my lonesome
till the hush of evening

79

then pick up those
warm plantain
with chopped
meat in them

80

how life back then just seemed
like some long pleasant and patient
plan having created your own private
and intimate kingdom from everyone
and everything which had been taken
and abandoned with some secret scarlet
senorita cigarette of a sun final farewell curtain
sinking over the spanish-chinese restaurants over on
delancey dipping down along the manhattan bridge
and connecting bum pa n.y.c. to bum pa brooklyn

81

the wild boys from the west side
playing softball in the asphalt park.
it's mother's day and he sarcastically
remark—"i see you're spending the day
with your moms!" he slides into second
base and they all pile on him. a sole-survivor
scales the center field fence searching for salvation

82

it was not until much later
you remember those times
some of the roughest times
like a crime or nonstop riddle

without the punch line
always on the road
searching for a home
always getting stopped
by a state cop on the side
of the road with a license
registration and insurance
from three different states
but always keeping it real
and humble and being
sympathetic and schmoozing
with them able to relate to me
letting me off with a warning
with winter blizzards falling
down all around me just as
abandoned and despondent
and down in the dumps asking
me about the social work field
not much i could say to them
and asking about police work and
the family and wishing them the best

83

those great big homes of the very
wealthy suburbs always with no
one in them silhouetted with that
dim din of brilliant opaque light
spilling in melancholy bleakness
strangely enough perfectly
synchronized with the
changing season

84

as the silence of those
distant rattling trains
rushing in and out

the radiant antiquated
anonymity of the station

85

living at that welfare hotel
in the mess and madness
and thick of it all my
lit matchstick room
you could scope
from the road
set right in
the corner across
from that department store
where they would change
the window displays and
scenarios during the holiday
season to best suit a certain
strata of population made
it all seem snug like a bug
safe and secure that dichotomy
and juxtaposition with the freaks
i was living with all holy half-crazed
and those higher than holy smug
stuffy citizens was so surreal
always kept hidden in the back
of my consciousness deepest
recesses of my soul allowed me
to get to know and understand
the superficialities (texture and
configurations and vain and
shallow injustices) and bullshit
of culture so much more the empty
and rotten core of folklore where
it all absurdly came from ghostly
lit phosphorescent purple elevator
going up the evening movie theatre
in the desolation of radiant melancholia

86

spent my days on the weekend
taking buses to the outskirts
of suburbia out of the city
over industrial bridges
where millions of birds
planted themselves
up on top girders
and felt i was
really able
to relate
to them
in mind
body
and spirit
with glistening
logs rolling down
rivers through
the mystical
lace cobwebs
of slick & sacred
verdant mountains
imbibing all
the universe
almost feeling
the seasons
change right
in front of me
to the two dollar movies
where i got picked up by older
women just as deserted as me

87

spent whole weekends feeding me chinese
while bathing me and going down on me
as if nothing mattered but that moment

everything
and everyone
who had left them

88

then dropping me back off
to the burlington northern
and making my way
back to the jack london

(made sense
and this to me
was real culture
and civilization)

89

that haunted house is really not so haunted at all
with its gorgeous monstrous sunflowers in front
and radiant river which runs through the back
of the backyard babbling beneath the white
birches to the mountains; dance steps on
the floor to billie joel's—"i love you just
the way you are" cha cha cha cha cha
the sugar maples have finally started
to pop in their blazing yellows on
the roundabout to the steeples
of the cathedrals lying flush
up against the mountains
where they keep the used
car lot and campground
and girls sipping at cock
tails out to break hearts

90

self-starter ghosts
aggressive self-winding ballerinas
a winding staircase going nowhere
young hooker virgins kissing in the barn
a whole town closed down due to drizzle
the only signs of life the delicious scents
and silhouettes at the diner and belfry of the cathedral
young boys and bums hanging out outside the barroom

91

your best companion the train tracks
running alongside the river and both
rambling away off into the mountains
in the long run everything vanishes…

92

in every perceived orphan and criminal
is a kid just looking to be rescued
(naive, innocent, wild, and blue)

93

first love in the language of yiddish…

meshugenah! meshugenah! meshugenah! meshugenah!
to be repeated much quicker meshugenah! meshugenah!
meshugenah! meshugenah! meshugenah! meshugenah!
train leaving station…"baby, you're the greatest!"

94

"when was the last
time you got the mail?"
she looked beautiful
after she shampooed her hair
blow-dried it and didn't comb it
looking out for the first snow of winter

95

every childhood
ended in candlelight

a certain kind
of suicide

96

satisfied (pleasantly stubborn)
you only listened to one side
your death bed will finally
be listening to the other
with a final sigh
walking wobbling
on the high wire
to the other side

97

home at last, home at last,
holy man, hallelujah, amen

98

that long lament of the laconic coyote
the domestic dog who always kept
an eye always stood by your side
now a centerpiece for lovely

family and daughters
who mourn and adore
internal now external vision
while dusks out here last forever

the tweaking between day and night
between the senses and seasons
like some sputtering candle
flickering off to the heavens

99

i think in the long
run in the end the great
massive sky at twilight
all inky & violet is gonna
just open up and turn into
a mess of starlings and take
off to the horizon no more pain
no more suffering—"know a good
place around here to get pad thai?
fried calamari?" draw bridge
opens on its own volition

100

i just need some place
to escape like some
bleary-eyed diner
on the corner where
it's constantly raining

and the waitresses
are nice and young
and kind and pretty
and after i've spent
way too much time
with my polish platter
and cup of tea gently
kick me out by the seat
of my pants and with
a slight chuckle and
wave say—"see you
next week" and you
reciprocate and just
naturally wave
silently heading
towards the falling
leaves and mist slipping
over the steeples of the
cathedrals and mountains
disappearing in the distance

the mist and fog
sifting and settling
shimmying in out
like some holy
and sacred
security blanket
intertwining the
skeleton and spine
of the jack pines
and sugar maples

101

every
one
needs
a place
to escape

like the path
the mist and

fog make snaking
down the mountain.
evaporating into day.

XI. Melancholia:
scratch & sniff prints for the upcoming apocalypse

#100

Gondola lost with lovers
missing-in-action never
heard from or seen
from again…

#99

Every time the bell
tolls it tolls for them
as well as murderers
and the myth and fable
of the silence of mayhem…

#98

The parrot suffers from
schizophrenia and tells
long drawn-out riddles
with no specific end…

#97

Young porn-freak-stud drives
to swingshift at dusk to work
the front desk at chain motel
up on top of the mountain…

#96

It's the mud season
and all the angels
and madmen
have come
out again…

#95

The hitchers and tourists
and sacred girls in sundresses
traipsing back & forth over bridges…

#94

So have the wild turkey
wandering from town to
town and season to season…

#93

Waterfalls thawing from
thick blue ice crystal
along slabs of green
granite like a miracle
like a new evolution…

#92

The hospitals
and halfway
houses…

#91

Juvenile residences
in quaint old new england
villages, who all seem barely
living, oblivious, completely
unaware of it, like ghosts to
each other between townsmen
and delinquents, really not
much of a difference…

#90

Dracula simply had insomnia
and bipolar disorder with
grandiose episodes
and at-risk behavior
unaware of what
he did the night
before...

#89

The advantages & disadvantages
of suicide pretty much the same
the same old sleazy men
playing the same old games
why you always loved the rain
why you always ran away
think if john loved yoko
would have also loved
kurt cobain...

#88

Who came up with the straightjacket?
think a pretty damn decent idea
but doesn't leave a heck of a lot
of opportunity for fly-fishing...

#87

Don't get too close to certain people
they'll only wish you the best for so long
then try to fuck you up mind body spirit and soul
trust me man, i've seen it all (what a brother will
do to you) the patterns of human nature and man

hackneyed punchlines (herd-mentality)
of the arch-nemesis and villain
that tutor who used to
plunder our refrigerator…

#86

Found myself hidden
at the bottom of one
of those big boxes
of *crackerjacks*
ripped myself
open and like
the mirror of a
nightmare looking back
wasn't much impressed
tossed myself aside
(the normal routine
and ritual of mankind)
and lost myself once again
they tell you you can't fight
the system why the hell not?
doesn't seem as if it make
whole hell of a lot of
difference or have
too much to lose
in the long run…

#85

If they were to ask
me any last requests
i'd say got any seltzer?
if not that bagels and lox
and do you mind if you can
cut down on the idle chatter?

#84

Remember every last single
one of them in your memory
and being like some savory
treat or celebration (of spirit)
or secret present suddenly
unwrapped in the moment
and will always be grateful
for their necessary presence…

#83

The origin of the tulip
of the red rose of the gladiolus
of the conch shell whose echo
radiates from the beginning of time
to the middle to the brilliant eternal

The origin of the rock through the window
with a desperate passionate message of love…

#82

The hx of
the new world
a bible salesman
and vacuum salesman

with profound personality
disorders desperately
searching for
redemption

#81

On-the-run and
bumpa da bumpa
to manifest destiny

to the horizon
to that pot of gold
at the end of the rainbow...

#80

Where do they keep
the bridges and prisons
and chinese cleaners
up on top of the hill?

You survive off baguette
meant for the bourgeois
left at the dewy doors
of dawn
the black
market stealing
ny sirloin from
suburban supermarkets
selling it back to the russian
hoteliers for half-price, donating
your books and bone marrow and
climbing up the pipes of whitewashed
hotels falling into empty vacant rooms
and vanishing into thin air like some ol'
time now you see 'em now you don't
black & white comedian mischievous
thief tom sawyer with gorgeous
sunrises and sunsets to die for

Someone
stole my bicycle
and ate all my chocolates

The transistor comes in clear
through the clotheslines of the pacific
with only a slight bit static from candlestick...

#79

Overly-responsible people just drain the hell out
of me and whenever i see them always seem to take
themselves and everything around them too seriously
as strangely seem to get so hostile and angry because
of what they delusionally deem and think and believe
(me to be or not to be jeeze-louise as serious as them
and not by coincidence these self-entitled legends who
come a dime a dozen and all follow the exact same patterns
are always the most arrogant and pompous of asses) while
instantly for me become the subject; subject to mockery

i take an instant diss-liking...

#78

Like those who always seem to boldly claim
with those clichés 'looking back at my life
i have absolutely no regrets' and not too
ironic those you trust the least and by
looking at them closely look like
they don't even trust themselves...

#77

Could never stand that hack
need expression if you cheat
you're just cheating yourself
yet what if you felt eternally
cheated right from the get go?
(the act of stealing and taking
back and claiming) the only
time i felt any sense of
meaning or identity...

#76

Those who make others feel like criminals
can't be close to who they think they are
matter of fact so far and when you look
close always got that look on their face
like they're nauseous or more accurate
grossed-out and repulsed by themselves…

#75

How to stone yourself
and become a better man…

#74

How to collect fallen angels…

#73

How to wash down robots
& buddha & bodhisattva
& black woman busts
& bums at the hydrant…

#72

How to clean & redeem
a filthy heart & soul
stray dog right
off the bone

how to interview ghosts….

#71

How to re-tune the trigger to the trigger
to the trigger to the trigger with constant
movement and observation (a repetition
to reduce the importance and significance
and original trauma to realize in the long-run
all trivial and irrelevant or as the brothers
stated—"ain't nothing to it but to do it…"

#70

The hx of
davey crockett
& billie the kid
& john dillinger
& abraham lincoln…

#69

The hx of all those maps
we shaded in with crayons
in social studies as kids in
which looking back were like
ancient & nostalgic parchment
from rivers to tributaries
to mountain ranges
to the great lakes
to the northern
and southern plains
to great indian tribes
like the brave and wise

sioux and lakota and cherokee nation
from the heartland to the panhandle
to the plush green lagoon and bayou…

#68

All taking on a keen mythology
through the shortcuts through
the pitch fences of plush green
lawns of backyards of suburbs…

#67

Natural hx for us
were all those
secret trails
and ponds
and brooks…

#66

All those seasons
falling and beaming
and skinned knees
and not getting home
in time for homework…

#65

All that guilt
& conflict
of not reaching
expectations all
wrapped up in one…

#64

All those first
& last girlfriends
& crushes & gossip
& rumors & drugs…

#63

Turning off the lights in the middle of the assembly
chucking party snappers and watching math teachers
dancing spending your formative years in detention…

#62

Not giving a damn about your future
and apparently not at all your present…

#61

Your report cards all chalking it
up to highly-intelligent and pure
acting-out and so much potential…

#60

A cross between one of those
single-cell organisms under
the microscope and discovering
fire beneath the sun burning
one of those ragged leaves
from the natural world
with a magnifying glass
when it all warmed up…

#59

I think if i ever get rich
gonna get one of those
mansions where no one
can see me like the roosevelt
estate (or was that rockefeller?)
in upstate new york and every morning
dive right out my window like one of those

perfectly-sculpted mexican cliff divers right
into my pool and will be my wake-up call

towel myself off and dive into my library
with the shutters open to the season
where you had all those secret
romances on the hudson and
discovered all those decent
seafood dives where it
was just you and her
and the foghorns
suddenly come
alive in the
middle of
the night

#58

Time eventually (when time
and mortality creep in) to return
home when they catch up with you
hit rock bottom and turn beat down
and blue guilty excruciatingly lonely...

#57

Missing the trainyards in patterson
jamaica, queens and the easy chair you
left behind beneath the stars in the over
grown courtyard in the lower east side...

#56

You pursue a master's degree in psychology
instead of being a mass-murderer on wall street...

#55

Meet the girl of your dreams
at your internship under the el
on jerome avenue in the bronx...

#54

Where the mafia got its
start and so did hip-hop…

#53

Make something of yourself
not exactly sure what
at some mental health
clinic in some depressed
town in new england
at the end of the train
tracks in the ghetto
now composed of
projects and
haunted
victorians…

#52

Which once held all the mines
and industry and movers and shakers
millionaires when a million meant a million...

#51

Group homes set up just outside the city
where they can't see you and
keep the zoos and bodegas
and college campuses...

#50

Methadone clinics
on polluted marina...

#49

Anger management groups
made up of cops
and gangsta'
bitches...

#48

Reading groups made up of a bunch of
little men with napoleonic complexes
and sexless resentful housewives
hostile and passive-aggressive
out to spit-out with venom
the opposite gender...

#47

That cathedral stuck smack-dab
in the middle of those filthy birches
right across the road from that hobby
shop both with weird eccentrics i got
my reservations about and guard up
for all the straight-up same reasons

#46

Not sure anymore if smelling
the crystal-meth labs through
the forest or if in fact maple
and molasses seeping
during sugaring season...

#45

You feen in getaway car
feeling like been waiting
for ages for so damn long
to make the grand getaway
and great escape never
exactly sure the right

the pure the safe & secure
time and moment that infamous
signal and feeling and emotion…

#44

The rest of the town
are a bunch of slaves
to the tourism industry
having to cow-tow and
defer and fulfill the fantasies
and visions of rich and wealthy
soulless caucasians always involving
some element of subjugation or humiliation…

#43

Like some dummy
and ventriloquist
convention unable
to make the distinction…

#42

She loves me she loves me not
bullshit and simply irrelevant…

#41

Marriage always a triangulation
between the past and future
and present...

#40

The best vacations
always with trains
in the distance
somewhere
between

the fog and mist
moving to the next
blissful destination...

#39

In america now for like vacations to like utah
they now show proud happy caucasian families
riding on horses through tourist spots like bryce
canyon and zion national park, but ironically later
on that night you find out from the debating intellects
and ideologues and sheriffs and governors that utah
is just another one of those shaded-in states which
supports and advocates for the death penalty and
now got this brand new option just in case that hocus-
pocus death potion doesn't knock them out, lickety-
split right on the spot, and they start to struggle
or suffer just a little too much, also for the convenience
and viewing entertainment of the victim's family through
that tinted plate glass window, can be dragged out to that
infamous yard with that infamous solitary chair and can
be whacked by the firing squad, and the prosecuting police,
the ones involved get first shot for the death squad, while
one of them is given blanks (so all of them, making it all
neat and tidy) can avoid any sort of guilt or conflict or possible
psychological damage so what's exactly wrong with this picture?

and what next? give the firing squad blindfolds and cigarettes?
would love to see a split-screen for the utah tourism industry
with these happy beaming caucasian families riding their
horses through the twinkling sunset of zion and bryce
canyon while some pour soul gets strapped down in that
solitary chair in the middle of the yard to meet his maker…

#38

A letter to all those very brave courageous republicans
who drafted that letter in the middle of those delicate
nuclear talks and negotiations i liken as some last-ditch
effort to try and embarrass and humiliate and demean
and belittle our president (after years in my opinion
of emotional abuse and spiritual neglect) like the
opposite of our original forefathers and statesmen
and the only image i can come up with are all those
clowns coming around the bend trying desperately to
honk out loud all stuffed in their little car at the circus.
As an aside: hilarious, when get an unexpected letter back
from that persian diplomat, who schools them and says
it appears as if you don't know a thing about your own
constitution, or for that matter international affairs
would have loved to have been there, having be-
come the punch line to their own jackass riddle…

#37

Broken up by some commercial for just another
formulaic film with liam neeson dodging fireballs
being taken hostage in some fiery plane out to save
the free world, could be a video game as well
really not sure (nor really think it would very
much matter) and then comes on the very
sincere and down-to-earth romantic middle-
aged erectile dysfunctional people we're all
supposed to care so much and be rooting for…

#36

Girl scouts with real-life werewolves
in the background be single mothers
seething cheated-on checking you out...

#35

Some cute tomboy and geek stud rolling in the mud...
she sardonically declares—"i'm gonna destroy you!"
he's a glutton & goes for the bait & provokes her
& of course she always gets the better of him
when the dusk suddenly shows & the stars
roll in; they lay side by side on the dewy
lawn at twilight as she plants a quick one
on his cheek & in the moment absolutely
nothing nothing in the world means more...

#34

Everywhere i turn they are putting up *dollar generals*
like a wrecking ball knocking down the coliseum
leaving a blind man and stray dog on the corner...

#33

Kickboxing across from the covered bridge...

#32

Geeks with buck teeth
bopping their heads
back and forth
singing the
love ballad–

"through the years
you never let me down
you turned my life around"

then fart the dueling
banjos from "deliverance"

at dusk they take
shortcuts home…

#31

The old sadistic french teacher
just looking to get her pension

makes the handsome
jock sob in the hall…

#30

It's all a cross
between being
stood up for the ball
and slamming doors

#29

He made pacts with his best friend
and next door neighbor growing up
in the suburbs that when they grew
up they would be bachelors and
move down to florida; he would
make the tuna fish sandwiches
while he would be the janitor

they were both obviously
diehard romantics…

#28

Spending their childhood hanging out
after school eating sicilian and the nice
sicilian boys were like second fathers…

#27

Their growth & development
spanned somewhere between
"everybody was kung-fu fighting"
and billie joel's love ballad "honesty…"

#26

The neighbors on the other side
were the nice jewish sisters
who said "if you show me
yours i'll show you mine…"

#25

Later on he writes a love letter
to his wife–"please pick up
some peanut butter and
a condolence card…"

i.e. to be the first husband
found with a fork and knife
in his head nun of that
hanging bullshit pills
taking out the whole
family keeping engine
running in the garage
but just at last getting
so sick of the whole
fucken goddamn true-
false mirage and found
in his easy chair like

2-3 days later completely
unaware just watching
non-stop weather with
a fork and knife casually
sticking out of his head

better to be seen
and not heard…

#24

He imagines all the non-
cheerleaders nude
on a platter...

centerpieces between
the past and present

thankfully at last
with no future…

#23

Eventually in the long-run
they will devour him
in a good way
and develop
crushes…

#22

He doesn't know what to make of it
and vanishes into thin air from the library…

#21

He always seemed to shine in intermission...

#20

Somewhere between the imagination
and what he sensed they wanted from him
as deep-down inside knew who were the
true-blue provocateurs, the true villains…

#19

Extra-curricular after school activities
was detention and somewhere deep
in the 'recesses' knew how much
more this counted; his fight-song
without even being aware of it–
"can't keep myself out of trouble"

#18

And learned in the long-run
not to trust that over-solicitous
aggressive population of the
goody-goody and very driven…

#17

He thrived in summer school
and became a scholar…

#16

Smoked marijuana
and made honors…

#15

You wait for mad genius
client real nice guy torturing

the prim & proper townsmen
(sometimes not) in the antique
shop behind the train tracks
while imagine bars in the back
of churches and them doing
a major jail break right into
the parking lot where my
first love angel rolls cigarettes
by the lake and big beautiful
bully female high school
basketball player hangs
out blowing smoke rings
beneath the thawing mountain
where they keep the radio tower
and the satellite dishes for the
telepathic madmen convinced
the government all symbolic
of big brother and everyone
who's let them down out to
get them; the haunted house
during the change of season
and when everything's melting
is getting renovated and more
dilapidated full of spirits and
haunted along with the black
cat and crooked branches
the freak who still lives
with his mom in his
coke bottle bifocals
takes off with her
in her pickup
while crows
come in for a
crash landing…

#14

When the weather warms
out come out of nowhere
like tree frogs the stray
echo of heels and pumps

the laissez-faire
call-girls and drugs
as people gotta get along…

#13

Those forgotten frozen
rivers of snow start to
become slabs of ice
moving miraculously
to the promise land
past the ole time
brick smokestacks
smoking in front
of golden capitols…

#12

The librarian
sings ghost
songs…

#11

Nightmares are a knife and mirror
seeing them come at you with a
knife in the mirror; at the heart
of all paranoia lies those fragile
and fleeting, sudden, shattered
bleeding triggers and all of those
deeply-embedded hidden secretive
truths or more like lies they try so
absurdly and desperately to hide
from you so in truth turns out may
not even be paranoia but something
far more insightful and hardwired
truer and bluer exploding in shades
of scarlet and muted paroxysms

(how the poor unconvincing
con-artists and actors try to
manipulate and pathologize
you to keep the act alive but
more so a fear of exposing
all their lies) more like your
keen perception and intuition
(and wisdom) and everything
you have learned from hardcore
experience forwards and backwards
and inward and much deeper and distant
to a place they could never even come close
to, penetrate or imagine even if they wanted
with their weak and fragile insecure behavior
and character played-out by deceit and betrayal
nightmares are everything you know about them
the knife and mirror and can't murder them
so says freud in his *civilization*...

#10

Is there not some elixir i can take before
i go to sleep which may help to decrease
the nightmares? yet recently have been
noticing every evening that foggy full
moon barely peeking like a thief over
the ridge of trees miraculously rising
and then perched proudly right above
the mountain which has proven to help
to feel a little less lonely and isolated...

#9

My nightmares are my dreams come true...

#8

Guardian angel is a crossing guard
smashing a stop sign over my head...

#7

The dream began from
the nightmare and
vision forgotten…

#6

Wet dreams came back to blissfully
surreally serendipitously haunt me
as somehow at such a young age
back in those days in our playful
half-crazed consciousness knew
and caressed and fondled me
the last days of school and how
in the heck could she have even
known (as perhaps was in all those
seductions and arching body language
and slow-motion motions of her perfect
shape and form to leave me awkward
and in awe to leave room open for
the imagination, for masturbation
at the end of some long impossible
period) couldn't wouldn't even
know how to pay back the favor
and still think of her every so often
when having trouble getting out of bed…

#5

What is sex without porno
and love without pillow talk?

#4

The academy
schmuckaditty
creepy-crawly awards
ho's showing off asses

and plunging necklines
and tin-foil monochromatic
smiles all with that same pose
acting seductive with head over shoulder

think i preferred when jean-paul sartre
refused to accept the nobel prize
based purely on principal
and political reasons...

#3

They got way too many
fake blondes in america

not exactly what i grew up on
not exactly what grew on the vine
not exactly two peas in a pod
as if they do all their shopping
on the home-shopping network…

#2

Talk show hosts become
as powerful as the president
reality show stars, the czar...

#1

A trail of postcards
sent out from the
burnt-out motel
with no return
address...

#0

Cuckoo clock's broken
and leaves us all a mess...

XII. A Fragile Childhood Strung Together By Chicken Bones

1,

Kid
    takes cover
        behind curtains

            with a mild,
                wild form
                    of depression

    wind
        skid-
            ders

            threw geraniums…

                            it is autumn.
                      Id autumn

2,

[angels]
    straycats
        Amen.

3,

What happens when you take
                a/man

                      child of genuine
                          kindness, caring

& compassion
    & constantly try to man-
            handle

      man-
         nipple-
            ate
              him?

                    (almost like ridiculing
                          with-
                            out/any

        cunt-
            sir

                    [f
                        con-
                            science

    or]

con-
    sequins

weak-
      links

      under-
          estimating

              spirit

                    & strength
                        "oi"

      con-
          vic/tion

                           socrates whispered to plato
                               who in turn taught
socratic method
      to both freud & dylan

how to address
      the madman...

      (the machinations
            of modern man)

        who comes at you
             with a dagger?

        worst of all his fake & flimsy
            (character flaws) & bullshit body language

                (i grew up on
                      the ball-

                            feel

on the
bored-
walk

      on stage,
          in prince/pall's office)

                in ditches...

      off the old adage–
          "big boys don't cry"

                                    getting swept-off porches

                                        in crime-fighting
                                            uniform

                    after literally
                            leaping
                                summer-

salting
     threw
          glass window

                            getting stitches
                                 & not shedding
                                                    single tear
                                        you couldn't even begin
                                    to under

                                            stand
                                                my visions

                        my woun/dead zen
                                        ab-
                                           scents

     of hope or fear

                    (my desertions
                        my abandonments)

                                    (*my wife couldn't*
                                        even begin
                                            to know

                                                    how much
                                                        i love
                                                            her)

        and wood think
                weed all this

                    down-
                            home

            up-
                    bringing

                                            i'
                                        d

eventually get stronger
                    yet in many ways

                            d-

                                        veloped

                            a/mour deep

        & fragile de-
                    mean-

                        or

                                turn in desperate
                                                detached

    of which

                            out-
                                of-
                                    touch

            witch
                    doctors
                                labeled
                                    as
                                        "attachment disorder"

and told them to fuck-off
            feeling damned

                              defensive/determined,
                                        drained & distant

                              appropriately paranoid
                                        & persecuted

finally with tears in my eyes
          really experiencing
                    fee-fi-fo-fum

                    fee-
               nom-
          enough!

               "of counter-
                    transference"

                              feeling once
                         again

                              man-
                                        nip-
          pill-
     late-
dead

                    taken advantage of
                              by false father-figures

          (here comes
               the judge

                    thief &
                         hustler!

o he's really
     a good
          kid...)

                                            did you hear the one...

            batmobile
                        stranded

                                    on the side
                                                of west-
                                                            side

                                                                        highway
                                                                                    stripped
    for profit
            by vultures

    & scavengers
            they're all under-
                        studies

                                    playing the roles
                                                of actors

                        always wondered if you slammed
                                    your head against
                                                the wall

                                                                                    against
    the floor

                            would this count
                        at all

        faw sum
                    desperate caw-
                                out

                                                too god?

    sum poor-
        ring
            out
                of da soul?

sum passion-
        net

    passion-
        play

        played-out
            prayer

                in itself?

        tom waits reminds us—

*   got to keep the devil way down in the hole*
*   down in the hole*
*   got to keep the devil...*

4,

                Still wandering,wand/ring,wandering
      literally spent your whole early to late adult
  hood wandering

  running away, escaping
        the phony-baloney
            poor influences
                if that's what you'd
                    want to call it

    you knew every
        street asylum,avenue,alley
            in sand-

                sansiminium
        man

  san francisco new-
           york

                          knew
                      awe-
                  lens

                        weather, and how
                            it naturally
"effects behavior"

                makes them desperate
                        & despondent

        makes them tender
           & meander

                    all the wild women
          in dark rooms

all the pillow talk
    which got you through

          picking up and getting picked-up
                      outside

              the raw rainy
                  movie theaters

                of poor-
                  ;land
                    or/gone

5,

    I have pondered
        generations&generation

                        lulled by the visions of television
             watching sex
      symbols

trying to catch up
      to their lipsynching

            to the shapes & shadows
                  of the sixties

                        leading...

                            (to no man's
                                land)

land of dead batmans
      to shimmying sequins

                      putrid pea soup
                          golds & avocados

      of the seventies

              greed of the eighties
                  which secretly
                        sinisterly

             bread
                bred a hole

     soulless species
           of "meanies"

                      [leaving you

dumb-
found-
dead

       & duh-
      ceased

 be-
   on

     be-
      leaf]

            have never quite recovered
                (believe me)

      to this very day.

6,

Global warming
    'round the way

       can i get an ol' negro spiritual
         or maybe something from down south
           down-home, detroit, chicago?

   just when i was starting to gain
some re/cognition

   god must be kafka

   & if we are all creations
      in his like end image

   i must be kafka's/guest
      gregor samsa, holden caulfield

         flipping a cat/log in backyard

                    looking at all the semi
supermodels

                                with the borderline disorder

                    who make breaking hearts
                                    an art

                                            charlie brown
    in his apocalyptic crown
                    with a resounding round
                                    of–"ugggggh! awwe why not?"

                        (whenever they show any of the old news reels
                                            they're
always moving fast-
forward

                                chuck chaplin at the hearst mansion
                                                    ruth
                                            rounding the bases

    great black & white orators from the trustbuster era
            ac/robots balancing on top of heads on top of newly-built

                                        shimmering skyscrapers
                        old gangsters
            shooting it up in chicago)

                                i mean what was the point of
                                                "culture"

                                    the wet dreams & worries
                            all the tests you crammed
                                & cheated on

    (#2 pencil)

                        slow-death local from the suburbs to grand central
                              dealing with all those obnoxious caucasians

        proverbs & cliches rammed down your throat

                              like–"patience is a virtue"
                all coming back to haunt you
to fuck you

                              you
                                    always "lived
                                                & learned" most

                                                when you took risks

& were impulsive

                        the darling boys next door
                              starting next world wars

                                                            i

mean what did mo/ham
dali go to
jail for?

                                          soulless cunt
                              in sunglasses
                        & cellphone
                                    pretending she's jackie o.
                                                & wasn't even born.

7,

              It is strange,
                        but in this boy's biography

                                                (in his early 40s)

                                    387

                                        he feels most insecure
                                    with the safety & security

interestingly,
    a thief
        in his own place

                (palace
                    of peep-
                        holes)

hollow heart
of suburbs

        (there is absolutely
            no one
                or nothing
                    out here to believe)

  needs the streets

        hell's kitchen,
            the east
                to be

in order to gain
    any real sense
        of belonging

                (release...)

        of reality
      of relief

                  peace

...grounding
to feel free.

8,

                       I have not been sleeping
                                  a hell of a lot

     lately

        & simply

                          need to be in a dark-
                                 end

                              room

                       & brewed
                  a/bout

      all the little things
 of life.

          what often
               some-
                   times

                    helps me
                        (in this fight)

                    to simply
                        start

         single-
           mind

              dead/ly

        sin-

     sear-

  ly

out of nowhere
      in midnight kitchen

            flapping my arms
                dreaming of flight

                      (like some sea-
                            gal)

      gradually rising,

escaping,
vanishing

          into the sky

   which always gets
        my heart
      ,my mind

              going
                  & going

                            beddy-
                              bye.

      for no particular reason
            in particular
                  you happen to notice

        your lovely radiant
              wife
                    the saint

                                                            that she is

            has put up an application
                            on the refrigerator
                                            to help out our babysitters

                to work in a sandwich shop
                                around the corner

                                        where one of the questions
                                                        is if you have.

                    ever pleaded no contest or been convicted of a crime?

                & start to fantasize & imagine
                                one of these fine
                                                15-16 year olds

                    (behind the counter
                            at the sandwich
                                    shop in this context)

        yet really know from
                        cold-
                                hot

                                                    ex
                                            peer-
                                                    ience

                    that in fact
                        when they get older

                            symbolically will commit
                                    some desperate crime of passion

             (but of course won't
                          address it
                                    as this

    or even know it
              as it all happens
                          in the instance

                                    wit the old "hit & run")

    & plead *no contest*
                  in the whole
                          half-

                                  baked
                          metaphorical
                  concept

                                    of marriage.

9,

                        Today we
                                  looked at a house in the mountains
                                                and old man whose
    home it was
        told our realty agent how bad he felt
                        that he didn't get a chance to clean up

                                    we of course said no problem

    and that we understood
                        and our only guess probably was

                                                that he was

a widower,
    wildflower

        cause the only thing

    which might have felt a little peculiar
                or left out of place

            was a great big pair of drawers
        which had been neatly laid

          on top his dusty bed

  like some rich-
      you-
        all

  from some old-
      long-
        lost

          lover-
            ghost-
              partner.

10,

    The neighbor's barb-
        er-

  cue smoke curling thru
    breezy screen window

        reminds you of the feint scent
          of your old tutor's tweed coat

    which always reeked

           distinctly of sweet pungent pipe smoke
                coming over the house most
                          because

            of *behave yourself* problems
          yet ironically he was the one
    making himself at home

        stealing the fruit from our refrigerator
and remember one of those terrible bleak

tuesdays
    or thursdays

           insensitively accusing me of something
                with his brash and "biting" personality

and me striking back a blow of my own–
        "you're a rotten asshole and just come over
                to steal our apples!"

                    his name was
                        michael plum
                            still
      lived with his mom.

  in retrospect,
      i turned out to be right
            cause a good friend of mine

                who lived right down the block

        said he did
            the exact same thing

     not even asking
         and making his way to the fridge

   (looking back it was
       so damn passive-aggressive)

             we both
              got
a nice hearty laugh
out of this

  having serendipitously discovered
      this while walking
        to school together one morning

    he eventually told me
      he had to stop doing acid

       cause he actually saw
         the numbers on his math quiz

in top hat & tails
   tap dancing off the page.

    when i decided to start "applying"
  myself

i practically
   aced it all

   ironically falling in love

     & excelling in proofs
       as though i was trying

    to logically
  & legitimately

                              "prove" everyone wrong
                    while at the same
          time was "someone"

                                        if you kind of get
                                            where i'm coming from
                    getting lost
     in all those logarithms & laws

                              & urine in your middle-ages
                                        having dreams
                                                  of strangely

                    frustratingly still
               not being able

                         to find your locker

                                        night-
                                             mares

                                        like
                                             dandelion

                                             detention
                                                       hall

                    of which you rarely
                              ever ex-
                                   helled or got closure

          the wild-
               victor/in

                         of summer school
                              which you all-
                                   ways passed

     with flying colors

the ancient stray
     aromas

    of fluff & peanut butter
      bologna & cheese sandwiches

           ...mangoes

  that kid who took
     all his tests
     all his quizzes

       with the assistance
         of in-depth, descriptive
             crib
notes
 as in my opinion,
   displayed great initiative
       guts,
        conyos (sp.?)

     coming from a long line of big irish families
   with a bunch of brawling brothers
  & everybody loved him

      ending up going to one
    of those good colleges up north

      wouldn't think twice
        about recommending him
  as showed a hell of a lot of
    drive & determination

& used to get a real kick out of him
   as i think we all thought if he had just
     made half or even a fraction of the effort

       to crack open the books

     but that was just him

                                        that was just tim

                    & look back
                              with great fondness & affection

        spirit,

[and couldn't hate on him
cause was always so quick
and slick with an abundant
amount of color and tricks]

                    as we used to get into these
                              great big mock brawls in the hall
                                        where i'd pull his shirt up over

                                        the back
                                              of his shoulders

    above his head
         & blind him
              then start swinging
                    for the fences

                    as our friends would
                              all gather around

                    announcing–
                         "and there they go!"

                    like all those great ranger/flyer
                                        rivalries of the late-seventies

                                   then pick up our un-
                    cracked

        books off the floor

    sweaty with shirts still torn
      smile & shake hands
        humbly admitting–

       "yeah, you got me that time!"

  continuing on to our next period.

11,

    You were the prince of bar-mitzvahs
        casanova at roller discos

   returning home blissfully,
      contented,
        exhausted

    romantic,
      passionate

       with your three-piece corduroy suit
         & tweed tie with soccer

players on it
  the theme to s.w.a.t.
    & latin hustle

      still bopping in the back of your head

  thinking this is what it meant to be a grownup
      probably preferred to be on the ball field

we all went home and masturbated instead...

12,

    Man on all fours on front lawn–
        "hey, what's your dad doing?"
                "he's checking for junebugs..."

      the difference of genders
          is what makes the world go around
              makes us humans get down

        graffiti reads–
          shorty & psycho
            eyes of a blue dog

both want to be left the fuck alone

      as you look through driving snow
        from the dazzling
          dreary

red hook docks

from the deep darkness
    of brooklyn

    cobble-
      stone

        out to the luna lone lady
          who stands stoic,
            solitary

holy
n' harbor

    who seems to have been through
      her fair share of drama
        healthy dose of damage

similar to your grandmother
          who lives at the last stop
                    on the 7

             out in flushing, queens
                     with a vacant view

                of old drunken
                      broken-

           down-
      trainyards

   where old puerto rican woman
takes care of her

     both not understanding
a word they're saying to each other

           as she repeats over & over
                  loudly

                   (as if she wasn't even there)
"i don't understand a word she's saying to me!"

                her best friend
                   a rose

            by any other name

        bee
      bee
   rose hirschleifer…

        till the end of eternity
          looking out from a bench

                                                                       from the boardwalk
                                                                           to the sea

                kind of interesting
                          as i too lived
                                      at the last stop in brooklyn

                                                               on *stillwell avenue*

      in coney island

                          (an usher in a movie theatre
                     hustling graveyard shifts
                driving a cab in manhattan)

    returning home all
             zombie-
                    eyed

                        drained
                          & satisfied

                                    down that long, empty
                                        deserted ramp

lamplight

           (like some sort of spaceship
                    of the damned)

        postmodern,
            haunted,
                transcendent

                        at last reaching
                              this lost lazyland

                of abandoned
                        artifacts
                                & phantoms

                                as all these funky
                                        yet familiar scents would smack

                        you right in the kisser
                                of stale beer

                                        & ammonia
                                                & roasted pralines
                                                        & salty ocean

                        while i wandered
                                down the wild
                                        wintery

                                                blasts
                                                        of brooding
                                                                boardwalk

                        every dawn
                                through the dead

                                                old blind men
                                                        & winos
                                                                & stray dogs

                just to get home
                        alone

                                & if i were to vanish
                                        into thin air

                                                absolutely
                                                        no one would know

                                                                    & that there
                                                                                        the

most lonesome feeling
in the world

                               (but got sort of used to
                                              & liberating as well)

               the only sound being...

                                         the shore
                                                   lung eternal roar

beating!
echoing!
crashing!

threw my window

               (got used to too
                     as some
                             soothing

                                     musical ritual
                                               ironically
                                                        kept me
                      from feeling so blue)

                 cracked open a little
                         above my mattress

                                   on the floor
                                                       my long
lost friend,
sports radio.

12,

        The people on my dead end
                all snake in the grass

          tattle-tales

    with very few tales to tell
  trying to one-up each other

          like some terrible
              trivial
                tale

        of rotten
          stale
            sibling

  kind of like those kids
      nerds

              who kissed ass
                & worked

    so hard
      yet knew

   you were always
     so much more
       clever & smart

           had mad heart
             & believe it or not
              much better

character

   brilliant film director
     jim jaramush
       from his mini-

                master-
                        piece

                        "down by law"
                                        quotes one of his actors
                                                        as saying–

                "america's like a melting pot
                        where all the scum rises to the top"

                                                time on the clock
                                        reads *man-o-*
                        man-o-shevitz...

13,

        Thinly-sliced hygienist
                        comes out

                                        of cul-de-sac
                                                for her swingshift

vacant,
homeless

                        from her whim-
                                sickle

                                                wrink-
                                                        killed

                                                                wild

                        nerd:
                                iness.

   kids return to dead ends
      on the back of dimly-lit
          buses

    insane,
 afraid

like leftover lobsters
    in their cage
      restless & crazed

           almost nihilistic
             all most in

      nietzschian way

   wondering about their fate
 (*these/those were the days*)

14,

     Spending whole summers
         holy summers

     camped-out on the roof
         of *the john adams*

    stimulated
   wasted
  overlooking
     12^(th) & 6^(th) avenue
      trying to take in joyce's

        dubliners, portrait, finnegans & ulysses

reading it not so much for content
                              yet mor/sel

                                        rhythm & cadence

          not understanding a word he was saying
                              but loving every second

             you did this too for kerouac & whitman
                         knowing somewhere down the line

                                             deep down inside
                                                  it would all

         eventually sink in
the summer

                                        the talking heads got big

                     (u2 were a fictional
                              character in the wind)

          & survived off tortellini & marijuana & sangria & chipwiches
                         whore-baths beneath fire hydrants

"red red wine..."

        your wife casually mentions:

                              "it's so funny
                                   sports radio
                                              's always
                 so fuzzy"

      today
         they're
             expecting..

408

isolated
     thunderstorms.

XIII. Sometimes They Make You Feel So Alone

The Case Of The American Existentialist: cultural notes
and clinical observations during the holiday season

1. some times when i think about the pure and pristine
perfect image and vision of the immaculate conception
even though i suppose i'm something of a believer i can't
help but to let my mind stray and wander and wonder and
consider the way of things these days and the way things
have always been and they're just so many more examples
and had way too many filthy and vulgar experiences with
actual aggressive competitive devils and betrayers and think
maybe just maybe there might be some dude or stud or gigolo
or perhaps even super that conveniently never got mentioned
(mean isn't the whole history of the world, whole history of
mankind really based on some deformed form of convenience?)
i think about the whole fable of how eve was created from adam's
rib but then who were their children and how did existence really
begin? did they have a lot of friends as well and even (more feeble)
enemies? when did people start becoming popular in cafeterias?
kid forget his clarinet and mother having to keep on bringing it in?
homo-sapiens or real independent thinkers start doubting themselves?
prescribed painkiller cause we got pain killer! when did they put
up rikers? rockefeller center? that girl in her little red dress skating
figure-eights fast-forward solitary contented right around the plaza
at christmas? when did blues come in 'cause that's always been
an instant panacea and made you feel just as good as any rapport
or talk therapy or woman? you spend your mornings out here
feeling like shit in the full-of-shit suburbs with all these mean-
spirited wannabe wheeler and dealers who thrive off passing
gossip and rumors (is not that the real and actual whole parable
and configuration 'in a nutshell' and wouldn't call it a coincidence
of the nature and final conclusion of the crucifixion?) left all by
your lonesome feeling like a fish out of water simply watching
your fish swimming all carefree and contented in and
out of the windows of the castle in the fishbowl…

2. to me think we've asked all the wrong questions like does god exist?
well to me that's all irrelevant and of happenstance if you kind of get
where i'm coming from and if in fact simply and always been a good
human well none of that should really matter but living out here in

the dregs of the desolate dreary suburbs am more inclined to ask do
people or whatever in the hell you call these specimens really exist?

3. why whenever i say god help me it always sounds so glib and sarcastic?
when i'm at my wits end and ends up like some hypothetical question?
job who eventually just turned to a madman; always the little shit
which gets you in the end. the recycled formulaic crap on television.
cross between feel good and frightened, feel good and frightened
feel good and frightened, feel good and frightened; these days
have a convenient psychotropic for practically everything even
if you didn't know anything was missing, and will make your life
all good again. they've invented and come up with new forms
and strains of diseases and entitled them with nice little silly
pithy acronyms. will hire you a very aggressive go-getter
(who will get you yours) if you've been infected by asbestos
just in case you happened to be hanging around any hanging
asbestos and didn't know it and they'll get them, and get
you your just and due settlement, then eventually show
the image of some middle-aged couple strolling hand in
hand alongside the ocean, seeming so free and happy
as though this should be your targeted goal to shoot
for for your destiny, or your baseline and control to be
happy, to eventually be middle-aged and happy-go-lucky
strolling alongside the beach; doesn't seem all that bad to me
only thing, these things never seem to happen to me or maybe...

4. all the devils out here on the dead end in the homeowner's
association literally a day after thanksgiving ends end up seeing
who can string up christmas lights first like some sort of competition
or representation of the caucasian in america acting as if (which is
the perfect and ridiculous paradoxical parable and parody of the blind
leading the blind white man)who is more righteous and virtuous
so tell me what's wrong with this picture?

5. sort of *murderfuckers* and devils
who slaughter the indian and black man
and then so delicately and eloquently string
their christmas lights up with their convenient
and fucked-up disconnect to show what a perfect
and peaceful pretty little culture i am? i think even
if jesus came back (*for goodness sake* on a heavenly
crash landing) all he could do was laugh and shake

his head incredulously and he was in no way shape
or form by all reported accounts a sarcastic man
just a normal and natural reaction pick up his
rucksack and then move on to foreign lands...

6. they nailed him like a butterfly to the board.
they always just seem to get the most colorful...

7. cowboy robbed & held up indian
when he was just minding his own
business after he came back in the
canoe with mountain & moon
"always on a mission..."

8. betrayal is in no way subtle (it is klutzy and the ode of the mediocre
and fake wannabe criminal) and if you been around the block enough
times and got enough experience with this life eyes wide open and
head over shoulder can see it coming a mile away before it
hits you before they even think or believe they can hit you...

9. i owe my wife everything and i'm still nothing.
yeah you could say there was a little damage
back then and am still in the seventh grade...

10. decadence is when you no longer know what to do
with your 'abuse of power' (or most likely never knew
what to do with it or had much to say in the first place)...

11. i always suffered from the psychological experience and phenomena
of once you get her what do you do now? what could she possibly want
and expect from me? and later on just realized it is the 'exacerbation'
hyperbole of the holy empty nothing and settled for a couple nice
scenes and episodes of sex (love making?) love (sex making?)
and necessary pillow talk and maybe good chinese

to realize we are all just leftovers...

12. mermaids on the barbecue...

13. has anyone ever done a primal scream during an interview?

14. me: out here like a caterpillar with a butterfly heart and butterfly soul
but impossible to evolve so unravel slow simply dissolve to a much
higher form they couldn't even begin to understand nor begin
to know and for that (forget about it) thank the lord!

15. you: i love you so and when i see these soulless lowlives
not treat you with all the respect i know you truly deserve
and who and what i know you really are (it gets me angrier
than it gets you) it breaks my heart like a window breaks from
the stray rock of an ignorant little punk who's never left the block…

16. them: out here in this filthy and vulgar suburb in this very 'insular'
and 'exclusive' and 'desirable' community they'll try to have you
and me doubt and question our identity our self-esteem but funny
got no idea where you and me and me and you are from
and give away their not so secretive secrets instantly and
got no idea what we got hidden up our sleeves turning them
right into what they thought they thought they could think
which now much to their disbelief can hardly believe…

17. goddamn with the whole natural process of evolution you sometimes
wish man would just turn the fuck around and return back to the sea
and whatever land he came from and a whole new race and culture
of species given the chance to evolve and grow and develop
and leave everyone the fuck alone; windows need washing…

18. i always hated life, life at the circus watching those
poor trained elephants having to line-up and lean-up against
each others shoulders, those psychotic clowns riding around
like a bunch of lunatics from the asylum on unicycles, barker who
i never really ever understood what his purpose was while waving
our lit flashlights around as a bunch of hopped-up lasso-twirling
kids from the dark crowd and just wanted to get back on the ball field…

19. america needs a new choreographer…

20. america needs a new stenographer…

21. commercials show the image of privileged white kids
greedily, primitively, barbarically tearing open presents
of the latest and newest technology and suddenly you
see them really love their mommy and daddy and

know may sound like just an obvious statement
but do they ever once make the connection
to jesus' birth and later on his crucifixion?

22. out here they control you with all these constant see-through
false offers. am sorry america but you feel more like the land of
false advertising and over the holidays just get more aggressive
and competitive. they say america is "great" and will debate
and will get up on stage (like some juvenile election in high
school running for class president but really comes down
to who's the most popular and just makes you feel smaller)
and so all this simplistic and strange shit of declaring we are
the greatest country in the world seems more like some sort
of defense or deflecting mechanism, and never quite sure
what they are talking of, mean the whole greatest country
in the world stuff, and the only thing i can come up with
is you can take off down the strip mall and can literally have
a burger king across from a mcdonalds and got the whole free
will and volition of what you'd rather get a big mac or whopper)
but i have had a couple friends from foreign places (middle
east, russia, iran, for example, coming from areas of pure
oppression and subjugation) who tell me and do sound pretty
damn sincere and convincing and i guess do kind of tell me
the same thing and more inclined to believe and trust them
coming from a more humble and self-effacing source, as
opposed to some great big schtick from some brainwashed
prick with their rather ridiculous and rabble-rousing song
and dance or punch line, which never quite delivers and
from the perspective that you can do anything and 'make
something of yourself' (always hated that expression when
you get down to the nitty-gritty and deconstruct it 'cause
why in the hell would i want to make something of myself
as pretty much hoarding in my apartment in brooklyn, ny
with leftover kielbasa on the counter and futon on the floor
which does provide me a sense of freedom and self-determination
yet so kind and compassionate, and will even offer me to clean up
but don't know cuz know not classic or clinical and actually the most
autonomous and independent and liberating phase of my existence
only just don't have a girl; perhaps maybe if they offered me one
i would and you'll see at the end of this that is where in my opinion
i believe all real self-motivation and passion in the long-run stems from)
and were always those kind souls which seemed so much more humble

and grateful and wished the best for them i guess like the ole existential
jean-paul sartre debate and dilemma of what you're gonna now do with
all your free time and freedom, as can send you into something of
a situational depression or vicious cycle, feeling proverbially and
symbolically 'unloved,' so what i guess it all comes down to in the
very end is the concept of love (of feeling loved and wanting and
desiring and giving and receiving love) fall asleep with the weather
on and it's the holiday season and the commercials are getting more
aggressive and competitive and they say america is a great country
and still not exactly sure what they're getting at and talking of...

23. life just seems to get colder and colder
know it ain't me think a man of the world
how every time during the holiday season
in america ain't sure what it is and can't
put my finger on it and never ever feeling
myself relating to it if you turn on the local
news just seems to be the same repeated
token and quota of rape and murder and
fire those police and ambulance lights always
flashing in the deep dark pitch-black night in
the same suburb or borough or ghetto priest
being robbed at gunpoint your heart and soul
being broken in to just to find right around
this time of the holiday season things
getting colder and colder and colder…

24. i want to go in the fetal
like those sticky figs all
wrapped in their halo

i used to steal a lot during the holiday season
some of the most memorable presents
for my family from the mall

left the who's "hooligans" on the bus…

25. our country seems something very much of a cross
between organized crime and organized religion
why very likely became something
of a disheveled criminal…

26. every time he comes to visit it's like getting
ready for an interrogation (but how does one
really get ready for an interrogation?) for
some grand sweeping judgment generalization
(of which he's totally out of touch) totally shallow
and superficial, re-feeding into that belittling
psychological repetitive damage loop-cycle
and getting swooped-up and swallowed-up
with all those awful and absurd triggers
in the vicious-abuse-cycle; (every form
of authority i have ever come into contact
with contained this exact selfsame element
of a futile, wicked abuse of power, as if lacking
some form of intimacy or affection, and passive-
aggressively, superimposing and transferring
it onto me, the personification of all things
soulless and bureaucratic, eventually simply
becoming satires, caricatures of themselves)
kafka, kafkaesque...how else would
you know him? how else would he
know himself in his sunday best
defending himself (from all the
spiritual neglect) not being told
what crime he committed, and
eventually takes it out on himself
and in the end interrogating himself…

27. sometimes in my opinion, ironic, fucked-up
there are not even depression(s) but complete
abuses of power from poor influences in ones
psychosocial environment; hitherto as such, it
might very well not be something organic or
a chemical imbalance, but simply just a lot
of bullshit and brainwash, and thus sometimes
a form of regression or even arrested stage of
development, a most necessary dynamic and
form of escapism, as well as a means to an end
while behaviorally providing and giving a little time
and perspective through 'desensitization' to help to
assist and support that isolated soul or fragile identity
and ego when all those triggers (and violators) come

flooding in so as to avoid a retraumatization until all these
very convenient assholes and schmucks wear off and hit the road…

28. a day after christmas ends the civil engineer leaves christmas tree
out on the curb for the garbage men like he's had it with the kids and
stays out there for at least a month or so until his very sweet and sour
pretty white trash catholic wife threatens him and gives him ultimatums

he has also done this too with a big pile of mulch…

it's no wonder i become something of an alcoholic
for a couple weeks just around this time of year…

29. the u.p.s. man comes around the dead end delivering packages
to the miserable housewives like some sudden sort of stud-gigolo
in one final and futile stab until the whole place becomes like
some kind of runway or landing strip for tchochkes and trinkets
and takes off to the horizon like some idiot cape-crusader to try
and fulfill some other shallow and superficial wish-fulfillment…

30. i think i was happier when i used to live alone skin & bones
as tough as they come and hustle the streets of portland, oregon
and used to just lie there bare and exposed without a care in the
world (well that's an exaggeration, cared way too much about the
world) out on that solitary table at the phlebotomist and brood
and reflect and wonder how i even got there and look up
to the heavens and plan for my next chinese meal…

31. weird weather these days
snow coming down in vegas
looking down from the mountains
of detroit on the shores of lake michigan
cautiously sarcastically giggling "gotta be
kidding!" all my best friends turned to perc
heads joined the army and started a family…

32. never understood that expression *whistling dixie*…

33. i would have liked to have been there around that
first morning after they pattycaked the pyramids
the egyptian dogs and scuttling iguanas
and all of life to look forward to

slapstick, vaudeville…

34. the traditional box of oranges
from your aunt down in boca raton,
florida gets dropped off in the garage

mailwoman sputters off through fog

phyllis schmutz sends her regards…

35. teacher with a drinking problem lowers her blinds
waiting for the purple pockmarked fog to swallow
her up and move from the tension-fatigue
syndrome phase to the mausoleum stage…

36. i don't care no one can tell me what to do or feel
(where to go and what's the deal) man i've been
around the block way too many times to hear…

37. i want to be wanted dead or alive…

38. i want to return back to the womb of my
lower east side mom before life crept in…

39. i wonder how frankenstein imitated frankenstein…

40. so with white man it's literally always a race against time!
a race against time! a race against time! erase again time?

41. the #1 movie in america
now the #1 movie in the world…

42. i don't know? don't all these feel-good films around this time of year
with their romantic formulas and ridiculous schmoozing where they both
never ever just seem to shut the fuck up seem to be about what a guy's
willing to do or try to do to keep up with a girl's fickle moods which
also includes her crazy chick girlfriends like some sort of ritual
tribunal you gotta be real cute and clever and charming to? and
if they somehow figure out a way of doing it and surviving and
making it through will have the honor of her choosing you
and taking you? i don't know; after these i just feel a little
worn-out and drained and need a drink and sets off a case

of the ptsd and trigger of feeling slightly played
and used; now *deer hunter* that was a film!

43. almost every single relationship got no closure
pretty sick thought if you ever stop to think
about it but urge you not to think about it
why maybe on a little later on in life
muted all those technicolor westerns
and watched them with the sound turned off
how dean martin got all of those leading roles?

44. your girlfriend's flirting with me
from the corner of her eye from
the corner of her lies cornered
in the corner of your crime...

45. genet had that look in his eyes like he never had anyone.
man i know exactly what that feeling is like. love that story
which went something like like jean-paul sartre had to plead
and pay his bail just to get him out of jail so he could finally
turn him from thief to writer and ended up writing one of
the best biographies of this brilliant lost soul of all time...

46. a home where the murderers reside
but actually ironically far more sublime
and keep up with the birds and tea
and their local sports teams following
that good old new york creed we never
started it but sure as heck will end it
things ain't always what they seem...

47. "killing time…killing time…"
what in the hell gives you the right?

48. may death be something of a blissful dementia...

49. what'ya do once you get over the rainbow?

50. every time my wife leaves her bloody napkin
in the toilet the first day of her period the first thing
i think she deserves somebody so much better than me...

51. orgasm/ejaculation the greatest thing
the icing on the cake of every boyhood
childhood delinquent action/adventure thief...

52. all existential angst is the cross between feeling
like you constantly want to be crying and be angry
stored somewhere between the upper chest cavity
and lower larynx and having no place for escaping...

53. taking the horrible slow languid local
from the affluent suburbs to grand central
really feeling like you never ever had anyone...

54. why just freaken caroling
during the holiday season
how about another evening
when i'm down & out & beaten
in the driving thunder & lightning?

55. frankincense & myrrh fluff & peanut butter
standing on top of the stairs suicidal as usual
what's new no different than any other
why tonight we only eat unleavened
never had anyone to look forward
to or for that matter backwards
why you very much became
a vagabond that fluorescent
carrot cake shop nestled
and tucked into the tenements
of jerome avenue in the bronx
right when the sun went down
starting to turn chilly and cold
at the end of autumn somehow
feeling most comfortable waiting
for the bus home to the glowing
bones of the castles of yonkers

56. see myself missing
on the side of a milk
carton been missing
for so so long being
poured never asked

to be born over my
flesh & bones milk
of human kindness
how does that go?

*glug glug glug glug
glug glug glug glug...*

57. just made me some of the best coffee
sometimes so necessary to make coffee
in the evening to warm up the cuckolds.
remember how they taught you how to
make crumb cake in home-economics?
here comes the mayflower! the mobsters...

58. yesterday erica was a monitor at the schoolyard
'cause one of the mothers was out christmas shopping
and said the second graders didn't want any help, that
they can do it all by themselves, not so much so with
the first graders or kind gardeners (is that what they're
called?) and there was this kid every time he kicked
the ball his sneaker flew off. when erica asked him
why he didn't tie it up he said it was a look...

there was a boy whose mom tied his sneaker
backwards with the shoelace around the ankle...

59. standing around the playground in waning dusk
watching your son while they are just so much more
well-adjusted and got so much more to say and offer
all these parents just hanging around with their pale
and pasty complexions who just look like slow-death
and been in some sort of eternal existential labor camp
and got absolutely nothing to say to them like when they forced
you to go to those school socials and just wanted to get on home...

60. what's next pepper spray the dr. pepper guy from the seventies
who was always found dancing euphorically all over the place for no
particular reason just that i guess he was drinking a dr. pepper and
it just suddenly made him feel happy beyond belief "i'm a pepper!
you're a pepper! he's a pepper! she's a pepper! (like conjugating

some fucked-up irregular verb) wouldn't you like to be a pepper
too? i'm a pepper! he's a pepper! she's a…i'm blind—dead!!!"

61. america never ever be a righteous culture
as long as we are ruled by our cell phones
car alarms and that fucken literal proverbial
casket door which slams three times (that
triggers our p.t.s.d. and fragile shell) when
we're just trying to unwind by our computer

kid purchasing extra megabytes at the mall…

62. every time just around this time of year seems like someone's
got to do something crazy at walmart to get themselves famous…

63. around this time of year it always seems like it's around the exact
same place where i turn off "a star is born" and "meet me in st. louis"
and the whole mystery to me is how did the rest of these movies go?

64. i remember "harvey" the middle but not the beginning
or end which is fine 'cause none of that is relevant and the
most important and germane parts in my opinion was where
his neighbors tried to alienate and ostracize and freeze him
out just cause he had a relationship with an invisible rabbit…

65. was one of the nicest and kindest outcasts (in the cast)…

66. reflection of trembling tightrope walker in sacred river
my mistake monkey much better swinging in from the jungle…

67. suicide people hanging silhouetted over urban terraces
looking longingly into the muted howl of the deep dark forest…

68. the mad scientist has been gravely misinterpreted
and underestimated and simply got mad passion and intuitive
and just wants to be left alone; picks up sunday paper, spits on curb…

69. the image or vision of a couple sales girls working on
mannequins in a department store window and both just
kind of naturally losing it and beating each other senseless
body parts limbs flying in the spirit of the season…

70. i hate that they put a bull's eye on dillinger's head
and made him public enemy #1. would so much more
preferred they do it for one of those romantic crooners
i could never relate to in the fifties as made my senses
so much more guarded and put up my defenses…

71. why is it i still find my earlobe
being eternally tugged by the gods?

remember that cat who used to catch bullets
in his teeth in the *guinness book of world records*?

i am a cross between a peeping-tom
and exhibitionist in the off-season…

72. i'm one of those you see in the random newsprint headlines
something like "boy found…canoeist found after 20 years
missing…" but after they find me don't have much to say
to them and just take off with their polaroid cameras…

73. on waiting outside super stop & shop for my wife to pick
me up my pain medication after pulling something lawnmowing…

and just check out those kids pushing those carts around the parking lot
simply minding their own business taking their time not complaining
just doing their job seeming more content than ever and thinking
man if there were just a couple more people around like that?

74. literally used to spend nights getting high
jumping over unfinished parts of bridges
that dipped down deep into the east river
waking up in brooklyn with a *chip on my*
shoulder and reflective blissful hangover…

75. you survive and savor leftover residue
from the dreams from the night before
out of sheer and dire need and
necessity just to keep you going
the wife next door who always
bends over and now sits on
your lap as you caress and
brush your hands up against

her breasts without her even
knowing it and then she does
and has got no problem with it...

76. this morning thought my wife's canceled check said something
like "monkey breath" couldn't stop doing half-crazed lollipop kid
from the wizard of oz with corncob pipe in jaw and wife saying
stop egging him on while my kidgardener eating crispies was
cracking up representing the lollipop guild with fish staring me
down cause going through some sort of mid-life crisis slice
of sliced bread on top the toilet and erica's got bronchitis...

77. weather's grateful modest humble
looking out bleary-eyed & tongue-tied
to the radiant sky from the porthole
of your office knowing the only thing
you can rely on the only thing consistent
is mercurial ephemeral change of seasons...

78. often i see birds as great spiritual creatures
and just stand there in my suburban window and
see them silhouetted way up high draped dipping
swooping swooning sailing diving far off in sky
far far away over the ocean in the dim opaque
autumnal change of seasons and really
do get that brilliant fleeting feeling
of escape freedom liberation flight
of ghosts of gods and can truly
understand that whole rare
wilbur orville phenomena...

79. movies that really moved me i knew once i walked out
the moving pictures nothing could stop me and lingered
and clung on to me 'butch cassidy, mean streets,
dog day afternoon, dead man walking, good
fellas and ghost' with that patrick swayze
disappearing in cold lamplight streets
in pawnshop dress shoes not quite
as lonely during the holiday season
to my weekly hotplate hotel room
with a view of the alley on the sea...

80. in every great sensitive artist they suffer from the insulting and
nauseating slings of critics and ends up (goes on) fulfilling the self-
fulfilling prophecy and it's just in how much he decides and how
far he goes with it the self-fulfilling and prophecy part if you
kind of get where i'm coming from...

81. today while i was in my office i hollered out neurotically to erica
and she just naturally walked in naked before she was gonna take
a shower and i went—"baby, beautiful you look like a model!" and
she just responded—"not when you're bleeding at dunkin donuts..."

82. when wife is sick as something ran afoul with our fowl
i turn the lights down low and say baby i'd like to
just be a lamp post to keep an eye out on you...

83. leaves never take their life
they just appear satisfied
in spinning and sailing
gently to safe ground
dappled in a crown
of golden sunlight...

84. the long purply branches from the pear tree
extending, reaching out to the windows of my home
in late autumn dusk allow and help me to keep the faith...

85. today we took off our ghosts late from the rainy branches
of apple tree. people out here race obsessively a day after
thanksgiving to put up their christmas decorations like
some competition of who's first to see jesus

yet there's nothing further...

86. grownups think what it is to be grownup is to always
say the right thing and give the runaround and be open-
ended somehow strangely confusing this with maturity
and being sophisticated and a sign of class and culture?

87. i'm confused? why do the critics and
vultures always seem to go after the kindest
and classiest people (i.e. present day president)
i mean what about the idiot who came before him

or is that just the natural everyday
mean-spirited fucked-up nature
of human nature to try and take
advantage and gobble up

leaving just
the skin
& bones?

88. the image and vision of jesus
but didn't he ever get to the point
with all his disciples and followers
where he was just like "can you
just once think for yourselves?"

89. seems like shakespeare really got (down) the whole
drama and trauma (thing) of "the drive-by shooting"…

90. my luck these days put a gun to each temple
to make sure i get the job done and the mother
fucken bullets hit each other and get reborn…

91. god there's still so much living i got left not to do…

92. open your heart like a slice of pie missing…

93. fish in fishbowl swimming like crazy
feigning for leftovers with that big glazed
turkey right next to him. i drop in a flake…

94. freud; got new theory that somewhere around stage or phase
in the beginning of early adulthood (somewhere between the end
of high school and beginning of college) usually somewhere during
desertion and abandonment 'feeling' between innocence and reality
our life suddenly becomes a series of triggers and not even being aware
of what is organically and cognitively and developmentally influencing
it and for that reason and that reason alone and selfsame configuration
leading us towards such a deep and inwards brooding and rumination
which naturally turns towards something of a situational (or even
for that matter environmental and social and cultural) depression…

95. it was weird this morning in the strange shift of seasons
suddenly seeing this great big bluebird with his big bluebird
wings bleakly raking up the leaves, while sitting back stuffed
in the deep dark hole of the bluebird box was his fucked-up
dysfunctional family all snuggled up watching sally jesse rafael

you wipe the dream dust from your eyes which has
derived a lot these days from real-life nightmares
of a ridiculous and repetitive non-existence...

96. watching *home shopping network* up on my treadmill and was thinking
how perfect would that be if they sold pistols? don't care what era, civil
war world war ii, russian, prussian, american, and the perfect poetic
justice to just get away from it all, not sure how that would work though
and how long it would take "yeah i'll get the nickel-plated..." will take
10 business days but what if i'm feeling alright by then? have a whole
new perspective? you turn the channel and find yourself turned on by an
overturned oil rig out in goffstown, new hampshire; makes me feel
warm and cozy all over

perhaps maybe just something i can connect and relate to...

97. you wonder what the first thoughts were of those astronauts
returning home in their space capsules from the moon? those dazed
soldiers on their planes from vietnam? the truck driver who drove
all day all night long delivering logs? probably the opposite of that
image and vision of all those things which push you over the edge...

98. the cul-de-sac dead end resembles the extension of some rumor
even the way it is geometrically configured and even more ridiculous
don't even have their shit correct in the first place a bunch of passive
aggressive neighbors of counter-transference acting-out and starting
drama to try and desperately (once in their lives) prove that they exist...

99. white man will try to one-up you with (false images of) virtue
what is wrong with this (self-serving, self-righteous) picture?
until you realize from consistent patterns and experience
which eventually will turn to wisdom turning the bullshit
and brainwash on him there's nothing further from the truth...

100. all the vulgar people
on the block who i know

all this tasteless behind
the scenes shit about and
obsessed with competing
and who's got the best
most christmas lights

i suddenly see right
before dusk is about
to turn to night a stray
branch start to fall from
way a top the windy pines...

101. sound of wife smacking wooden spoon
against the cake bowl suddenly triggers
the cops rapping at my front door

i've lived way too many lives
folklore something like living

somewhere between
the law and the lord...

102. i wanna live inside one of those giant crayola crayons
which used to lean back in the corner of my bedroom
when the seasons would change season
outside my childhood window...

103. how to make cornflakes & bananas…

104. how to cook with saffron…
taking the slow canoe with mom's best friend
through the lilypads of the lagoon who comes on to you

i swear it's true and i am considered the criminal
these emotionally neglectful people who never
got to know me even ther-a-poo-tized me

i wonder if i actually took her up on her offer
probably would have been treated like
dustin hoffman in *the graduate* like
i was the aggressor or the provoc
ateur and sold me down the river…

105. conjugating irregular verbs

je suis   nous avons
tu es   vous avez
il est   ils sont

when you coming home?

106. language tries to cat chup and cap ture t hought
but does though t evertry to catchup and capt ure language?
(all the time!)& thusthe clar/ification why'awl contra/diction
(s)of commun/ication (a fineline &not much ofa difference be
tween declarative&Aquestion trying to makes ense of thep :ast
present whilewressling with theconflict ofwhether to forgiveorforget)

we are very,alone inn:thisex
dance/ &denial so muchmore

a functioninglaw wit an obsessive/compulsive
component too:it of codes&roles to allow/us too

move:on
totell us
who
we are

night:mares made,up of doughts&feers
&dreams some:wehre? between truth&dare

if i could havedone itawlover a/gain woodhave invi:dead
completelydifferent guess to:my:wedding (they were
shakesperian&plot/in a saint joking no/notwhy all:those
pathedick&petty:things thee immurderbard tells us Asigh
clinically&reality-based conspiratorial&perse:cuting as if i
hadn't done enuff suff:ring to make it& reach my fate&dest
knee) e/ven my,self asdone deserve her knowonlykidding!
howmuch arewe ruled? by hour an:xie t(ease)
and howthesis made:up from ad/
vice we weren't evenasking

man i only get to know:culture
from those first couple:moments

first:instincts, first:impressions, first
:smells and first:visions, not spending
too:long in it, as it loses all its spontaneity
& substance (like one of those:relationships
that gets:repetitive & none of you have the:guts
to end:it & just continue it for some,strange,reason
probably having something to do with 'the brutal, futile state' of
mortality like survival instead of living) so just enter the cosmopolitan,
& sophisticated,metropolis & ruins,of,culture then just get right,out,of,it

ihave)this(finer:morelucidimage ofgod
afterglobal:warming&it,all,goes,down…

everything they always prom:ised mewit flat/ry
(n/ever asked ironically theyoff?redme) be:came
the roots&symptoms&disease to the beast:of:betrayal

u blowthem:off more/so frumbor.ingpat:terns
than haven'tany thing todew with the hard/enedsoul…

107. thief broke into my home
stole my five o'clock shadow

when the cats away the mice will play
what happens when the mice are away?

skipping staticy sound of church bells…

108. always found myself far more the canary who swallowed cat
as they'd chime in look what the cat dragged in and i'd instantly
retort who you talking about me or him leaving them defensive
speechless with blank expressions hating me for my rapier wit
hating me even more at those decadent pool parties in affluent
suburbs exclaiming i was flirting and trying to take their women
which was probably only part true at least the first part as always
found life to be pretty damn absurd and ridiculous and empty and
useless and this always seemed to pay off no matter the results and
suppose in to the concept of instant-gratification the denial of existence…

109. girls always seemed to ask that eternal, rhetorical question
"do you like what you see" and it was only until much later on
you realized they didn't really want you to answer or respond…

110. today i found myself real down and out down in the dumps
and just out of nowhere started going "hot ptezl! hot ptzel! get
your hot ptezl!" from the old garden where all the brothers
used to smoke marijuana in the blue seats and amazingly
keenly found got me right out of it instead of all this new age
rich white girl yoga buddhist able to afford 'holy and sacred'
photographic trips to india "get your hot ptzetzl! hot ptzetzel!"

111. every so often feels in my recent life
people trying to steal shit from me (for their
basic intrinsic jealousy and insecurity) and then
because of that basic intrinsic jealousy and insecurity
being the little men and bitches and shits they are
follow the exact same predictable pattern
of trying to sell that shit back to me...

112. i don't know? can one really argue spending the rest of your life
being a dope addict (i mean the advantages far outweigh...) while just
watching the hallmark channel or weather channel or rick steve's taking
you around the world keeping a very close eye on your stamp collection...

113. would have loved to have been with paul revere
that deep dark evening in his glow-in-the-dark bastion
in the twinkling new england trees of lexington waiting
for the british to come in; imagine the adrenaline?

imagine the sense of pride & duty & do or die mission?
heartbeat mixing with hoofbeats and just around
the bend where all american history began...

horses sniffling...

II. Fluff & Peanut Butter

Do you really remember growing up?
your past?
how you grew apart?
in some soggy pasture
peeking through
peeping tom curtains?
torn & tormented?
misinterpreted?
how did your role model
& probation officer treat you?
your tutor? girl who cheated on you?
did your sister speak to you?
who were your heroes?
your villains?
gods & muses?
who had more of a profound & lasting influence on you?
who did you really think was gonna' save you?
your father? savior? selectman? lantern man?
best friend? moon? star that never left you?
lamp on in your mother's room that always
led you through because you intuitively knew?
grilled cheese & bacon & slice of boston cream pie
in midnight diners with best girlfriend from the rhineland?
do you remember the patches of drizzle that incessantly
fell on your melancholic island while hearses crept up
misty mountains past the car wash & tanning salon?
do you remember the end-of-the-world boardwalk
lost in the wisp of the wild winter of coney island
where all freaks took flight to a forgotten land of hasidim?
some sort of postmodern pogrom made up of the spirits
of dead scholars looking to be redeemed & reborn by
the rise & fall of radiant rhythms of a vast regenerating
ocean where sword swallowers & fire eaters & stray
dogs & winos secretly spent their off-season?
do you remember all those whimsical
women who showed up after the storm?
the dolce vita girls set up for revenge & folklore?
do you remember your fantasies & nightmares?
the scorched orchards & hustlers' porches?
the fastidious fishermen who eagerly reeled

in rainbows while their wives woefully
wept polishing the silver with their sorrow?
were you engulfed by sunflowers, mother's
gardens & the compulsion to be a criminal from
an authority figure who constantly put you on trial?
your most lucid reflections
in times of trauma & real-life
acquired pawnshop paranoia?
is this what it said
on your report card?
the seductions & alienations?
the anger management? altercations?
cat-calls, keyholes, convictions & karma?

Do you remember the rivers of pleasure you paddled
to avoid judgment & feeling beat down & battered?
were all those things that made you feel flattered the only thing
that really seemed to matter while everything thereafter idle chatter?
cheated out of a childhood & cheating throughout childhood
literally, unwittingly robbing all those who had robbed you
labeled with infamous, stereotypical, absurd half-truths
such as—"at risk," "oppositional," "defiant," "vulgar and
crude," "attention-seeking," "wise ass," "the class clown,"
"never amount to..." & somehow finding a way of making
it through, surviving, coping & rising above the abuse, like
brando in streetcar, proving all the doubters wrong, turning
hand-me-down blues into a rousing lapis-luzi indigo psalm?
how could they possibly call you "passive-aggressive" when
you simply were responding to feeling eternally put down?
do you remember getting turned-on by card tricks, flipping
cards & prank phone calls relying solely off charm convinced
the cruel world was simply a series of false alarms? what were
your rationalizations & reasons for a sarcastic call-to-arms?
why you pushed buttons & had enough one-liners
for a comic slapstick delinquent epic poem?
what were your forms of freedom
& how did you make the distinction
between reality & rebellion? abandonment,
guilt & glamor? glowing guillotine at the end
of the rainbow; that ghostly road where no one
seemed to go, yet meant so much more than you
will ever begin to know; the smell of mother's supper

which scurried down the hall swept you up & saved your soul!
did your existence become more drama than detention hall?
how did you like summer school? the summer?
the period, the play, the phase, prison that followed?
can you feel your mind starting to open?
to crack up, to crack open just a little?

Upon further reflection were not your
finest experiences in the schoolyard?
did not all metamorphoses get lost
& found with princes' & princesses
& a crumbling queen keeping guard?
is not this what revelations are made of?
dreams & nightmares?
the slaughter & foghorns?
compare this life to survival?
customs, rumbles, smells & forms
what happened to all those feelings
& beliefs cherished as a child?
the confessions & contemplations
dramas & quarrels
compromises & bargains
obscure seductions & offerings
you found it so hard
to make sense of?
to get rid of!
secret glances
& blatant avoidances!
nausea & romances!
the pouting & petals!
madness & marigolds!
manifestations!
manifestos!
sincerely feeling
every season come & go!
the sensations! its glow!
and tender toes tumbling
to the fragile folklore of fall!
your soul burst open like a rose
like a rock through the window
sweeping down some long-lost holy ghost hall!
those wonderful & weird smokestacks & steeples

that rose over the raw rainy roofs of recess!
the brooding & bridges & beloved birches!
the barking bitches, snobs & snitches!
guilty conscience & consequences
caught amid auditorium announcements!
dramatic entrances & disgruntled exits
always far more significant than any
of the shallow semantics spewed
from soulless teachers! promises
of imagination which required absolutely
no permission, sacred sacrifices, your visions...

Are you still wasting away in some surreal school lobby
waiting for the second coming or maybe simply just the first
or at least the three stooges with all those mad magical muses
who were far more sincere & shrewder, sincerely not mad at all
much more compassionate & clever than any of the useless drivel
dribbling from the status-quo who acted self-righteous & untouchable
exactly like their title, as you still feel just as restless & ready to go
(to grow, to glow) where all that seemed to really matter was to be-
long? do you still wish & wonder where the heck you belong coiled in
counselor's office like some common criminal hoping for "guidance"
most likely being escorted (tugged & paraded) by the sadistic dean of
discipline wishing to be saved, to be rescued...dragged down some
holy hollow hall past the lost & found...trophy cases...science lab...
water fountains...custodian...loose librarian...dramatic auditions
in the auditorium...u.s. army draft board snickering at last supper
tables in the cafeteria like con-artists with smirks & scowls & you
with your famous halloween hoedown pose like it was the end of
the world...could be the holy land or hell with an unconditional
radiant feeling of hope when your cup truly did overflow with
kindness & charm & punchlines so dry they always seemed
to be choking & shaking their heads muttering about *your
potential* like some buried treasure that they'd use against
you wondering why they tried to stick the rapier right
in your backbone when you kept them all bawling...
hysterical...fucking cowards that they were...never
had a mean bone in my body, did i mister?

Are you starting to become one of *those* people?
lost & lonesome in a civilization seeming to lack
any kind of consensus or 'collective unconscious'

of ethics & morals? kindness & compassion? scruples?
do you sometimes feel as though you missed out on
that "stage" of development whatever or wherever
or whoever it might have been, that class or lesson
where they told you you no longer needed to be loyal,
sincere, or accountable & may thrive simply off of attitude,
to be single-minded, competitive & aggressive "no matter?"
like that nightmare where they told you you didn't graduate
because you missed gym as if the dreamcatcher had broken
from some whimsical wind? had you hoped & prayed
that betrayals & contradictions were simply mere coin-
cidences with an easy out and even easier explanation?
(thrust into an existential crisis in which past friends
& acquaintances for no apparent reason became strangers
in an absurd drama that never ever seemed to really happen)
did you take it on yourself & develop a personality disorder
where they stigmatized & pathologized
& labeled you a pariah? do you believe in
the concept of before & after, the here & now?
that you will be saved by the holy cow, ice cream
man, american flag? (oprah? al roker? bachelor? survivor?
process of elimination, sacrifice & slaughter to land soul mate,
companion & perfect partner?) the wind & fog? town or suburb?

Always most puzzled by those things attributed to culture
(cafes & cellulars & churches & college) enraptured
at where populations choose to settle, on bridges
behind billboards, over highways, in the canyon
those barns & silos & steeples & trees which turn
to geometric silhouettes of gentle antiquity, as your
restless & fleeting thoughts intuitively turn inward,
outward, flushed against the blinking belly of a firefly
evening, ignited by the midnight blazing wings of a crow,
solemn howl of a seagull when the sun disrobes at strip mall
low self-esteem angel dusting off profile, cautiously glancing
over shoulder, diagnosed with "attachment disorder" instead
of searching for rightful owner battered by butcher's brother
the monstrous baron *munchausen*, put them all together &
got father-figure who marched out on mother & daughter...

What happened to those good ol' heroes brandishing blazing bold axes
who used to shuffle in spirit & turn bowlegged, bright-eyed & muscular
into the thick-wooded wilderness to chop down a lock of the warlock's
forest for daughters & mistresses & stake-up hearty, healthy houses,
hugging the banks of gushing, glorious rivers; scarlet doors & stainless-
steel steeples shrugging home all charley-horse, cranky & contented
to pharmacists' porches of pensive & piping glowing lanterns; slice of
shepard's pie bubbling in oven beckoning coquettish & pathetic blushing
ballerinas & their pudgy ancestors for a biscuit & gravy evening of
bingo? that holy haunted home of raggedy rundown industrial spindles
on the border of madness & freedom spinning to the heavens with a
whole town engulfed in the shadows of state hospital curtains? hooded
phantom parks at sundown of rundown down-in-the-dump mutton-
chop beat down wraparounds? mannequins who kept an eye out
on all the secrets & rumors that really never ever changed at all in
the bustling center of a forgotten town? monument with his rifle &
long black cape draped over a place that now seems missing-in-action?
the neglected wives & unfaithful husbands? music teacher & adjustment
counselor? old timer with alzheimers directing traffic, like some insane
crossing guard that has lost his mind right at the wrong time, inside,
outside ancient dusty brick alleys like the fine flaky sugar of donuts
sprinkled through the twilight (spending his time pondering the
peculiar pendulum of time woefully wondering & worrying about the
passing of days literally counting his blessings in the rain)? forgotten
railroad discovered to still wind & make its way over black licorice
buddha river? deserted diners & down-in-the-dump drive-ins? that old
play dough factory when frozen blue seas seemed to stretch endlessly
through the rib-caged, knock-knee barbed wire trees & senile old
fishermen lost all their dreams trading in their sanity for memories?
will the stray scent of chimneys somehow deliver you right back
to everything you forgot...classrooms, bedrooms & secret haunts?
those lost ramshackle strip malls composed of bowling alleys, tombstones
& used-car lots? everything, anything & nothing you could possibly want?
to return home in the eternal dusk where golden bats flash through
flickering forests as you know you love the misses, that is the bare
bones of it, when on some cold winter's night the stars beam bright,
like some spiritual blanket enveloping all those brutal experiences of
cruel existences that were so exotic & distant, stoic & tragic, stirring
up memories like magic? might there be nothing left to do but to paint
the garden chairs for the spirits? for the miraculous moon? for the breeze
& leaves? for the subtle and sneaky thief change of seasons?
for the mean loneliness which always pervades your being

& never seems to leave you? for the dwarf apple trees?
for the sea & seagulls? for the cornfield & crows?
for the bridges & church bells & battered girls?
for the stars & shore? for the grapes & graveyards?
for that final solemn snatch of sun which illuminates
the bare bones of maple-sycamore turning heaven-
ward to holy hunks of horizon that bless the ocean?
for your soul which sluggishly opens like a rose
down the bleak snowy highway heading home
where signposts read *horseneck, fogland,*
holy ghost road? do you remember
how you used to hang out
& swagger in flannel?
where's the schoolyard
stud & seductress now?
what have they all become?
accountants? pharmacists?
truck drivers of glistening
freshly-cut sappy logs
like those lincoln logs
lumbering toward long-
lost holy destinations?
delivering psychotropic
medication through
the haunted silhouetted
mountains when all the
madmen are sleeping?
to all the institutions
& detention centers
& group homes
& old age homes
unable to leave the homes
of their moms or sainted
loved ones? dead dad
houses at the end of
dead end cul-de-sacs
when self-destructive
& suicidal siblings
finally hit the road
content now just
to mow the lawns
of parks & prisons

churches & graveyards
staggering up & down
through the town?
tugboat captains?
topless dancers?
do you really remember?
do you really recall?

III. Views From The Twin City Motel

1, how to defrost rock cornish hens
2, how to wake up without suicide ideations
3, how to make friends with your enemies and enemies
    with your friends like the difference between god and religion
4, how to develop a crush on your wife's
    snow globe and glass animal collection
5, how to during those long days of marriage
    fantasize and dream about past old borderline
    girlfriends with eroticism and maddening erratic behaviors
6, how to die a happy man not getting to know the neighbors
7, how to be grateful for that geometric barn of the seasons
8, how to observe that apocalyptic sun coming in from
    the movie theater over the purple-gray mountains
    to the eternal swamp and lagoon of your
    deep-down blue and brooding ruminating
9, how to feel forgiven and forgotten by spare image
    of a toll booth at dawn somehow representing
    all life-transitions and state of flux
10, how to deconstruct and decipher and turn
    that bartelby the scrivener infamous line
    "i prefer not to, i prefer not to" into a rap
11, how to paint-by-number your whole life
    and existence and assign specific shades
    and colors to different parts of the picture
    breaking down all devils and developed
    resistance while reaching certain levels of
    truth and faith, revelations and redemption
12, how to be a criminal for just trying too hard
    and caring too much and them thriving off
    other's hardships; those down on their luck
13, how to become a petty thief just to sublimate your
    moods and how they try to make you feel about you
    (beating them at their own game and don't exactly
    seem anymore so cocky, confident, and cruel)
14, how to have them believe you when you don't even
    believe yourself and believe in yourself so much more
15, how to look out for deer and moose and bear
    on the side of the road they're always talking
    of never seeing them and that now you see 'em
    now you don't mythology meaning so much more

16, how to be content and proud looking out from clean motel room of the cottage onto the strip mall from your window of the twin city motel

IV. Motel Reflections (the makings of a misanthrope)

Ruin 1:

Once again you forget your sneakers
but your wife being the saint that she is
has stuffed a pair of orange-blaze shorts
and gold cut-off shirt into your sports bag
and you climb up onto the stair master
with your shirt & shorts & colored socks
& penny loafers getting in your workout

Ruin 2:

Back in those days when you used
to runaway to places like san francisco
and reno you used to love to fill the tub
with very warm bathwater, fix a highball
from the mini refrigerator, then once you
found your long-lost center would start to jerk
off to girls you had lost somewhere down the road.
this was your homage to them, paying your respects
and then delaying as long as possible, getting out
squooshing your face and tugging your earlobes

Ruin 3:

It was only until much later
you were able to discover
it is much better to have no
support system at all than a
bunch of mixed fruit and nuts

Ruin 4:

When you get out you start to think
maybe the best thing simply is to

be married with lovely little lady
rubbing your aching feet after
some long crazy day at work

Ruin 5:

Your wife telling you how she really only wants you
to be happy as you truly know deep down
inside this is a veritable impossibility
almost even feeling guilty as though
betraying (for keeping it a secret)
and her being so innocent
and naive and sweet

Ruin 6:

i.e. Back in the day they used to have these
half-crazed streakers with untamed afros
high-top sneakers suddenly show up
and streak across your tv
now a lot of stalkers
and serial killers
trying to make
the scene

Ruin 7:

Outside your window in reno
is the crossroads and winos
breaking bottles against
the *burlington northern*
your skyline shattered
damaged a long time ago

Ruin 8:

Terrible tourists bring with them their all-knowing attitudes
and hollowed-out ship in a bottle privileged and entitled souls

most often from places like new york (more like the upper east
side more like some suburb) and for some strange perverse
reason always feel the absurd and pathetic compulsion to
want to challenge you due to most of them being meek
little men with fragile male egos who appear lost and
miserable yet playing their see-thru roles of loving
fathers money earners and heads of households
who have brainwashed their wife and bratty clones
who none of them really know or even care to know

Ruin 9:

At the front desk she's too self-absorbed with her schtick just as sick
in playing roles when you've already told her several times in a row
you'd prefer to pay with cash as opposed to a credit card

by the fifth time she finally opens her fucken ears
and suggests i pay with cash. you feel
like hitting her over the head
with a gideon's bible

Ruin 10:

The paint-by-number faux-influenced
pastel floral and pastoral pictures
on your wall with never any room
for the imagination at all always
make you think less than more
inevitably causing you to
somehow think more

Ruin 11:

Always end up feeling starving
due to feeling excruciatingly lonely
crows crooning outside your window

Ruin 12:

America engulfed by soulless clones
gabbing away on their cell phones
(spoiled brats on walkie-talkies)
everything now's about buttons!
buttons! buttons! buttons! buttons!
nightmare come true as car alarms go off
back and forth like the infamous banjo duel
from *deliverance* while innocent bystanders
simply walk past doors and the wind blows

Ruin 13:

I can't stand these motherfucking motels
with people slamming doors making a hell
of a lot of noise drunken in the hall having
come to the conclusion a long time ago the
louder they are the less creative and original

Ruin 14:

If this is what it means to have a life
i so much more prefer those without one
who simply walk in their doors and shut the fuck up
you with orange rinds, pork fried rice, and wine on your
queen-sized bed, hopefully with a muted ballgame turned
on somewhere in the midwest preferably st. louis vs. chicago

Ruin 15:

As all you can do is turn to hard-working
& honest & heroic pugilists duking it out
in the center ring all alone one on one on h.b.o.
who don't have a mean bone when you know
the true killers & criminals & cowards
& clones are right outside your door

Ruin 16:

The pharmaceutical salesmen...
cunts at cosmetologist conventions

Ruin 17:

Hesitant once more like hamlet
not sure whether to fight or run
feeling a little cursed like job
wondering why you're always
the one poor soul with the
one devil kicking your chair
at the movie theater one room
where all you ever wanted to do
was to simply relax read
and even recite haiku

Ruin 18:

You even start believing those defeatist
proverbs—"just can't seem to catch
a break...how trouble always
seems to find me…"

Ruin 19:

And start to feel
a little sympathy
and gain a bit
more understanding
for the alcoholic
and adulterer
and junkie

Ruin 20:

You stand buck-naked in the middle
of your motel room in front of the mirror
like some madman praying for a miracle
as though pathetically pledging allegiance

Ruin 21:

Sleep naked in the fetal position
not so much for the obvious reasons
but more so from what your ex-convict
con-artist 'man of constant sorrow' acquaintances
taught you so as to thwart stabbing or rather 'jigging'
of any necessary vital organs by enemies while sleeping

Ruin 22:

You start thinking out here on these long days on the road
would it really be such a crime or sin or so wrong to have
some stranger, some girl, sleep with you, i mean would
that really be so much a betrayal (as we're all such
slaves to semantics and spoon-fed morals) while
you feel so alone and she's so alone and might
even be considered in the context of a full body
workout, not just the physical, but also mental
& emotional & psychological & spiritual
working out not just your gluteus maximus
& inner thighs & buttocks & gluteus but all
those other very significant & neglected internal
organs such as for example the mind & heart & soul

Ruin 23:

This time you're with your realty agent
checking out homes who you know is really
lying through her teeth but really don't so much mind
the stories and constantly telling you about her fiancé
and that he is a lumberjack as you think she might be

fibbing just a little cause she is a little scared of you yet
really don't care so much cause she's a truly fine and
kind girl and had a rough life with an overbearing
husband going through a messy divorce

Ruin 24:

Always hated the checkout even
after you've paid for your room
finding it to be so frustrating
and futile and just wanted
to get on the road like after
some domestic quarrel
and having to go back
and review like some
exit interview when you already
know exactly what had happened
and simply just want to move on

Ruin 25:

As she just stands there in her
very formal pose pre-packaged
dialogue, wrinkle-free clothes
when you know all she really
needs is a nice little spanking
and then maybe following up
with your own line
of patronizing and
placating questions–
"how was it for you?
is there any other service
we might be able to offer you?
is there anything else i might be
able to be of any assistance with?"
and she's got those big blushing rosy
cheeks and bashfully feeling enlightened
and liberated with a natural glow says "no"

Ruin 26:

When you take off at least you
know you no longer feel alone

Ruin 27:

Some big moon still blooming
over a mountain in the morning
where they have signs which read
things like *moose crossing* and hear
there have also been a hell of a lot of
coyote and deer spottings even baby bear
nibbling the glistening pears of backyards

Ruin 28:

Where you don't dare think of disturbing
them or scaring them as you more
so are a part of *their* world

Ruin 29:

Golden pears
dangling from
branches of pearls

Ruin 30:

Your realty agent who told you
the most dangerous times for deer
and moose crossing the road is dusk
and that you can see the deer more so

because their eyes
light up but not so much
the moose who will simply just set
themselves up to get themselves struck.

you start thinking there's a beautiful and simplistic ignorance
to all this like the native-american or ancient egyptian's
intimate concept of regeneration and reincarnation.

you even remember as a kid watching those shoot 'em up westerns
and worrying and wondering most of all what happened to the horses
not really so much the humans that being both the cowboy and indian

Ruin 31:

Make your way past
"the last gift shop
in new hampshire"

Ruin 32:

A gigantic snowball moon still looms
over the etched-out ruins of silhouetted bleary-eyed
bristly purple-blue mountains of vermont just waking
up where your agent told you they got hit pretty hard

Ruin 33:

And your heart starts to open up
when you take the long empty
lonesome highway home
down through the bosom
bone of big burly mountains
& bridges & lazy hazy faraway
smokestacks where all the fog
& smoke & steam from factories
& chimneys & cities & lagoons
& lakes & mountains of being
all seep & stream together
in a great big heap
of holy firmament
& thankfully can't see
a thing *a think* a head of you
as you're enveloped & encased

& drowned & bathed by draining sunlight
finally taken away to a place they can't find you

Ruin 34:

Time ceases to be
you cease to be
add & subtract
these things
& you got
exactly
the absolute
zero infinity
of reality
which is
your perfect
(non-)identity
& true self
finally free
to creep out
of the haze
a new entity

Ruin 35:

A slanting sun at dawn coming down from the mountain
feeling like some sort of good old nice warm toasty buttery bagel
a fog like fresh-cut powdered sugar donuts that melt in your mouth

Ruin 36:

Inspector clouseau conked-out on the side of the road
pleasantly tinkering & toiling in his tiny little telephone
truck, rearranging & primping his puffed-up disguise,
handlebar mustache & big cigar & bifocals whistling
whimsically pretty pithy phrases & suave one-liners

Ruin 37:

As you head home reflectively
tired & hungry & alone

Ruin 38:

Past great cathedrals of cities like dripping sandcastles
with belfries where bells are supposed to be...
keyholes, seaholes, teaholes, soulholes

Ruin 39:

When you finally get home
there simply sits a bottle
of pink bismuth liquid
right in the middle
of your kitchen island
which reads "pain relief"

Ruin 40:

Rest-
(less)-
in peace.

XIV. Character Analyses:
How Juvenile Delinquents
Sleep Like Creatures In Hibernation

1, A clinical case study of the "human" heart throb

I've decided i'm gonna stalk david hasselhoff
not necessarily for any reason in particular
like sex or violence or for whatever
reasons stalkers stalk stars but just
think what the hell has anyone
ever thought of stalking the hoff?
and more off from a psychological
and sociological point of view
to find out what his everyday
routines and rituals include?
his daily activities and moods?
how he spends his downtime?
how he spends his uptime?
what his vices are?
what his virtues are?
and just hang out there
on the downlow all calm
and snug like a bug in a rug
with my wrinkle-free stakeout uniform
on in my *hertz* rent-a-car maybe chowing
down one of those new fancy-schmanzy
fast-food gourmet burgers from *wendy's*
i'm hearing so much about which seems
to be a delight in every bite and might just
make my life seem a little more worthwhile
with tears streaming down my face coming
to closure and making sense of arrested stages
of development; fuck all those hi-tech instruments!
don't even seriously know what the hell they're used
for anyway what ya call them? androids? smart phones?
but maybe some good ol' time polaroid camera you used
to pull out like an accordion picked up at a pawnshop just
off the strip mall hopefully shooting long distance or if not
get a close-up in a slow drive-by shooting right outside one
of those sleazy and seedy vegas casinos he's starring in doing
his very earnest and heartfelt and sentimental renditions of such
old time soft classics like "band on the run" or who was that?
starsky or hutch? "don't give up on us baby"
glen campbell's "rhinestone cowboy" to make

the whole herd of middle-aged women swoon
until my cheap room runs out way out at the end
of the strip where they don't even have ratings
or guest comments and find out how in fact
we have so much in common and how our lives
in many ways really do intersect and are not that
far apart or that much different both a bunch
of used and leftover good-hearted losers just
trying to make it or make a little sense out of
this poor and wretched existence and trying
to contribute something positive to culture
like jimmy walker *kid dyno-mite*! just barely
keeping our head above water scared shitless
of our mortality after our 15 minutes of fame
has finally run its course for like the 10th time
in a row just like those dazzling bulbs of the
casinos on the strip naturally fading and going
out and camouflaged with the sun and clouds
when the drunken intoxicating evening turns
to the bleak morning, hungover, aimless, empty
not knowing a single soul but in a strange and intimate
way (motivated, forward-thinking) having a place to
go lost and alone within the absurdity of anonymity

2. A clinical case study of the elevator operator

Think i'm gonna apply
for one of those jobs
working as an elevator
operator where you
just stand there all day
& do absolutely nothing
think i'd be pretty good
at something like that
at doing nothing
being one of those
old timers like one
of those relatives
who would always
just show up to family
gatherings you never
knew & what they did
& never said a thing
but reserved & keen
& always with a kind
look on their face
& grin & for that
reason liked them
better than all
the others
i'm gonna apply
for one of those
jobs as an
elevator
operator
& just
stand there very
prim & proper
in the corner
in my charcoal
gray suit rubbing
up against one
of those spit-
shined spittoons
or silver domes

loaded up with sand
where they stash
all their leftover
cigarette butts
& secret & taboo
issues & problems
& paranoid plans
never got the chance
to get off the ground
got the chance
for closure
or for that
matter
fleshed-out
in one of those
schmaltzy
buildings
in manhattan
usually around
the diamond district
or garment district
or one of those
very high rise
upper east side
condominiums
along the river
minute by minute
day after day
season by season
make small talk
in the mellow
madness of
the muzak
& schmooze
with strangers
as with that i've
always thrived
& excelled at
at being
something
of an existential
hustler in the midst

of the nothingness
(getting to know
all those rich
& spoiled
codependent
helpless daughters
who are always in crisis
who need & appreciate
me more than their own fathers
eccentric old maidens who half
the time silent & half the time
blaming & having explosions
old money howard hughes
characters who never leave
the lobby or their apartments
& in the family passed down
from generation to generation
those old jewish immigrants
wearing their same modest
& humble tweed jackets
& haberdashers
& galoshes
literally
wearing
their heart out
on their sleeve
early to rise
& always
the last ones
to leave getting
older & older
shrinking
smaller
& smaller)
i think i'm
gonna apply
for one of those
elevator operator
jobs as feel
i've always
had the
penchant

& charm
& gift for gab
& not wanting
to get too close
to them
always been
like that
a natural
at that
at coping
& surviving
& excelling
& thriving in
the nothingness
but my luck like
everything else
these days
most likely
who you
know or
unionized
or hire from
within (usually
having nothing
to do with within)
or some form
of nepotism
i'm also thinking
& considering
one of those
tugboat or
lighthouse
positions

3, A clinical case study of the telemarketer

I wanna
have sex
with one
of those
very
driven
pledge
drive
women
& see
how truly
sincere
& earnest
she really is
how far she
is willing
to go for
the cause
what really
goes on
behind
closed
doors
if her
non-verbals
& body language
actually match
& meet up
with her
body language
non-verbals
how giving
& generous
& passionate
& creative
or something
of a control freak
& has a whole

list of do's
& dont's
(even
directions
& lecture
right on
the spot
if you
should
happen
to take
chances
& cross
into un-
chart-
hys-
teria
how
neu-
rotic
breaks
down
to lack
of erotic
& episodic
guilt &
conflict
for being
neurotic)
hit the road
& leave
a check
right
on her
night
table
maybe
a little
stickie
tickler
on the
clock-

radio
thanking
her for her
patience &
participation
& please
no need
to call

4, A clinical case study of the innskeeper

I want to be an inn
keeper at some
half-crazed
half-sane
haunted inn
around the way
(with a high
murder rate)
maybe might
be a slaying
here & there
yet all part of
the ambiance
& atmosphere
people who've
mysteriously
disappeared
no questions
asked as
the town
& villagers
& politicians
want it that way
& keep it all on
the hush-hush
& keeps down
the taxes
& good for
the tourists
& even put up
historic plaques
to sentimentally
commemorate it
while all a part of
its fabled history
gossip & rumors
& gruesome
ghost stories
a log always

thrown on the
rip-roaring fire
(along with other
things in this life
which prove to
not be worthwhile
not needed which
leads to brooding
and self-loathing)
& plush beds
prepared with
fresh-dipped
chocolates
fresh crisp
sheets
& hospital
corners
& when
the cops
& coroner
show up
infamously
conveniently
botch it up
as get
a special
discount rate
or even comp
for friends
& family
due to nepotism
& the percentages
& guest comments
during the off-season

A family-run business
based on word of mouth
& reputation & who you
know & of course once did

5, A clinical case study of the witch

The witch opens the door
to escape the folklore...

flicks on electric fire
and sparks a cigar
checks the clock
on her coffee maker
and recharges vibrator
takes chattering teeth
out jaw and gently lets
it fall to cocaine mirror
screws off splintered stilt
and sticks it in hole
of floor leaning it
up against door
to keep out all the
hookers and whores
composes curses for
the sleazy and soulless
neighbors then goes on
to pray for bad weather

the witch opens the door
to escape the folklore...

man took off on her
on a motorcycle
to new mexico
and now stores
her sex symbols
and super heroes
in shoe boxes in
her walk-in closet

the witch opens the door
to escape the folklore...

all her daughters have left
her who once were gorgeous
tomboys of the neighborhood
radiant and rambunctious hoods
who used to spit
sunflower seeds
into each other's
hair at sunset
now simply
going through
the motions
going into
the fortune
telling business
with cheating
husbands
who have
all left them
(this tradition
this rendition
has been passed
down from generation
to generation as they
now shuffle through
the lower east side
suspicious on the sly
with glowing cat eyes
powder-blue suits
tap shoes
and dangling
roses having fallen
for much younger girls

the witch opens the door
to escape the folklore...

getting back to daughters
they have all become
parasitic and vindictive
or what the abusive
psychiatrists call it

passive-aggressive
having turned on each other
competing on every other corner
wasting away in windows, aloof
and apathetic, catatonic on
cell phones, picking at their
beauty salon nails with swaying
palms and pastel views of paradise
chewing on pork rinds
while all you hear outside
are their bastard boys cry
—"you don't don't know
what you're talking of!"
right below
blaring globes
which read—
"fortunes to go"

*the witch opens the door
to escape the folklore...*

all her sons become dope addicts
either in jail or underground
having interestingly
been found dead in alleys
or having robbed a string
of friendlys upstate
having become the
punchline for all
the inmates
having once
been seen
screaming
at sisters
beneath rainy
movie theaters
in brooklyn—
"i'm not proud
i'm a junkie!"

the witch opens the door
to escape the folklore...

pulls out a batch of fresh-baked road kill
straight from the oven, lights a candle
and while half-blind, and now numb
all over from what life has wrought
her, stands dazed in a haze
watching the radioactive
sun squinting through
pine needles, window
cleaners high up above
cleaning the panes
of the sanctuary
and slaughterhouse
factory with thieves
stealing the cable
of next door
neighbors, then
starts to go through her
obsessive-compulsive
rituals of kissing every
souvenir and tchotchke
in her rent-controlled
hole-in-the-wall
as the only
thing which
makes her feel
safe and secure
and hasn't
betrayed
or deserted
or taken off
and proceeds
to turn on all
the game shows
with those road kill
sandwiches and mugs
of carnation instant breakfast

*the witch opens the door
to escape the folklore...*

and sees a sudden gaggle of crows
stalking a coyote in her backyard
thinking to herself—"no one ever
seems to leave anyone alone..."
now feeling at home, contented,
demented, even convinced she's
lived a pretty charmed existence
or about as well as can be expected

6, A clinical case study of the dominatrix

I am going
to turn the tables
on the dominatrix
and rip off her outfit
and give her a spanking
aint never gonna forget
with little baby girl gasps
and squeals, then gather
up this bunched-up peeled
off sex appeal, and carefully
delicately fold it up and send it back
in a neat little package to her mother.
this redirection or life-transition
will turn out to be a very profound
and crucial, significant turning point
in her existence, as she too craves
the structure and discipline, growing
up with an extremely overbearing and
domineering, manipulative father figure
thus resulting in always feeling guilty, hollow
and vacant while could never ever come to grips
with not meeting his grandiose and unrealistic
expectations, consequently overcompensating
and taking on the role of domination in hopes
of healing all that hurt and pain inflicted, as
evidenced by being an unwilling victim to
psychodynamic patterns and vicious cycle
of this characterological narcissism and
dysfunction. she is a good/bad all-american
girl, hard-working and diligent, who presents
as highly intelligent, one might call her driven
for the exact selfsame reasons, even a genius
and go on to run her very own successful
beauty business, focused, self-motivated
and self-determined, using her charms
and manipulation to marry a wealthy
doctor or lawyer, naturally evolving
to ironically become a "virtuous vixen"
attending all fund raisers and functions

bearing 2-3 kids, yet what proves to
be significant, found hanging in her
deep walk-in closet, which always
provides a nice reminder, is not so much
the transitional object of that infamous
wedding dress, but more so the leather
outfit, mask, boots, and whip, going
back to a period and time when things
seemed just a bit more free and innocent

7, A clinical case study of borderline disorder

After my borderline girlfriend broke up with me
for the last and final time after she had asked
me to marry her a million times i heard she
started going to those 12 step programs.
she had never had a drinking problem
but think this helped her to reframe
things and put things in perspective
and somehow in a very perverse way
felt flattered but this was what most
of our relationship was like in a sort
of really fucked-up and damaged way
and i am not ashamed to admit i think
i miss it a little bit. i wonder where she
is now and been thinking these days
of the image of considering attending
suicide funerals. the girl i went out
with after her was a rich girl from
michigan and met her in my
second year of internship
and would spend the summer
bum-rushing all those gourmet
shops in new york city handing
out those free samples and
would stuff her face and
then just storm out of
the place heading back
out down the avenue
not by coincidence
never once with
a thank you
or sense of
appreciation
and interestingly
speak all intellectually
and erotically but when
the time really came for any
type of affection or intimacy
ended up quixotically sleeping
all alone in her bed while she

slept on her pull-out sofa
in her very exclusive upper
east side high-rise condo...
sort of ironic as she was to die for
and had a great head of flowing
hair and called herself a zionist
and things could have just been
so simple but always made things
so complicated eventually doing
stuff like coming out of the shower
with just her towel on draped around
her soaking body deliberately engaging
me in casual conversation on her sofa
knowing and being completely aware
of what she was doing spreading open
her legs revealing her whole big wet
deep dark dripping monstrous hairy
pussy and what's a guy to do and
felt like the whole great maddening
perverse and perplexing metaphor
for women or at least girls like her.
she eventually asked me how i
felt about her cranberry curtains
and when i offered her my heart
felt opinion seemed to ruffle
her feathers and get very
offended and said the job
had not yet been completed

8, A clinical case study of the juvenile delinquent

As a kid couldn't stand
and still can't stand
matter of fact could
never stand those
expressions such as–
don't play with matches
don't run with scissors
don't talk to strangers
while fuck it had never
thought of it and grew
up playing with matches
running with scissors
and talking to strangers
as think even became
a more complete
and well-rounded
(whatever the hell
that is) upstanding
citizen because of it
symbolically sitting
lotus-style cutting
out my cut-out
figures while
sitting in
front of
a burning
blazing home
and casually
gabbing away
with a whole
slew of strangers
all except for
that very new
and strange breed
of self-motivated
and single-minded
and goal-oriented
power-walker
vigorously

pumping their
arms like a pack
of nazi foot soldiers
with expressions
of constipation
to their targeted
goal & destination
yet in retrospect
when it truly came
down to it didn't give
a shit as every grownup
i had ever come into contact
with was a complete hypocrite
(of this they were quite consistent)
with their own agenda full of blatant
contradictions and really had no
other choice nor saw a conflict
in acting-out against every
brutish authority figure
even having friends
trying to swallow
whole bottles
of lysol
because
they felt
filthy about
themselves
lowering bottles
with suicide notes
down building windows
(you talk about
reaching out
for help!)
so tell me
is it really
such a crime
to have lived and died
by playing with matches?
running with scissors?
talking to strangers?
as i thrived off danger
a creative imagination

humming lotus-style
in front of a burning
blazing home
snipping away
cookie-cutter clones
and in many ways
as a grownup
am proud to say
at least in this way
have never grown

9. A clinical case study of the 'gentle giant'

It's strange, i always experience the exact same reality…
and to be brutally honest, have become completely bored
by it (even a little hostile; that's usually what happens after
the same repeated behavioral patterns of people who come
up with ridiculously inaccurate, absurd and exaggerated
conclusions about me; have even had partners i've run
into on the street and we'll start strolling down the avenue
and casually mention—"i feel bad for you, i know you, and
it's like every dude wants to try and fight or challenge you"
and in the moment, means the world, and instant validation
for someone who has always felt so damn alone, never quite
ever really having a home to call his own) and so yes i fit into
that unenviable, anatomical, physiological category of that of
i suppose you would call the "gentle giant" who doesn't have
a mean bone and heart of gold, perhaps that convict just let
out of jail and they instantly judge or become scared of but
about as nice and sympathetic and compassionate as they
come, and maybe you might just see me somewhere in the
not too far off distance across from some diner or basketball
court, doing pull-ups on some stray summery corner streetlight
in the lower east side, all by my lonesome, in perfect fighting
shape, flesh and bone, not an ounce of fat, raw and muscular,
and eventually after all those nit-wit know-it-alls, who don't know
their ass from their elbow, impulsively, consistently, make the exact
same wrong conclusions, appearing more so scared of themselves,
while find out deep down inside i'm a romantic at heart, and after
just getting sick and tired of these exact same repeated behavioral
patterns of them, now somehow, repulsively coming onto me and
wanting to be near me, or even, believe it or not, fall in love with
me my first and even for that matter, last instinct, is to want to
just instantly crawl right into that so-called proverbial hole and
be left the hell alone; the final fate of that of the mistaken gentle
giant with the desire to go into hiding with my transitional-object,
isolating, and staying away from 'strangers' trying to get way too
familiar (the ones in my opinion, of true-blue crude and vulgar
assault & battery) for purposes of sanity and self-preservation

10, A clinical case study of the american doll

Holiday season not too far off down the road
as they have started showing those commercials
for the *flesh-colored* dolls with the psychotic
blinking eyelashes and chords that you yank
from the nape of neck like some transitional
object for schizophrenics while you ponder
about the effects and influences that this
has had on the 'modern american woman'
on the 'grownup male,' little boy who's
wanted to say—"shut the hell up!" for
so damn long *proof:* used to have
this uncle i was so fond of who
used to play with who went gay
and it was discovered one day
by a mother whose reaction
was not so uncommon
back then and completely
blocked and later made
no mention a whole
drawer full of
barbie doll heads
and his father who
supposedly was this
very stoic and handsome
gentleman and quite the lady's
man yet as opinionated as they
come always with something
clever to say constantly drilling
into his boy's brain how the female
gender was the far more dominant
and aggressive of the species.
sometimes i can only imagine
him self-consciously (not even
knowing what he was doing)
slithering through some toy
store in the late 50s snapping
the heads off barbie dolls and
when you think back in a kind
of nostalgic and macabre way

is not this classic americana?
(likewise can only imagine
the reaction of the toy clerk
when he came upon
and discovered this
sudden sort of
andy warhol
repetitive
mass murderer
image or pattern
and what to do
and make of it?)
turns out he did become
quite the "male stud"
who all the ladies
fell *head over*
heals in love

11, A clinical case study of j. morrison

Jim morrison blue eyed bartender is let go jim morrison
social worker and innkeeper takes off from below blue
marquee in the middle of nowhere somewhere between
the country and outskirts of the city somewhere between
the foreign and familiar ring of foghorns and churchbells
on cobblestone feeling so alone right at home in the drizzly
dusk jim morrison down on his luck wanders home after
a night out in jail in the bleak and blue bleary-eyed break of
morning through bail bondsmen and law offices and strange
neon postmodern boulevards jim morrison feeling blue let go
from hitching on the side of the road with sawed-off machine
gun back to his bungalow jim morrison blue tears streaming
down his cheeks in those brilliant muted home movies playing
role of both slave and savior (slay and save her) some children's
therapist calls him up after he just gets fired something his wife
has urged him to do several times and get back to his writing
while the child psychiatrist provides him her undying support
as turns out most likely has fallen in love with him and declares
she will miss him and will keep on calling to check in on him
bit strange and awkward and first time in his life not feeling
uptight despite being flattered (as feels sincere and compassionate
while to him doesn't really matter but to her appears devastated
and saddened) and thinks maybe perhaps it was just those long
messages he used to leave on her answering machine and most
likely turns out was dreaming and fantasizing about him in that
motel just down the stripmall and be just the man for the job
even though she's a single mom and knows he's spoken for
but perversely being the opposite gender may be what makes
her respect him that much more and what attracted her to him
jim morrison falls back asleep somewhere between dream and
nightmare at last muttering mantras under his breath as really
didn't want any of this to begin with with headlights at night
from the newspaper trucks beaming through his window like
a jailbreak like jesus at the stake like a mistaken identity like
an insane slaughterhouse like the mad million burning stars bal-
ancing over blushing barn fragile and forgotten out to do no harm

12, A clinical case study of american hx

Abraham Lincoln
tall gigantic svelte
silhouetted under
his top hat drops
his mug shot
haunted in a
state of shock
turns quick
to the left
down river
to the dead
where they
are all piled
up in alphabetical
order outside the
movie theaters
and brothels
and pickle
and porno
and piano
shops where
a mechanical
mannequin with
a sarcastic smile
like some inside
joke only she
is privy to and
stereotypical
shrug of the
shoulder
in the chicken
wire window
is playing
joplin nonstop
and abe just goes—
"fuck when's this
gonna all stop?"
heads down
the stripmall

of desolation
where you can
smell roasting
bodies and
roasted
chestnuts
where they
keep the
used car lots
and electric
werewolves
going off
at all hours
in the forest
on the border
to scare off
all the tourists
and strangers
where the
cheerleaders
are fornicating
getting fucked
by frat brothers
and mascots
soon to become
state senators
and the everything
must go madmen
liquidation blaring
bulbs flashing
on and off
with macabre
mascara
masquerade
parties at
the all-night
diner right by
the meat market
where they keep
the drag queens
and tough looking

cookie-cutter
motorcycling
homosexuals
right before
the dawn
right before
the sun comes
up and the bagel
shops open and
sweep the flour
from the floors
with leftover
electric roses
from the casanovas
blinking on and off
left on the lonesome
docks where the mafia
make a name for them-
selves by the brooding
river of blaring foghorns
and tug boat captains
with tourette's disorder
get familiar and like
some war hero who
has been abandoned
by his troops for no
apparent reason
(most likely for
his bravery and
courage like jesus)
dips his dark foreboding
ominous graveyard figure
into the freak sideshows
a fine line between
apocalyptic and
prophetic and
looks forward
to a brave
new world
goes to pick
up his prescription
of heroin at the pharmacy

and with one rare glimpse of
hope heads up to the balcony

13, A clinical case study of wonder woman

Today after
a long day
of existing
decided to
put on one
those old
reruns of
wonder
woman
muted
with a
caption
on the
bottom
which
read–
"wonder
woman
meets
the baroness
von gunther"
& how
i thought
man how
back then
things were
so much more
ridiculous
& innocent
& thought
back to
my child
hood in
the seventies
how i always
found my
self getting
into heaps
of trouble

& worrying
& thinking
the world
was gonna
come to an
end but look-
ing back
back then
didn't seem
half bad a
matter a
fact so
much
better
(& self
soothing)
& thought
about linda
carter in her
red white &
blue uniform
with that killer
bod & that
truth lasso
& how she
did that slow
motion bionic
turn turning
from what
looked
some
thing
like a
librarian
with her
hair up
in a bun
to wonder
woman
& imag-
ined how i
wanted her

just to lasso
me up & toss
that truth lasso
around my bones
& with a boner
would confess
to her how
i wanted to
bone her or
just as least
be the mother
of my children
& you know
looking back
back then
when i
was sure
the world
was gonna
end things
didn't seem
half bad
& there
was really
so much
more to
be said

14, A clinical case study of superman

Wonder if superman
that being clark kent
ever just got to a point
where he got sick of it
all and didn't want
to change the world
didn't want to change
into his superman
uniform anymore
from his
brooks
brothers
and bifocals
and blocked hat
lazy and lethargic
more so disoriented
dysthymic mildly
depressed stagnant
looking more like
a cross between
ratzo rizzo
and elastic man
the man of steel
feeling forgotten
stolen with steely
glazed over
eyes and malaise
of a putrid pasty pallor
slouching in that phone
booth on the filthy slushy
corner of hell's kitchen
outside the automat
of devil may care
businessmen
and dope addicts
with all that steam
from the subway
seeping up from pot
holes and sewer tops

and just in a sort of
faraway catatonic daze
nodding off nodding away
dome dropped dreaming away
a kind of hamlet bartelby
the scrivener for the ages
lois lane driving him crazy
constantly moody playing games
with his feelings and emotions
and now experiencing something
of the 'fight or flee' phenomenon
stuck with the trauma of whether
he's coming or going and throws
himself, without knowing, into
what he believes to be the safety
and security of a self-imposed
isolation (he can't get out of)
decompensating and desperate
feeling a false sense of comfort
locked-up silhouetted detached
and distant in that phone booth
of his coiled in the fetal position
with pained expression and only a
swatch of his starch white shirt torn
off and a bit of that blue and gold
muscleman leotard superman
lettering showing through
bemused confused clark kent
bent more so on just being
'a mild-mannered man'
as opposed to always
having to save the planet
and do something beyond
the call of duty and not
in the job description
something heroic
and savior and
save her and
save civilization
as when it all comes
down to it just appear

ungrateful and thankless
and don't ever give a damn.

XV. A Bundle Of Blues

-1

the patterns of history & civilization
prove very much to be triggers
from social and cultural and
psychological and spiritual
man's petty absurd cruelty
to man where the symbolic
becomes quite literal
and literal symbolic

0

one wonders if government and politics
is as bad as it was in greek and roman times
as in my opinion a comparison may be made just
in much different ways (but when you think about
it really not so much) while all forms of subjugation
and lies and betrayal and deals and abuses of power

why the rise of the great philosopher (& rebel & scholar)
all having to go into hiding or put on trial by the devils
pleading for their beliefs & ideas & rights & lives

1

words speak louder than actions…

2

wouldn't it just be so nice and refreshing (and validating)
if just once, once, bush said—"i think it was a real mistake
to get us involved in iraq and afghanistan" and apologizes
to the american people as well as all the innocent victims
in those regions, but i guess from a psychological and
behavioral point of view these are the 'types' of people

who never ever once (in their poor and pathetic lives)
ever admit they are wrong (god forbid) and will live

an 'absurd' existence of pure (and impure denial)
even go so far as in the short-term and long-run
to become compulsive liars and criminals. it is
important to view this horrible and ridiculous and
tragic period of american history not just simplistically
from a political point of view, but from a psychological
model of a spoiled and privileged and entitled child
with consistent, characterological patterns of poor
impulses and insight and judgment, just trying to
please and get approval from his archetypal heroic father
(figure and turns delusional) while he and his advisors
from the structure and configuration of a dysfunctional
family unit with scapegoats and manipulators and provocateurs
and past histories and those who aligned with who and those
who got bullied and alienated and broken lines (and fine lines)
of communication with its collective distorted thought pattern
developing interestingly into delusions of conspiracy *and* grandeur
moving on to con the american people and con the con/stituents
and con the con/gress and everyone and everything which got
brought down in the long run by this scumbag "son of a gun"

3

imagine churchill wiping his mug off
after one of those yalta conferences
with one of those wet warm towels
they used to give you at the end
of those feasts at one of those
good ol chinese restaurants

(why do theodore roosevelt
and andrew jackson never
get talked about?)

4

i think kafka lived in one of those
pure plastic capsules and saw
it all from the poor helpless
portholes of one of those
beatdown bubblegum machines
surrounded by other plastic bubbles
then some punk random stranger
slipped a quarter in and he'd go
tumbling down against his
own will and volition forced
to have to figure it all out

this is how he developed
wisdom and a sixth sense

jean-paul sartre's novella
"nausea" was contagious

5

yah say shalom yah say shalom
say shalom eloheynu yah y'israel
well however that song goes…
made me feel a little less suicidal
as people got these ways of making
you hate yourself combining years
of remedial french hebrew school
and allen ginsberg confessional
say shalom eloheynu yah y'israel

6

Abstract:

these days recently almost everything
practically and impractically has been

penetrating my sleep cycle of dreams
and dream if only it happened maybe
a little bit more frequently in reverse
and dreams not the dreams of dreaming
but those other dreams touched my being

Psychology:

i hate the fact that i hate the facts
that there are no facts that's a fact

Philosophy:

the fact is there are no facts
and i hate the fact that i hate
the fact there are no facts in fact

Specifics:

liars hate it when you know (or find out)
they are liars as deep down inside (pretty
shallow) through paranoia or their own
distorted form of reality (insecure and
fragile identities and egos) go on the
defensive then not by coincidence
become awfully offensive…

7

i feel shot like a bottle shattered
up atop a tree stump by bonnie
& clyde barrow with time to kill

8

does pumpkin just ever tumble over
pick himself up pull himself out
of the pumpkin patch because
he's dead tired rest his bones
by the rambling river looking

forward to the season
right below the mountain
across from the haunted motel?

i look forward to my subconscious
finally catching up with my nightmares
which will one day be my best dreams ever

9

"joey you saw i got seltzer
for you before! i'm putting
my foot down" always liked
those kids who tried to make
a clean break for it out at
the group homes and spent
the remaining hours of your shift
searching the dusk early evening
of suffocating thick dense trees
didn't get paid enough...broke it
to my wife tonight for the first time
they put me in one of those classes
in my freshmen year of high school
for delinquents and kids who couldn't
keep themselves out of trouble as the
junior high school counselors made it
all sound so good and special but like
the first day when we looked around
and recognized each other and knew
each other's m.o. figured out what was
up believe only class i really excelled in

10

i should have gotten a letter of recommendation
for college from my detention hall monitor–

"don't give my taffy to the schizophrenics!
it was a gift from my sister!"

vote mitt romney for the ticket
vote hillary clinton for the ticket

fuck it has anyone ever attempted
to assassinate them before it...

or at least toss those leftover rotten
tomatoes they used for spanky & alfalfa?

reminds me of one of those relatives i'd never
think of talking to at a family get-together or function

11

i remember when i was at one of those
high school house parties way back
in the day like when the parents
would take off to their second
home out in the country and
always order in one of those
great big kegs (which i suppose
was *our* second home) and saw
one of those untouchable impossible
wasp girls just looking and admiring
herself dancing in the dining room
mirror and thought how could i even
begin to compete with something like that?

12

i had been having a really good rapport
with my wife going back and forth and
when i decided to go into the kitchen
for a bologna and rye sandwich had
saw where her car had left the garage
several hours before and it was crows
moaning through our window. don't
think i'll tell her about it as pretty
much had gotten closure…

13

why whenever you are going through such maddening
overwhelming conditions and circumstances all beyond
your control but putting up a damn good fight and defense
in the struggle and never give up they will always just show
up to your door always with the most loving of intentions
and say such crazy shit like i didn't want to tell you this
have a friend of a friend of a friend and had my cards read
or will rip out horror/scopes straight from the bullshit paper
or declare with great conviction i found out our birthdays
don't mesh or stars are not aligned and you're like what
the fuck i need this now? how is this in anyway helpful
right now at the present time like going off into battle
with some lying sheisty palm reader from the avenue
who just gets paid to rip you off and prey on your
most fragile instincts and emotions and feelings until
all you're forced to do as always is fulfill the self-fulfilling
prophecy as really tried so hard and diligently to persevere
and go straight like billy the kid or butch cassidy sundance
that kid you grew up with from the neighborhood screaming
at his sister in the driving pouring rain passionately half-crazed
beneath the marquee of the movie theater—"i'm not proud i'm a junkie!"
which right about now able to relate to and feels pretty damn liberating…

14

recently
not really
have had
a fantasy
of one
of those
beautiful
and sleazy
aristocratic
southern belles
in her hoop dress
with a slight glimpse
of her pale buttocks
even have her parasol
up with her whip tucked
in and deep thick humidity
and magnolia seeping through
the shutters trust me have
been there and done that
with some of the cutest
insane jewish girls
from the suburbs

15

everyone's always grooming
and primping their kingdom

(a bust of joseph stalin
with delusions of grandeur
sticking up from the garden)

like eternally stuck in some dentist chair
          with one of those drills

      never quite exactly
being invited to the ball

      nor reaching
the promised land

don't know anyone out here
& never felt more a stranger

16

criminal sneaks through
tall stalks of flowers
but turns out falls
in love with them
as all you see
is his silhouette
with head embedded
deep in the stamen
then steals away
to the shadows

17

i think i want to take a tour
      around those frank lloyd
wright homes
      where they around?
the midwest? michigan?
      chicago? buffalo?
and just ask to be left the hell
      alone a former shell
of myself and curl up in the fetal
      position all by my
lonesome on one of those long
      solitary benches
with straight lines during sundown
      and order in take-out
any place which delivers
      perogies? blintzes?

18

amerika when the fuck
can i show up and do
a surprise visit
to *your* home
with ten-gallon
and guns ablazing
and show up to all
those pussy coward
sheriffs when they least
expect it and chuck them
and pile them all up
in the holding tank
and leave them
like those lobsters
in some fish tank
and make fun
and ridicule
and bully them
then feed them...

19

history of this country's a crime
as don't fool yourself still runs
by a herd-like mob mentality
an obvious and see-through
and predictable trend where
people desperately try to fit
in and cater (and acclimate)
to that privileged and entitled
mediocre and majority baseline

20

there was a reason
for organized crime

coming from a very unfair
and unjust disorganized life
like some fucked-up
dysfunctional game
of musical chairs
and you do the
hokey-pokey
and you turn
yourself
around

21

always seemed to make a name for myself
every time someone tried to steal
my name from myself…

22

always wondered when they
delivered those washers and dryers
does it also come with the gorgeous
puerto rican housewife with the smile?

power of advertising...

23

is it just me (know it's not)
but does it not just seem like
the whole world's melting away
and breaking apart while arrogant
and aloof suits at ball games are
busy on their smart phones texting
away and american online providing
all these tips and suggestions to

pour coca-cola in your fertilizer
to help your garden grow?

24

always curious about that whole scenario
when they put you in front of a firing squad
and ask if you have any final wishes or requests
as they always seem to go for the blindfold
and cigarette and wonder if they give them
the chance to smoke it or just hit them up
in mid-puff. since i'm a non-smoker for
no reason in particular would request
a hebrew national with sauerkraut
and relish and like the zen-buddhists
said would be the best hotdog ever.
of course if that was not available
a fast-food order of crab rangoon
and ask if they might be interested
in sharing maybe possibly forgetting
their reasons for blowing my brains out

25

is our hole ancient history
culture and civilization
the magical kingdom
down in disney world
florida? cinderella
with her breast
implants and
donald duck
the dope addict
with a chemical
dependency
problem?

(all-inclusive
made to feel
exclusive?)

our royalty kanye/kim kardashian
and another new scandal
brewing of nude selfies?

everything spawned
from a college
cheerleader's
pussy?

26

always find myself picking up hitch hikers along the road
and pretty nice and down-to-earth people and will take
them for miles on end or as far as i can take them
as totally sympathetic and not just about their car
breaking down but their life breaking down
and family breaking down and i was exactly just
like them and it's scenes like these where have
always felt closest to culture in these interludes
and moments and even now any chance i can
will head and crossover the border to check
them out check out that second language
you were mandated to take a long time ago
and now find myself rather fluent in remedial

27

why does it always seem like those
who need and require peace and solitude
the most have the hardest time in finding it
and eventually may even be put in the pathetic
unenviable absurd category of undesirable or violent

28

cul-de-sacs dead ends homeowner's associations and suburbia
are like really bad predictable strolls through overly-manicured
neighborhoods of nepotism as ironically have always
felt far safer in very dangerous unfamiliar areas

29

it's strange but every culture or religion
or group or organization who give
the impression linguistically
of inclusion (or some sense
of belonging) always in the long
run turn out to be so judgmental
and alienating and only take in
those specific people with similar
like traits and characteristics
(and resemblances) which
will give it its 'good name'

30

pain,
shame,
sane,
saint

i've lost my strength
lost my memory
what'cha say?

31

every quote on quote human being i have ever met
who self-proclaims themselves as being so religious
have always found them to be so full of hypocrisies
and contradictions and not by coincidence overly
punitive and parasitic and thus in conclusion
realized the fine line and huge difference
(schism) between character and behavior

the greatest crime i have found in man
is his ability (more accurately inability
to justify) the disconnect (and blatant
neglect) between morals and ethics
and everything they have claimed
and said and disingenuous promises
and actions (complete lack there of)

32

funny to start off they're always
so much more attitudy than you
and then when you come back
with an attitude of your own
because of their attitude always
act dumb like what did i do?
and don't know what hit them
and with their ridiculous and
higher than holy disconnect
always so far from anything
realistic and act like you're
the one with the attitude
the nature of the know-it-all
who doesn't know their ass
from their elbow and the traits
and characteristics of a very
uncultured culture who des-
perately through attention-
seeking trying to have
you think different

33

at my funeral i just
want there to be drizzle
i don't know maybe a couple
my old girlfriends the only ones
i felt really went out of their way
to really get to try and know me
(and were just as abandoned and
deserted and in need of a rebirth)
maybe a couple my sister's boy-
friends who i guess played the
role of older brother figures

triggers and true
love just as lucid

"lava spills just a mile
away from subdivision"

guess i don't have too many regrets
how they forced me to learn a second
language although i never really used it

34

wouldn't it be great
if people were like
your local library
and docked a
nickel or dime
every day late
when didn't
return a call
or didn't
return
a call
at all
or simply
disappeared

into thin air
for no apparent
reason would put
a whole new spin
don't you think
on the dynamic
and experience
of desertion
abandonment

the best thing
about childhood
were friends
who appeared
to be there for you

35

it is great to hear children's truths (whose
beliefs always so true to their conviction)
and means so much more than what adults
try to persuade (and convince) you as truth

36

are the people
in the haunted house
just as haunted too?

37

the sign along the side of the road
reads "pain ahead" snicker to myself
going–"tell me something i don't know"

jim morrison in
the background—
"unhappy girl..."

38

you drift through tourist towns
while through hard knocks
and experience have
learned to naturally
ignore them as
they're all simply

repeated cookie-cutter
cowards who just greedily
take and got nothing to offer

feel like the expression
'the white slave trade'

39

g.i. joe trooper
literally standing
in sun glasses
and uniform
and ten-gallon
secretly hiding
in the shadows
of the shrubs
of some
front lawn
in this very
quaint historic town
pointing his radar gun
right at your car when
you're just picking up

speed to accelerate
to try and get out

what the hell is this all about
and who are the real criminals?

chuck d said–"america
is set up to trap you..."

40

freedom (is what it feels like)
to finally be left the hell alone
when they don't know you
and finally get home...

XVI. Suburbanization: a wasteland of illusions

Catatonic father just sits there
in his favorite chair and stares
out the front door of his home
at the same paint-by-number lawn
especially loves looking at the same
shadows at the same telephone wire
which naturally drapes itself down
from the telephone pole and gets
lost in the forest while the kids
on their play date play all around
his home who have simply grown
accustomed to accept and know that
it's just him being him. he thinks and
dreams of his wife's ass which he
has learned to love and always has as she
comes storming up the stairs like gestapo
complaining and demanding something
of him gets up and goes out to the dump

*It is of importance to note that a man's labored
breath on his death bed keeps almost the exact
same rhythm and cadence as a woman in labor*

Wife pulls car into garage like a mirage
like she's done millions of times before
and not sure if it's because of the safety
and security her presence provides
or deep down inside really loves her
(in many ways can't live without her)

*It is of importance to note that a man's labored
breath on his death bed keeps almost the exact
same rhythm and cadence as a woman in labor*

Presence in relationships (in marriage…)
is 'practically' everything and all that subtle
spiritual stuff in the subconscious which helps

to assuage and ameliorate all the acquired
and what has turned to hardwired damage

*It is of importance to note that a man's labored
breath on his death bed keeps almost the exact
same rhythm and cadence as a woman in labor*

They come in whipped by life and now try
to find a new pathetic way to be whipped
by a wife. i used to really like those bars
in the montana night not too far from
the indian reservations where with
the last call would rap it all up
like a doggy bag and give you
the rest of your remaining
beer in a cup to go

*It is of importance to note that a man's labored
breath on his death bed keeps almost the exact
same rhythm and cadence as a woman in labor*

I look at the rain in my window
and wonder if i brought myself in

i love it out here in the mountains
the cloud formations and know

they're probably getting
something far more
serious up there

witch whipping in the tree
and an american flag
across the street

doing the same thing
with a tractor parked
perfectly beneath

*It is of importance to note that a man's labored
breath on his death bed keeps almost the exact
same rhythm and cadence as a woman in labor*

There seems nothing more damning
or strange than living out here

Wrap me up in the veins
of a rainy orchid

I miss the accents
of runaways…

*It is of importance to note that a man's labored
breath on his death bed keeps almost the exact
same rhythm and cadence as a woman in labor*

Don't know if it's just me but i love polaroids
from the sixties and seventies of innocent
(no so innocent) jewish girls dragging
canoes during the season of summer
camp down to the lake with their
long milky legs and colored socks
and sandals on and long chestnut
hair to the mountains turning away
from the camera with very natural
hard-working expressions maybe
all collectively murmuring at one
time "portage" turning away
knowing (but not wanting
you to know) o you pervert
you're taking pictures for
the yearbook glad you
got my best side

*It is of importance to note that a man's labored
breath on his death bed keeps almost the exact
same rhythm and cadence as a woman in labor*

The transitional object (the stuffed animal
for example) was invented for the toddler
and child as a sort of vehicle of safety
and security as well as even slightly
an object of object permanence
but if analyze certain such
similar like objects more
closely in depth and in detail
may be used for practically every
stage of growth and development

*It is of importance to note that a man's labored
breath on his death bed keeps almost the exact
same rhythm and cadence as a woman in labor*

You may very well find and not by coincidence
your dreams hidden and burgeoning in that phase
of your arrested stage of development. you may also
find believe it or not and can even be some time after
that initial arrested stage of development another arrested
stage of development (what life and existence does to you)
which psycho dynamically may be trying to make sense of
the original arrested stage of development all for the sake of
reflection, self-awareness, clarification, and some sense of closure

*It is of importance to note that a man's labored
breath on his death bed keeps almost the exact
same rhythm and cadence as a woman in labor*

It is my contention that commercials
and advertisements do more to cause
and persuade me not to buy the product
as have always perversely viewed sex
and violence with a certain amount
of individuation, independence
and intimacy, sex and violence
to a certain extent as lasting
within the moment, sex
and violence in retrospect
for all intents and purposes
with silence; sex and violence
has never sold me of course
only if we're talking about
the whole other thing
has always left me…

It is of importance to note that a man's labored
breath on his death bed keeps almost the exact
same rhythm and cadence as a woman in labor

How does one become a hurricane specialist?
i want to become a hurricane specialist
think be a kick ass hurricane specialist
and gonna put in an application
for hurricane specialist as wonder
if my social work credits will transfer
over watching all those pastel colors
swirling around el paso acapulco
pressing all those buttons
and circling concerned areas
with my very stern and earnest
expressions and body language
and my tight muscular health
club abdomen and pectorals
starch white pleated shirt
and clean slacks
and clean look
making small talk

with all the pretty weather women
with my million-dollar smile
and very clever one-liners
then comes on commercials of dancing
black families ('cause of course all black
families dance) around generators by *kohler*
and a milf living happily after with her
new state of the art vacuum cleaner
and of course the jolly green giant
with his cough medicine complexion
yes i want to be a hurricane specialist
that's what i want to be a hurricane specialist
how does one put in for a hurricane specialist?

*It is of importance to note that a man's labored
breath on his death bed keeps almost the exact
same rhythm and cadence as a woman in labor*

Suburbia is like
some really fake shit
some bullshit sibling rivalry

between little man with a napoleonic complex
and his archetypal twin with a savior complex

obsessed with territory and boundaries
and from a zen-buddhist perspective
never satisfied with what they got

trying to one-up their neighbor
never once appearing content

*It is of importance to note that a man's labored
breath on his death bed keeps almost the exact
same rhythm and cadence as a woman in labor*

Leaves fall out here
like paint-by-numbers
on a souvenir postcard

*It is of importance to note that a man's labored
breath on his death bed keeps almost the exact
same rhythm and cadence as a woman in labor*

Could put a bullet in your head
and feels like no one would know
or even care or even for that matter
be aware which in fact feels even scarier
like those archetypal symbolic characters
in a nightmare you thought were supposed
to be there for you and just continue on with
everyday creature-of-habit routines and rituals

*It is of importance to note that a man's labored
breath on his death bed keeps almost the exact
same rhythm and cadence as a woman in labor*

Communication for this lot
of 'human' beings does feel
something of a foreign language

or something they were never
ever introduced or exposed
to and thus become 'absurd'

and rather fragmented
vessels of a distorted
thought pattern and
reactive behavior and
even clinically delusional

*It is of importance to note that a man's labored
breath on his death bed keeps almost the exact
same rhythm and cadence as a woman in labor*

Anything that may threaten
or cause them to stray
off this straight (and
narrow single-minded)
path they become
very paranoid
and defensive
and guarded
and hostile

*It is of importance to note that a man's labored
breath on his death bed keeps almost the exact
same rhythm and cadence as a woman in labor*

It does become something of a fascinating
and paradoxical phenomena and intriguing
too how those neighbors we never see or
come into contact with often strangely
enough may make more of a significant
connection for the exact selfsame crude
and vulgar petty and trivial behavioral
patterns and routines and rituals already
mentioned or the reasons or non-reasons
(of perceived non-reasoning) for absence
and thus develop more of an aesthetic feel
and flavor for the forms and images of homes
of hedges and shrubs of the shapes and forms
and configurations of lawns of where they
extend to and go to (maybe even bringing
us all the way back to all those spiritual
memories and experiences and historical
transcendent feelings of early childhood) and
leaves *so much more room* for the imagination

*It is of importance to note that a man's labored
breath on his death bed keeps almost the exact
same rhythm and cadence as a woman in labor*

I live on a block of a lot of leftovers and losers
(and don't in any way mean to sound negative
or pejorative) people who wander through
dim halls silhouetted when the sun goes down
high on codeine medicine, stray and pasty bald-
headed geeks from the library who still live with
mothers suspiciously skittering down the dead end
perfectly primped poodles who just stand there staring
straight ahead while their wild masters dead to the world
do control burns and never wave at you, piles of chopped
wood simply left on front lawns in front of garage doors
under a full moon cradled on top of the bare branch empty
apple tree, neighbors with luxurious tennis courts who never
leave the forest of backyards and like idiot zombie-explorers
can't stop compulsively chain sawing down trunks
while standing on gigantic mountains of mulch
american flags whipping in front of every home

It is of importance to note that a man's labored
breath on his death bed keeps almost the exact
same rhythm and cadence as a woman in labor

You know it's a bizarre and perverse phenomena
but the more i have found myself surrounded
by splendor the more i have found myself
detached and turned off from my emotions

It is of importance to note that a man's labored
breath on his death bed keeps almost the exact
same rhythm and cadence as a woman in labor

Shangrila can exist only in the mind
and exactly where it should stay
if you ever experienced the real
true-blue (functioning) and ways
of people out here; the horrible
juvenile politics and protocol
and nepotism and social system

and psychosocial environment
and pathetic and absurd ways
people get viewed and judged
and how weak and conformist
they actually are
when an allegiance
can literally change
(loose change?) in
the matter of a moment
based on insular and ignorant
narrow-minded resemblances
on the periphery of an erratic
exaggerated thought pattern

It is of importance to note that a man's labored
breath on his death bed keeps almost the exact
same rhythm and cadence as a woman in labor

Suburbia was created and set up and structured
to provide an even (keel) functional and idealized
baseline for safety and security and (social and cultural)
state of being to provide 'a sense of normalcy' but with
all this repressing and suppressing everything kept
in and kept down (all this lack of communication
and avoidance and confrontation) all these gossips
and rumors which all ultimately eventually turn to
secret taboo could be nothing further from the truth

It is of importance to note that a man's labored
breath on his death bed keeps almost the exact
same rhythm and cadence as a woman in labor

It becomes awfully queer out here how they identify
the seasons by lights and decorations and store-bought
ornaments they put on their front lawns as some form
of *giving the impression* to welcome but strangely enough
feel the opposite phenomena of not feeling anything at
all and the experience of feeling 'distanced by the familiar'

estranged and alienated and a sense of non-belonging
and in their obsessive need to one-up and make them
look the best and get them up first are also actually
absurdly depriving themselves of all the instinctive
and intuitive and visceral senses and sensations
and spontaneous elements which make them (the
seasons) distinctly different inherent and magical

It is of importance to note that a man's labored
breath on his death bed keeps almost the exact
same rhythm and cadence as a woman in labor

She fidgets delicately, desperately
with a sign which reads "scream"
for halloween that gets moved
back and forth by the gusts
of wind on her front lawn

It is of importance to note that a man's labored
breath on his death bed keeps almost the exact
same rhythm and cadence as a woman in labor

Childhood was those little
leftover *light bright* bulbs
scattered in the shag rug
of your closet lost and
forgotten in the suburbs

It is of importance to note that a man's labored
breath on his death bed keeps almost the exact
same rhythm and cadence as a woman in labor

Sometimes marriage
in tying the knot really
feels like tying the knot

by the way how the hell did
they come up with that one?

*It is of importance to note that a man's labored
breath on his death bed keeps almost the exact
same rhythm and cadence as a woman in labor*

Too much superstition
or becoming a slave to it
or letting it take advantage
becomes something symptomatic
of a cult-like status (or the prodromal
phase to the traits and characteristics
of magical thinking in obsessive-
compulsive behavior) or just
a really poor religion with
loopholes in it which will
never ever pay off
in the long-run

*It is of importance to note that a man's labored
breath on his death bed keeps almost the exact
same rhythm and cadence as a woman in labor*

The neighbors are involved in secret
undercover clandestine maneuvers
and do do or die missions planting
the same stump on different parts
of each others backyard as originally
started when some natural force of nature
spontaneously and suddenly rolled it over
without warning to the other's territory
and plot of land and now when the sun
goes down based on severe paranoia
the persecutorial and conspiratorial
kind and having no idea how
to communicate or clarify

plan and plot different ways
to get back at each other and go
back and forth with that stump
like some fucked-up *les miserable*
kafkaesque torture or camus eternal
myth of sisyphus; one's a lawyer
who's very punitive and the other
a chemical engineer control freak
and an overbearing perfectionist

It is of importance to note that a man's labored
breath on his death bed keeps almost the exact
same rhythm and cadence as a woman in labor

The games grownups play
are always of the most boring
and obvious kind like that game
of opposites like that game of
telephone always a staticy line
like some big fake pretend act
nothing affects them but always
appear to be working and trying…

It is of importance to note that a man's labored
breath on his death bed keeps almost the exact
same rhythm and cadence as a woman in labor

How much more heroic we were as children…

It is of importance to note that a man's labored
breath on his death bed keeps almost the exact
same rhythm and cadence as a woman in labor

It's funny looking back at my past
i have been loved and hated
for the exact same reasons

and strangely enough but
really not strange at all
view these individuals
and source of criticism
with the exact same
sense of ambivalence

*It is of importance to note that a man's labored
breath on his death bed keeps almost the exact
same rhythm and cadence as a woman in labor*

You get so sick
of having to prove
you are not a criminal
when you have a heart
of gold and soul
even more giving
getting judged
by this absurd
narrow-minded
lot of rigid
miserable
caucasians
the masses
arch-nemesis
and the lone
(st)ranger
and individual
who goes it alone
without even
knowing it
a super
hero

*It is of importance to note that a man's labored
breath on his death bed keeps almost the exact
same rhythm and cadence as a woman in labor*

I find
myself
lost
some
thing
of a cross
between
gepetto &
pinocchio
looking for
a father
figure
with
no
where
to go
getting
into a
hell of
a lot of
trouble
without
a mean
bone in
my body
searching
the heavens
for a punchline

funny they deported chaplin
during the age of McCarthy...

It is of importance to note that a man's labored
breath on his death bed keeps almost the exact
same rhythm and cadence as a woman in labor

I very much disagree (yet in most ways do)
with the hypotheses of the old time sociologists
(the archeologists?) who speak about the advantages
and disadvantages; about the differences of suburban

and urban living, as when it really comes down to it
spiritually (even non-spiritually) has absolutely
nothing to do with any of these types of things

*It is of importance to note that a man's labored
breath on his death bed keeps almost the exact
same rhythm and cadence as a woman in labor*

Why i constantly find myself moving…

*It is of importance to note that a man's labored
breath on his death bed keeps almost the exact
same rhythm and cadence as a woman in labor*

XVII. Assembly Not Required: naked psalms

Sob #1

i trust those most of a mocking tone
yet watch they don't turn their back on
you or perhaps do i have that backwards?

Sob #2

1, all i've ever wanted is a red head
2, opportunity not to walk on the moon
3, both of my dreams have come true...

schmuck on wheels…more apropros
asshole status-quo please don't bring
your goddamn phones to the game!

Sob #3

wiping the dream
dust from my eyes
might just take solitary
stroll from lower east side
through a city of sighs
through bleak weather
all the way up to hell's
kitchen to catch one
of those $2 fliks
spend the whole
day there with
the bums
& winos
making
small talk
ad-libbing
always the
best way to
spend the
holidays
and make
a name
for my

Sob #4

marriage is a game
by *milton bradley*
where every so often
the pieces go missing
but if you look deep enough
may find them hidden with
in the shag rug and replay
it on some windy driving
rainy day and it all comes
flooding back sentimentally
used to know this black
girl from the ghetto loved
her and she used to carry
hot sauce around with her
in her purse wherever she
went and would instantly
conveniently whip it out
whenever she needed it
for the gizzards, fried
chicken, seemed to
make a whole hell
of a lot of sense
all of these things
discovered some
where deep in
the shag rug
after that
absurd phase
where you
feel left out
and you're
losing
it all

Sob #5

what if in fact we find on mars
it's not something romantic
and glamorous we imagined
like aliens but more so
just a bunch of kvetches
like that breed of wives
complaining about
their husbands
or species of husband
complaining about their wives
getting sick of each others habits
and just getting on each others nerves
the repetition and regeneration of sleazy
and corrupt politicians beauty queens
and prom queens and drag queens
and drama queens always just out
of reach alienating the rest of the status
quo population soulless schmucks killing
each other off all for the sake of vanity
and privilege and entitlement and religion
a whole social and bureaucratic system
built on the worst features and tyranny
of human nature and pathetic and petty
shit like sibling rivalry and something
shakespearian, and like always based
on natural human instinct and the need
for sublimation have to turn elsewhere
like pluto or neptune or somewhere else
in the solar system even better yet turn
further inward to that mythological fabled
deep hole dug all the way to china or
that miniscule and melancholic little
boy on the moon fidgeting restless intense
brilliant with obsessive-compulsive traits
and characteristics just trying desperately
to meet his impossible to please parents'
expectations now spraypainting
whole new oceans and galaxies

Sob #6

how you find yourself
cracking-up way before
any sort of punch line…

Sob #7

it took only 15 years of marriage for my mother-in-law
to finally admit to my wife–"he's a pretty nice guy"
as she responded–"he means well." when i asked
her for her hand in marriage she said–"if you ever do
anything bad to her i'm coming after you." go figure?
she used to threaten her a lot too. what's the opposite
of a male-chauvinist pig? i know there's a term for
it…what happened to those warm towels you
used to bury your head in after those chinese
feasts? i want one of those before i reach
the promised land. grab a handful of those
chewy mints and stuff them in my pocket

Sob #8

on my death
        bed
i want to wear
      one of those
double-breasted
old faded 1970s
dungaree vests
with the torn
patches on
them, a pair
of polka-dotted
sheets fading
away to stan
getz playing
the girl from
where?
wherever
she's from
don't really
matter much
with a bunch
fake mourners
like jack tripper
slapstick comedian
from 3's company
pretending to be
crying ringing
a wet sponge
and it all flow-
ing time to drop
the disguises
deeze guys is
jesus strangely
enough all
coming in
the form of
hollowed-out
acquaintances
passive-aggressive
never ever quite

following through
on promises which
made them the worst
sort of stranger worst
sort of coward could
never quite figure?
logs lollygagglng
down icy river
of seasons
making the
acquaintance
of holy
emptiness
turning to
the brilliant
symphony
of foghorns
what next
in amerika?
coming out
with those
sweet tarts
on a rope
o no preferred
the punch line
to bazooka joe
stan getz going
        solo
or was that
    chet baker?
  curly
reading
  elegy

Sob #9

it all ends up so damn
kafkaesque & dostoevskian…

        better yet stated, stop your kvetchin!

Sob #10

think one of those boyscout leaders
should run for president. just think
always be in that perfectly pleated
navy-blue uniform with that gold neck
tie and beanie. if worse comes to worse
knows how to tie the perfect knot pitch
the perfect tent and cut the perfect trail
and find his way out if ever gets lost
when times get rough. they say we're
looking for someone to try and win back
the confidence of america. well i ask
you what more can you ask for?

Sob #11

the comediennes have arrived to the opera
and river is finally thawing through town
where the witnesses hang out somewhere
between the haunted house and firehouse
rapist has been released on good
behavior from the state hospital
and an announcement comes
out in the paper and cable
and school board
and superintendent
and they all breathe
a collective sigh of relief
when they find out
he'll be moving
further up north
towards north country
where they got
an opiate problem
and keep the colleges
and swamps and prisons

america's an industry within a vision...

Sob #12

i feel like one of those old
ancient wooden china dolls
left on the mantle and the more
you twist her open another one
comes out smaller more hollow
yet am able to hear every tick
of that grandfather clock
the delicate dust collecting
on each piece of furniture
the texture of shadows
of each season passing
in front of the window
the lagoon taking
on shape and form
and sounding like
some haunting symphony
when the sun goes down
a bird's eye view of the beautiful long
distance runner moving from town to town
the resurrection of ghost bones underground
and wish there was still some morphine hanging
around from the saint whose stray dogs keep
a close and thoughtful eye on him for when his
days take a turn for the worse and start to go downhill

Sob #13

alex rodriguez
is like the *bp* spill
not particularly believable
and like america with its
idiotic convenient amnesia
we're supposed to fall for
all these very down to earth
and sincere images of how
they're now doing so much
to restore the environment
and keep the gulf clean
(clean like what?
a clean syringe?
and forget about
all those many days
in between and all those
other negligible multiple spills
and having to see like those
after school specials on *cnn*
of it gurgling nonstop out of
control with no end in sight)
like a-rod signing baseballs
for *the harlem boys club*
of america as humble as pie
and a slice of the american
dream and if you believe
any of that bullshit
i got a bridge

Sob #14

you see your existence
      making some shoestring saving catch
                      while having to put up

    with all the futile bullshit
of all those
    asshole alcoholics

           throwing haymakers
                in the bleachers

    making a spectacle
& names...

existence in america
      is rain, recession
           better yet stated

mild-depression
and post-disco

Sob #15

my client has got one of those pathologies…
where he is so precise and meticulous and manic
and detail-oriented and obsessive-compulsive
with language to the point at times of tedium
and can be a little maddening and happened
to mention today how that show *chips*
from the seventies was one of those
shows you'd watch when there was
nothing else on and couldn't help
but to laugh under my breath as
couldn't agree more and thought
what if could apply this metaphor
to life and existence all that leftover
shit which we try to make the best
of it; ponch and john riding side by
side down that nondescript california
highway on their motorbikes freely
exchanging ideas and just airing
out their grievances and issues

Sob #16

if happiness were to roll on
by would i be able to identify
and recognize it? would i be
able to swipe and snatch it?
perhaps even fondle and
caress it? cradle it like
an infant and say this
is what happiness is?
or would it be more subtle
and undercover like *the circle
line* rounding manhattan in
a thunderstorm and those two
old hags actually mother and
daughter, exclaiming–"that
mookhead stole my drambuie!"
soaked in rain slamming the taxi
on each others ankles while outside
looking in, what existence (mortality)
in the long-run always seems
to gradually boil down to

Sob #17

decided since every one's running
from the democrats and republicans
i'm gonna just throw my hat in the ring
when no one's looking and won't put it
out over any one of those forms of social
media (don't even know how to use them)
but be one of those real annoying people
always mumbling under their breath always
driving you crazy and not quite hearing them
as believe this would be far more effective…
(true test of the emergency broadcast system)
and a real man of the people not representing
a republican or democrat or aristocratic tea
bagger or pompous populist or progressive
proletariat or self-proclaimed independent
or lone libertarian but as an agrarian with
a taste for the schmaltzy life somewhere
between *miller high life* and "schaefer
is the one beer to have when you're
having more than one" as ironically
always found myself getting far more
done and home from bars way before
dawn so much more safe and secure

Sob #18

they don't make movies
     in america anymore
  (sob!)
it's all about shock value
    (not a hell of a lot
of value in that)
or some truth
or dare game
of flinch tag
      un-
    aware
it's all one
long slow
methodical
mundane
apocalypse
(witch has
already
gone
down)
   think of
     the last leader
        you have respected?
all of my heroes
     have been deported
           & assassinated

Sob #19

sometimes when i'm feeling really low
        low down in the dumps
    out here in america
i think back to those luscious
smells of the sweeping ocean
after long weary exotic travels
and pilgrimages of necessary
escapes coming off the ferry
in the mediterannean not
knowing a single soul
but in that one moment
paradoxically feeling
like i know it all
for future
and
real-life
dangerous
adventures
what it straight-up
sincerely means
to be a realist
and fatalist
and true-
blue born
and bred
romantic

Sob #20

cary grant gazing
lost and alone
worn-out wasted
from the porthole
of his tiny little
clean tiled room
reflective contented
inward melancholic
stoned still with that
to catch a thief ascot
technicolor striped
stud gigolo cabana
outfit on to costa
del sol corsica
shores of sicilia
"no more mafia"
scribbled on white
washed blanched
sea-splashed beach
zen-buddhist like
in the moment
knowing at least
he's made the effort
to try and know
and see it all

XVIII. On The Hx And Deleterious Effects Of Advertising:
101 principles in psychological stanzas

1

they appear to glamorize
the mild and the mediocre
the 'middle of the road'
people in tv commercials

2

who always look so excited,
alive, satisfied, contented
over their smart phones
as evidenced by their affect,
expressions, and non-verbals

3

what it means to be complete; an extension
to their identity (and what would they
do without it?) be so lost and alone

4

like some real-life parable of object-permanence
or transitional-object to the heart and soul
of the virtual-reality-netherworld

5

soulless subcontractors to 'the promised land'
who make breaking promises (mathematical proof
of opposites, 'betrayal') an art, as no one has to really
be accountable (just read the small print) dance of devil

6

the middle man (the see-through salesman)
has all the power as aforementioned does not
really need in his dialogue to be 'accountable'
to either the client or his 'co-workers' as can
superficially claim 'convenient amnesia'
after the initial 'engagement' and 'connection'
has been made, or what they like to refer to
as 'communication' (the opportunistic vehicle
or medium to 'gain an advantage' combination
of false promises and proclamations) and then
plays the instant convenient role of 'anonymous'
while the customer in the short *and* the long-run
completely disempowered in those selfsame 'spiels'
(sort of sexless and soulless sex appeal) to brainwash
them with pre-packaged dialogue, ultimately leaving
them confused and disoriented 'at a loss for words'

7

it all fits into that blank space
of the script of the telemarketer

8

they're all telemarketers
as trained with videos
multiple-choice tests
and if climb the true-
blue ladder of success
conventions out in the
manifest destiny west

9

which if get lucky
may include such
'choice' destinations

like boise, salt lake city
palm springs, california
somewhere around phoenix
the republicans out in utah

10

and appear more safe & secure
wearing the exact same uniform
using the exact same dialogue
with the exact same dreams
of 'living happily ever after'

11

a member of the masses
with their mortgages
and retirement

12

all about competition
and how you can
manipulate language

13

somehow they mistake
this for some sort of
(hierarchal) class-system
(1 college?) 2 culture 3 religion

14

confusing something rigid
for righteous, higher than
holy for something sacred

15

exclusive chartered members
of the theater of the absurd…

16

required to get at least an 80% on the test
and to remember every psychotropic med
which will reduce stress and bring about
chemical equilibrium for grandiose episodes
every ingredient which goes on the warm and
cold sub and what to do when the percentages
drop low and how to manipulate the rates
of rooms for the 'busy' and 'slow' season

17

will even rapidly increase the cadence
of speech and spike the volume over
your tv/radio so you don't exactly
get it (an explosion of smallprint)
and like soulless and punitive
authority figures say provide
this (to cover their *assets*)
all for litigious reasons

18

no behavioral techniques
could possibly help or rescue
you from this technical behavior
made to screw, and screw with
your mind, heart and demean/or

19

trained (with role-play) to placate
'the frustrated customer'
and keep them 'happy'
so they will continue
shopping...*as we
want to keep...*

20

worst thing speaking to any of these
mechanical monotone automatons
over the phone who are trained
always to say the right thing
to make the customer happy
which always find so much
more offensive and insulting

21

and if been around the block enough
learn not to feed into it, turn the tables
on them and give them a true taste of
their own medicine, which always jars
and disorients them and plays them out
at their own semantics; even a repetition
of their language scares them, as so out there
and triggers and reminds them that 'are on to
them' and know their false 'games of pretend'
while angry enough to mock and ridicule and
you got experience and know all their tricks

22

another wise idea to instantly ask for a supervisor,
get names, times, receipts, and model numbers
as for the most part due to human nature
only respond to 'natural consequences'

23

if they happen to present with features
of a human being remind them of your
history (can even check the computer)
how much you sincerely are a frequent
customer and patronize their establishment

24

if they remain dehumanizing
and indifferent continue
your counter-argument
as merely sticking with
your true-blue conviction

25

where with their false rhetoric
and inherited psychobabble
need to be reminded they
are there to serve you and
not the other way around

26

advertising feeds off the fragile
and vulnerable (in some ways
the disillusioned, in others,
delusional, like the pimp
to the prostitute, like
the drug dealer to those
who feel so lost and alone)
giving a false sense of belonging,
security, 'sanctuary,' and instant
panacea, illusory sense of 'home'

i.e. what happens through trial & error
when you discover the 'good christian'

is just a liar and religion (all those things
justified) like some form of organized crime?

27

the puppet master pulling the strings
in the background like some false
apotheosis father-figure (dangling
the proverbial carrot) pressing buttons,
pulling levers, not quite honest, which
triggers (often not even necessary the triggers)
the worst lies and blatant obvious betrayal of all

28

rape (having to keep your
guard up) in the long-run
becomes a form
of wisdom

29

survival becomes like constant trial and error
divided by trials and tribulations figuring out
who's full of it and who isn't through repeated
patterns, symptoms, traits, and characteristics

30

dummy becomes ventriloquist
and the ventriloquist dummy
in our collective unconscious

31

call it suburbanization…
call it privilege and entitlement

32.

and so it seems when it all comes down to it
just a piece or slice or ratio or percentage of
the american dream% the american dream%
the american dream% the american dream%
think how silly that sounds when you keep
on repeating it and honestly don't even know
what that means 'american dream' and maybe
was just out that day they were teaching it
and sincerely sure as hell don't want to be
a part of something or someone else's dream
sure as heck not one of those phonies who always
seems so damn sleazy with some sort of scheme
or trick up their sleeve and make it abundantly
clear they don't want you to be part of their dream
as to be a member of this team are required to act
exclusive and mean and to keep the great illusion
(the thought pattern/delusion) alive and in order
to function must in real life give other competitors
and 'the perceived enemy' a sense of non-belonging
(what kind of dream is that? and seems like the theme
to every nightmare ever been a part of or not a part of)
"the candidate" looks like one of those useless fools in
high school who was real nice to you individually and
then when they were around their crew (cluck clan)
pretend like they don't know you and to be cool
start slinging cruel demeaning insults at you
as if exchanging insecurity for identity
these species all seem make-believe
as repeat that over and over again
and sounds so much more linguistically
and phonetically credible; make-believe
make-believe, make-believe, make-believe
no that's ok i'll pass (i'd prefer to fail) and
really don't want nor need to be a part of
any one of these see-through superficial
dreams especially the type (and hype)
which deems one beholds and buries
the worst kind of traits and characteristics
of human nature and personality full of every

possible contradiction, self-interest, and hypocrisy
that always inextricably made one feel so empty and lonely

33

one can measure the topography (and nature
and aesthetic) of a town or neighborhood
by the mentality and presentation
of its used-car salesmen over
your local television station

34

their aggressivity and herd-mentality
projecting man's basic and funda/mental need
for control and power and sense of belonging...

35

this may also be applicable
for the weather woman
and her small-talk
and innocence
and ridiculous
riddles

36

the literalism of the rest
of the local news team
(whose wooden expressions
and body language) indicate
that they never ever
seem to quite get it

37

like a blind date that went
bad from beginning to end

38

ex: one wonders if it would be far more
positive and productive and efficacious
if they interview one of those gorgeous
seductive cheerleaders who really moves
the masses and believe be far more indicative
of what really goes on behind closed doors on
the college campus than one of those middle-aged
ranting madman coaches pulling his hair out
his head and taking the team along with him

39

the wives forced to be saints
and put up with them; with their
mood swings and erratic behavior
their ultimatums and superstitions

40

if they interview the ball boy
and that pretty, hard-working,
all-american girl who provides
them a dry towel and water

41

the hot pretzel
cold beer kid…

42

a behind the scenes look at the life
& times, everyday existence of
the drooling jowled mascot

43

the scalpers and drug dealers...

44

a flooding of images and rhetoric
has taken over and never once in
the real world matches real-life situations
or for that matter, crises and celebrations

45

a role-reversal where all caucasians
act dumb and harmless (the slapstick
comedian) and the black man, intuitive
and humble (the straight man) for
the punch line to the riddle

46

who was it? phyllis diller? the old brilliant neurotic comedienne
ironically said present-day television with its myriad of constant
flashing images (its flooding of sound bites and nonstop
distractions) makes her feel instantly nervous and agitated

47

sound effects and special effects in no way, shape,
or form prove special or effective, merely recycled

and formulaic, and diluting the overall baseline for
independent thinking, perception, and imagination

48

turning them all into idiots
keeping the zombies talking

49

van gogh sliced off his ear
for all the right reasons

50

all the wrong people got famous…

51

tesla mutated found muttering to himself on the steps
of the ny public library the night they were giving
out awards to thomas edison and his old cronies

52

likewise the projected and perceived social and cultural baseline
(having been over-exposed, manipulated, and supersaturated)
has backfired due to the fact that everything is so objectified
no longer having the ability towards perceiving or analyzing

53

in the late-afternoon when we used to watch cartoons
now commercials of very earnest down-to-earth women
matter-of-factly explaining their issues during intercourse

54

whimsical caucasian middle-aged couples
and their sweeping scenarios, acting all
romantic and liberated, as they apparently
found a breakthrough to erectile dysfunction

55

reality shows deliberately set up for physical
and emotional and histrionic confrontations
and showdowns with contrived and shallow
reactions (which got its 'do or die' derivation
from the ghetto) to try and trigger a reaction
as they all have the exact same cookie-
cutter gestures and body language

56

5 ways you can cry
(you can sigh
you can lie)
and if you do it
this way you may

manipulate the reality audience
so they might sympathetically join
in in this life-changing transition
as well as force a catharsis
and boost television ratings

57

two dueling phenomenona...
in the wars in iraq and afghanistan
the media was not allowed to show any of the fighting
or images and carnage as if none of this existed at all

58

a little later on when the arab spring came to be
they said there were issues and conflicts with meeting
up for the protests and rebellion and overthrow of governments
as they threatened to turn off their social network; picture this

59

i guess the whole point and purpose
in the theater of the absurd trying
to make it difficult to picture

60

and if in fact we are a sum of our choices
i must be my furniture and appliances
and #1 leading lawn equipment

61

the real creed in america
live comfortably ever after

62

who came up
with that expression
"mild-mannered man?"

63

soft drink will decide what kind of man you really are
if you are human (or alive) or happy (and a star) and
decide between *doing the dew* or to *obey your thirst*

64

i.e. he was supposed to represent
the everyday all-american father
with the wife and two children
even turned him into a cartoon
version turns out he was knocking
out his underage girl rape victims
with something of a bill cosby concoction
now *subway* as some defense-mechanism
or form of deflection are telling us it's their
50th year anniversary (know it really isn't…)
and can get 50% extra meat on your sandwich
if should happen to remember or help to forget
it all or just another form of instant-gratification

65

the production co. spends a full day
focused and fixated, picking up all
the necessary equipment to make
sure it all looks real, representing
your real-life casual scenario of
'freedom' devoid of any issues
conflicts, worries, or problems

66

the opposite of any hindrances
or obstacles, happy and euphoric
to last for your 30 second slot for
the american viewing audience

67

archetypes come to life, while
perfectly-sculpted boys and girls
from the health club along the sea-
shore frolic without a care in the world

as not too ironic tossing (perfectly-
sculpted) succulent shrimp into
mid-air, then in one fell swoop
scooped into a dish of butter

68

attempting to capture the moment
both looking not coincidental similar
all to make our miserable lives seem
just a little better, less crisis-oriented

69

the production co. spending thousands
of dollars to cater for the models and
actors and producers and directors
and backers and assistants and
electricians and makeup artists
all with some sort of personality
disorder or self-imposed addiction

70

child stars who don't want to be viewed
that way anymore turn themselves into
instant sex symbols (overcompensating
becoming impulsive and promiscuous)
having no problem stripping off their
panties and brassieres for the public
in front of the camera, while later on

71

conveniently become holy and sacred
(wanting to be viewed and perceived
as such) doing commercials for yogurt
and the homeless and animal cruelty

and the mentally-challenged during
high-holy season to get your money

these are their life *stages*
of growth and development

72

they now have very earnest and caring
and compassionate expressions, as now
the spokespersons as if 'they have been there'
and made to look all sincere even a little nihilism

73

those who appear to get respect are simplistically
those who get good press (like a cross between
duress and largesse) through the ancient art
of nepotism as if buying and purchasing
and making deals for one's reputation

74

and often some of the biggest and see-through
hypocrites full of contradictions, opportunistic
and aggressive having become so hardwired
in their personalities (and behavior) with
rationalizations not even aware of it and
will instantly change their allegiances
to however it best serves their self-
interest and works to their advantage

75

this proves adventitious as well
in the context of the work place
the psychosocial environment

and even the family unit which
includes immediate and extended

76

while it's all about style and presentation
rarely having anything to do with loyalty
or substance as ironically even tragically
the individualist or independent thinker
who doesn't fit into any of these convenient
structured categories or groups of culture
is seen as a threat and ostracized and
alienated for simply not being cookie-cutter
and conformist and a slave to spiritual fashion

77

more accurate, social and cultural
and psychological subjugation...

78

they say that clinically, instinctively
one cannot remain angry for more
than 12 seconds. i *beg* to differ!

79

a matter of fact would like to perform a clinical study
to exhibit and prove how tv (no longer sure if the pre-quota
of affected and made-up computer-generated violence is for
a movie or video game and if that would even matter) can trigger
post-traumatic stress disorder and multiple forms of retraumatization

80

push 'the citizen,' 'the common man'
over the edge, but they always
refuse to go to the hard data

81

as our great leaders
watch the same tragedies
repeat themselves over and over

82

the self-fulfilling prophecies, self-deprivation,
self-mutilating, and self-destructive behaviors

83

so you were in this calm state, feeling great,
trying to get things straight, and literally got
to mute it and turn the opposite direction
so as not to jump straight out your skin

84

what happened to the ole time exhibitionist
in his trench coat (with his sudden and spon-
taneous spur of the moment machinations)
who tried to turn on a flock of women?

the palpitation of pigeons...

85

and so looking back at later-adolescence
we were so pumped and enthusiastic when
they came out with that romantic safe and
secure concept of "love exciting and new…"
which always turned out so boring and blue

86

then transporting those miserable middle-aged
married couples who always seemed so spent
at the end of their rope, uptight, and wound-up
involved in constant power-struggles and issues
of trust and betrayal followed somehow by some
transcendent fantasy which would mystically
and magically heal and redeem their being

87

being whisked back to some innocent period before it
all became so damn clueless and complicated and more
so found yourself conked-out, passed-out, somewhere
right in the middle, like waking up from a diabetic
coma down-in-the-dumps dragging yourself down
the hall and off to bed to experience true 'escapism'

88

while your seductive older sister was torturing
boys at keg parties in real psychodramas
getting involved in testosterone battles
(paranoia and suicide ideations)
absurdly, desperately, trying to
prove their undying love for her

89

and knew the only thing that could really save you
which somehow felt like true-blue truths and could
relate to was *the battle of the network stars* or that
poor madman schnook hurtling down the mountain
(and got you every time you saw him) at breakneck
speed tragic out-of-control in *the wide world of sports*

90

you find out in later life
that most entrances
are like exits and
exits entrances
in the literal
and palpable
and spiritual
and meta-
physical
world

91

how you learn so much more
contemplating between phases
and life-transitions as if gaining
insight, perspective and wisdom
into 'the theater of the absurd'

92

not only the actor but
also audience member

93

as if suddenly being awoken
from a deep sleep in the back
of the car by your mom, over-
stimulated after returning home
from a night out on the town in
the bad part of town on broadway

94

culture and reality becomes
everything you parse from these
conscious/subconscious experiences

95

the difference between
the dream and nightmare

96

how to maintain a green lawn...

97

how to maintain your soul...

98

how to maintain your cool
and sanity and not implode
on the dead end with so many
devils who really don't wish
you the best and discover
the neighbor's got nothing
to do with anything biblical

99

personification and microcosm
of the worst things to have to do
with half-truths (which has absolutely
nothing to do with truth) and human nature

100

maureen delgado "your plains flooding
insurance expert" tells you as the sea
level rises so too do your premiums

have you or a family member
been diagnosed or died
from mesolthometia?

like some punch line
to a rhetorical question

"these are not actors
these are real people"
as if any of that
would matter

101

it's also of interest and
some importance to note on a
historical social/cultural level
(a good and decent paradigm
and parable) when considering
the nature and influence of the
media or advertising, or even
for that matter, 'propaganda'
looking back at all of those
old nostalgic black & white
newsreels, which may have
provided a healthy dose of

inspiration and self-motivation
(and maybe perhaps what 'turned
on a nation') was how for example
fdr was able to transform himself
and just stand up with all that charm
and courage in front of those crowds
and tv cameras during that phase of
'great depression' (and never once
complain about his condition)
to give a good impression...

XIX. Those Final Stages Of Growth & Development Eric B. Erickson Failed To Mention

stage -10

i want to be cloned
i want to be stalked
i want my clone
to be stalked

i want to stalk the stalker stalking my clone
then everything might just seem right again

rake up the leaves and clean out the barn
who was it nietzsche said–"i believe
i was born a very old man..."

stage -9

when i was born
they knew i'd be
so much trouble
they didn't pass
out cigars they
simply passed
around the blunt
and those warm
towels from old
time chinese
restaurants
and then
the neighbors
used to come
around to our
porch to watch
me eat burgers
from my high chair
i swear and gather
around to see how
many i'd down
in one sitting
little later on
that summer

went tearing
through my
kitchen and leapt
straight through
the screen door
howling–
"superman!"
remember them
scooping me up
stitching me up
on the operating
table in my football
uniform refusing
to take my foot
ball helmet off

stage -8

women, wives will
go on the attack
i want to be
the first man
to walk on
the moon
and never
come back
bialy crumbs
like the stars.
in the morning
i turn on strauss'
waltzes which always
somehow remind me
to never give up
al weiss from
standard
& poors...

stage -7

think i know global warming
by our cactus flower coming
out 3 times this year usually
comes out just once (feels
like a new sort of creation
or evolution with no need
to debate it) 68-75
dgs. mid-october
in the mountains
the radio tells us.
that little cartoon
character from north.
korea has come out
of hiding, seems like
if ever the right time
a pretty good time
for that second coming
always telling us about

stage -6

what doesn't kill you
makes you stranger..

stage -5

i want to stick my head in a plastic bag
and suffocate myself and say a prayer
and just before about to drop dead
let out a mad hallelujah and amen
and whether my wish comes true
or doesn't really not so much
the point or question...

stage -4

in all those ol' black
& white films full of
preppies in their
beanies caroling
to the heavens
i was the buffoon
behind the garden
wall bawling hysterical
mumbling under my breath
with my slice of pizza with
everything on it and a brown
paper bag full of shit ready to

light it on fire right on the doorstep
of the aristocrat's daughter i sincerely
loved as didn't know how to express
myself nor offer my hard(end) soul

i think later on at my funeral
i want to hire myself to play
the harmonica without that
whole schmaltzy band
behind me and those
cute jewish cousins
in their sky-blue
evening gowns
and sky-blue
mascara

with their
white-leather
pumps from
the island
who no
one knew
who they
belonged
to and later
got turned
on to heroin

only showing
up to weddings
and bar-mitzvahs

i'll be the one
stealing glances
at you across
the room
blowing
spitballs
at you
don't pay
me any mind
for a good time...

finally going off
on a long yodeling
jimmy rogers solo
as if finally figuring
out the rest of
the lyrics to
the song
or even for
that matter
some of
heart
& soul

stage -3

tasteful nudes
       & some
              not so tasteful

        of old girlfriends
   scattered all over
the walls

    of the haunted house...

  there is absolutely nothing
        haunted
    about this home
  just how he simply
chooses

    to live & die & get by
  in his life & feels
far more apropos

    than waking up
      to the same awful
        routine & ritual

of the morning paper
& cup of joe & keeping
an eye out on the weather

stage -2

those lady bugs
circling the skies
doing nose dives

i sincerely find
to be the finest
of companions

(more than any
one of those fake breed
of phony betraying humans)

why thoreau turned
inwards towards walden
whitman holy beloved nurse

to those dying boys
in the civil war arena
kerouac to desolation angels

who was
on the
$2 bill?

stage -1

doctors dropped the ball on ebola
and now they've scheduled an
all-out news conference for all
of america instant pop-up tribunal
like the McCarthy trials and will
tell you how humbly sincerely
sorry they are and all the news
casters from the rival networks
are gonna get on to assess and
analyze how sincere or insincere
they were like all those multi-
millionaire athletes way after
the fact (because of natural
consequences) apologizing
and asking for forgiveness
from the amerikan public
as opposed to more
apropros their nuclear
family unit all written
by their lawyers and
public relations

stage 0

i'd like to invite over every land
lord and henchmen superintendent
slumlord would be an understatement
who try and truly prove you do not exist
no heat for winter pure neglect never
a return phone call for everything
breaking down for the rats
the fucken rat bastards

invite their asses over
the phony (stingy and greedy)
motherfuckers for wine and humus
and when the drunken devils are laughing
aloud clinking glasses put a bullet in the back
of each one's skull spit on them sicilian style
and drop these fucken jackals off in the forest
for the wolves to devour and give them a burial

only fit for a coward...

think the first night i'd finally rest well
not have any more of those nightmares

stage 1

feeling this morning a true-blue case
of depressed and down in the dumps
finding it virtually impossible to drag
my ass into the shower all of sudden
saw my son's green freezer-ray gun
in the bathtub from the night before
and thought doesn't that say it all
and it was all good and an instant
cure-all and do hope he's having
his action-adventures in school
playing king of the hill
all those pretty little
fourth grade girls
with crushes
on him
pulling him
into that blissful confusing
stage of the fight (whether
to engage) or flee (or run)
phenomenon anywhich way
don't think he needs to know
yet about the awful hostile passive
aggressive phony and bullshit grownup
world and will have him hold out as long

as he can and of course will be there for
him when it all goes down and happens
and explain to him how they're not worth
a dime and come a dime a dozen and all about
those action/adventures and green freezer-ray gun

stage 2

it's an interesting phenomena
how to see a therapist or have
someone clean out your wood
burning stove pretty much
comes out to the same
charge as much
the same job and
absolves and resolves
and solves the exact same
problems helping you to get
things back on the right track
to somehow function
and suppose reignite
the senses and warm
up your heart and soul

always a fine line
the blushing girls…

stage 3

liked myself much better
when i was in love and fell
in love with my first love
and after we broke up
(around 17 years old)
to find in my mid-
forties still have not
yet exactly recovered

stage 4

would it be ok in my forties
to get in touch with my old
time pediatrician/mortician
and even though i know he's
good and retired (and maybe
the last one i perceive is not
a liar) as from what i heard
retirement driving him crazy
driving golf balls into that
great big golf net of his
he's got planted in his
little suburban side yard
and just rap with him for
a little while to ask him
how things are to try and
just make things right again
like of course that great big
fish bowl with the tropical fish
in them when used to just hear
the repetitive soothing gurgle
of bubbles without being
aware of it and always
a fresh stock of lollipops
popping out of that little box
he'd keep in the waiting room
as seems somehow in the long-run
fated and doomed to wait there forever

i do know why my olfactory senses
are the most keen profound triggers
as its delicious aromas (d)instinctively
cut through all the bullshit and rhetoric
(all the cognitive conflicts) devils use to
make your life confusing and complicated

stage 5

i do remember when me
and a good buddy of mine
who used to work at *rko
warner video* in the upper
west side when going
to video stores was still
in and the in thing to do
and had nothing left to do
in your lonely life (a matter
of fact met some of my best
and most beautiful girlfriends)
as it was a platform and culture
and used to get into these great
absurd brilliant futile debates
about who was a better (or best)
american director martin scorcese
or stanley kubrick (somehow leaving
out woody allen?) of course myself
taking martin scorcese something
which could not be debated
as of such different subject matter
sensibility and so silly but when looking
back so damn nostalgic and necessary
and somehow sentimental and relevant.
when the district manager took off
(one of those very serious schmucks)
i used to like to do surreal shit like
put up "viva las vegas" or was it
"blue hawaii" starring elvis and
anne margaret on the great big
screen hula-hooping and surfing
flashing and beaming onto the hot
sweltering streets of new york city
which seemed to really bring in
the customers as opposed to
that required list which was
mandated like "uncle buck"
or "honey i shrunk the kids"

i think we both got fired
just a little bit later...

stage 6

"to the bat pole!"
what happened
to that lost episode
where they tried
to crawl upwards
backwards
(inwards)
back to their
original selves?

stage 7

wouldn't that be totally insane...
half-crazed to hook-up for a blind
date at a bowling alley and think
in most ways would really get to
know what they're about and their
personality. i remember after my
wife and i had just been engaged
we met up with a good buddy
of mine and his fiancee for
a double date at some alley
in the village as we had
all been through thick
and thin and the trials
and tribulations in
trying to get though
and getting our masters degree
in social work at *yeshiva university*.
he was an orthodox jew and a relatively
decent dude from brooklyn and a couple
years later i had called him up to see how
he was doing (in many ways too to try and

figure out things and how i was doing) and
turned out as he told me half-embarrassedly
had a couple of kids and going through a divorce
and now living in his sister's basement as his wife
had repeatedly caught him obsessive-compulsively
after work in the whee hours during sleep cycle
as had asked him to stop secretly doing porn
over the internet, guess just didn't want
to stop it and enamored by the concept
of speaking to completely anonymous
girls and moms who would turn him
on while their kids were around; sort
of ironic cuz he always got special
treatment and favoritism over me
cuz was always seen as a nice
jewish boy and i was something
of a bad boy, something i never
really was but impossible to fight
the stereotype and so just didn't
and just said fuck it; ironic all those
ultra-orthadox girls who used to come
on to me and call me in the middle of
the evening (and used to claim higher
than holy boundaries to however it best
served their needs, having something
to do with their religion which was also
my religion) as was very convenient for
them (cuz guess seen in the same 'light')
and of course i was some kind of rebel
and used to i imagine provide them a
certain amount of real-life support and
compassion and guidance which never
got recognition. i still like that image
and idea and notion of meeting a blind
date at the bowling alley as suppose
in more ways than not without even
being aware of it tells you a lot
about people and how it's all
about instinct and how it all
lasts in the moment i think

stage 8

i remember those times...
were some of the roughest times
always on the road searching for a home
always getting stopped by a state cop
on the side of the road with a license
and registration and insurance
from three different states
but always keeping it real
and humble and being
sympathetic and schmoozing
with them able to relate to me
letting me off with a warning
with winter blizzards falling
down all around me just as
abandoned and despondent
and down in the dumps asking
me about the social work field
as not much i could say to them
and asking about police work and
the family and wishing them the best

stage 9

will there ever be a specific
point in my life like the final
stage where they literally
throw in the towel and
wave their arms and
say he can't come
out no more! he
can't make it
anymore!
and who

would that be?
my wife? sister?
god? my coach
in the corner?

probation
officer?
and simply
creep out
through that
trapdoor in the stage
and return to the vast
hazy blissful unknown
as simply can't continue
the act and to live
like that anymore?

Stage 0

i want to know the distinction
between the buffalo and the bison
from an anthropological and historical
point of view; want to know when and
where buffalo met its demise and extinction
and why the bison is still around thriving
and do they still cohabitate somewhere
around the great plains? those stray
places on the map we never used to
really know about but loved to shade
in from a nostalgic and escapist
cognitive-behavioral perspective
during elementary, taking solace in
those tributaries taking off to the horizon.

XX. The Drug Trade

2:32

Out here it's not at all a fear of the unknown
but a fear of the known as crave the unknown
and really want to get to know it so much more

3:00

What grownups think is grown up
some of the silliest shit in the world

3:45

Everyone's always giving me tips
and wish they would just give me
one big tip for everyone giving me

tips as when it comes down to the nitty-gritty of it
they're all just a bunch of see-through hypocrites
of self-interest talking shit far more in need of it

4:01

All these specific positions they always act so suspicious
and that they are going to perform a full and extensive
criminal background check (to check into if you are
a criminal) but can assure you from true hardcore
experience all these supposed clinical supervisors
and managers with their constant clinical abuses
of power and hypocrisies and contradictions
crossing over of boundaries and confidentiality
are the greatest criminals you can ever imagine

4:05

All these fucked-up idiot rules and regulations and forms
you are forced to sign as if america just aint got no
common sense or judgment no more like don't
pick up hitch hikers along the side of the road
when delivering psychotropic medication
as back in the day actually think i might
just have because they told me not to
as idealistically for very good reason
was so oppositional while i chatted
with some selfsame young runaway
kid i could really relate to; the best thing
about any of this trip about any of this shit
with a van full of morphine and methadone

4:14

They only seem to do their jobs
when they're kicking you out
and showing you the door
then suddenly become
awfully official
and professional
and responsible
funny how you
really impressed
during the interview
then for some strange
reason started ignoring
you and treating you
like some sorta burden
like the opposite of
descartes' proof of–
'i think therefore i am'
by the way who the hell
said i was even asking?

4:16

Upon reflection introspection
when i am feeling really low
low down down low on the
down low in the morning
after a night nightmaring
with the winter months
coming in i think
when i used to take
my kid out to that blessed river
rambling through the deep forest
mountain trees during the summer
and everyone would just hang out there
young lovers mothers with their kids singles
pretty women just dropping by to get a soak in
remember this beautiful young girl who couldn't
have been any more than twenty-years old looked
like a single mother with her son just sitting on top
this big bare boulder right in the middle of the river
with her gorgeous milky body long lengthy legs
and long silky black hair draped down her
shoulders to the contours of her bosoms
(down the shapes and forms and bodice
of her bikini) pensive brooding her head
hung down low into those long alabaster
popsicle stick legs like some brilliant
perfect specimen or insect then for
some reason all of a sudden after
all the reflection and brooding
eventually decides to pick up
that anatomy of hers and with
her kid jump straight in and some
way anyways that gets me out of bed

4:23

Very old kind retired men simply sit at long metallic
laboratory tables in the pharmaceutical room (hidden
in the back of some bleak nondescript industrial park

in the back of some stripmall in america) plopped
right across from each other separating pain killers
then stuffing them methodically and melancholy
into those bubble wraps casually discussing
the macabre and messed-up, fucked-up news
through the midst of natural stream of consciousness
dialogue like some bad joke or punch line with some
anti-climactic build-up hey did you hear the one? did
you hear about those 8 bodies which were discovered
in north carolina as if just a natural routine and ritual
and happenstance of everyday living and don't even
think about it (like once more one of those mysteries
and riddles and finally figuring) the other one not
having much of a reaction 'cause can't quite hear
him and this natural pattern and rapport and routine
and ritual going back and forth continuing to talk
and not quite hearing each other about such
awful absurd matters going on in america

4:25

I usually get my sorry i'm a fuck up
or thank you i am grateful and love
you so much gifts from walmart
as looking back think i got such
stuff like a straw cowboy hat
waffle maker, couple of those
feel-good dvd's out of those
discount bins where you just
stand around like some old
man all day over his ice hole fishing
some oompa-loompa in his jumpsuit
collecting asbestos or some dope
addict nodding off for hours on end
into his netherworld of never never land
or just something real thoughtful and practical
which i think actually she seems to appreciate
the most with simply a bag of those plain bagels

4:30

The perfect happily ever after people
are in fact quite angry and hostile
looking to out-do one-up neighbor

never ever buy into the mythology
like a college coed who presents
all natural and holy and only
fucks certain fraternities

you need an escape plan(e)
from the phony-baloney…

4:33

Aristocrats seem to make a living
giving the impression of living
spending a hell of a lot of time
on their clay courts courting
but nothing much ever seems
to happen and don't seem
to have too much to offer

they all appear brainwashed
through sexless/selective

drunk responsibly…

4:34

Suburbs milk & cookies
witch has gone missing
and all that is left
is the moon beaming
the difference between
quiet and silence and
kindness and violence

always in all ways
sneaking over that
border of the fine line
where all rumors start
with no ending cause
there never ever was
a true beginning while
all things supposedly
and ridiculously heroic
betray and contradict
itself with fake and
overcompensating
absurd role playing

4:35

*

Great thing about the senses
there's no reason to sense it
or the fact of the matter no
reason to make sense of it

*

Why is it those so punitive and puritanical
always somehow see themselves as spiritual
and those spiritual made to feel like a criminal?

*

Realistically there's nothing realistic realistically…

*

I think i think i think
therefore i ain't if you
kinda get what i'm saying?

*

Could never stand such statements like—"charmed i'm sure."
"i'm sure i don't know" just as frustrating and futile
like eternally getting ready for the ball
and never ever quite showing up

*

Decadence is those who have lost their
will to be creative or never really
had much of it to begin with...

4:38

It's all like one of those decadent
richard burton & elizabeth taylor
theater of the absurd he-said she-
said 'much to do a bout' films out
here where the lawnmowers never
shut the fuck up drain you and all
end up doing themselves in cause
they're all so clueless and unaware
and out of touch with their emotions

4:45

They have already been gobbled up by the roses
inconsequential whether or whether not replicated

4:53

It's like setting up for some elaborate carnival
without the spontaneity humor or adventure
and resembling more so some picture
perfect postcard for the sacrifice and
slaughter no one ever shows up to

Dusk

Why not mow the lawn high on opium
vroooooooom! rooooom! ruuuuuuin!
so sick of the boring cliched argument
about marijuana and how it's straight
from the soil and all natural and when
was the last time you ever saw anyone
high ever get violent well what about
the poppy when was the last time you
ever saw some good ol' lost and lowdown junkie
getting angry or hostile nodding out on the corner
somewhere in the middle of nowhere at the end of
the world on the corner of eddy and mission in the
tenderloin district in good ol san francisco falling fast
asleep on the real true blue great lawn under the holy
moly sun with views of the pacific ocean and golden gate
and alcatraz birdman just hearing the feint sound of lapping
buoys and shimmering echoing foghorns far off in distant
lands of china and hong kong japan far east western land
with nothing to look forward to nothing to look back on
as if any that bullshit manipulative linear order brainwash
ever mattered at all hey by the way did you hear the one?

nothing in the mailbox
except shadows and a caterpillar
homespun and homegrown and if you
look closely enough the rare delicate details
of a snail wedged and embedded in the crevices
of the school not so different than that dope addict
with the opiate problem vanishing into thin air on
the corner all having something a little to do with

the mother earth and evolution and all those things
which just sort of show up and crawl in from shore

junkie mowing his lawn
going along for the ride...

5:02

I want
to swim
under
the pond
the swans
are gliding on
during the down
pour when the com
murders are driving
back and forth from
the city to the sub
orbs and when
i am sure
they r good
and gone
leave them
couple bags
of croutons
and order
in from
those
good
ole
young
sicilians
i grew
up with
hanging
out with
after school
when i was
supposed

to be doing
my home
work
like
father
figures
for good
natured
delinquents
when
i felt
like
i had
nowhere
else
to go
feeling
eternally
lost & alone
guilt-ridden
down in
the dumps
watching
the day
turn to
dusk

6:02

All i ever cared about
was returning home

to my sanctuary for
fried chicken meal

just the smell of some cheeseburger
streaming from the window of farm
house in the corn on a river at dusk

no leftovers
ashes to ashes
and dust to dust

6:03

Standing in the mud room
in the thunder with the winds
coming in absolutely no reason
to leave and no reason to go in…

6:05

I want to do all those things
required for suicide maybe
even give it a try but never
quite follow through with
it and wonder if someone
might apply these same skills
doing the opposite dynamic
for something of a rebirth?

6:07

Hopefully death
will be like the denouement
of tension-fatigue syndrome

the end of this fucken delusion…

6:11

I would have
wanted sid vicious to do

(along with his i did it my way)
everything's coming up roses
as a sort of double-feature
double-header with
a curtain call of
zippety-do-dah

always a good kid
and wore my heart
out on the ballfield

6:12

Sign blow silo
wedded mountain
simply announces–

reuben
espresso
shakes…

7:00

Loved those commercials
back in the seventies

which made absolutely no effort
towards political-correctness

as when it comes down to it
who in the hell really wants

anything political or for that
matter any correctness, like–

"i got pabst blue ribbon on my mind
i got pabst blue ribbon on my mind"

"schaefer is the one beer to have
when you're having more than one

schaefer is the one beer to have
when you're having more than one"

as if trying to turn the whole public
and status-quo into pavlov's dog

drooling and feigning
and when you think

about it is there not something
rather nice and comforting about that?

7:05

It's funny i don't get tempted at all
by any of the drugs i carry (just feigning)
over the bagels lox creamcheese i grew up on

7:06

Funny all i seem to hear somewhere
on the radio station in the background
is led zeppelin barely audible but know
absolutely every guitar riff word by heart
when i drop off the drugs to the great big
foreboding, spooky, haunted institutions

7:07

When i get my first paycheck
i'm gonna get my wife a couple
those sundresses hanging off those
torsos in front of the secondhand shops

in the depressed towns (not so much
depressed towns) of new england

7:08

Yet it's all so strange that whole range
of once really charming dusty towns
in vermont that suddenly got struck
with opiates like what the fuck
some gorgeous and pure
down to earth ivory girl
plunging a needle in her
arm for kicks or just to
forget it in some bare
edward hopper room in
a farm house in the corn

7:46

Every night we seem to run
into these very nice and kind
well-dressed religious brothers
who seem under the influence
of brainwash and ask if want
some information about god
or our savior or jesus never
quite sure which one while
are delivering meds to the
old age homes in these very
quiet and bizarre somber
postage stamp suburbs
yet are pretty polite
so sorta tell them
thank you anyway
but are not interested
and just delivering psychotropic
medication and the same routine
and ritual appearing to happen

on a nightly basis as they vanish
to their dark backyard and their
darkened home and all you see
are the lights go on in the basement
with some strange continuous sound
of a chain saw and a recording of
church bells like that soundtrack
from that 1950s film with bing
crosby and what's her name
what was it called?

8:12

Lake champlain! lake champlain!
in the deep-down navy-blue breaking
bleak majestic romantic dusk evening
don't think i'll ever complain again!

lake champlain! lake champlain!
one of the prettiest rivers and lakes
of all time in all of america always
appearing like winding to never
never land laying flush against

the iridescent and pristine span
of the adirondack mountains
stapled up against the horizon!
don't think i'll ever complain again!

lake champlain! lake champlain!
always seeming to just show
up miraculously out of nowhere
somewhere over your shoulder
around the corner holy & haunted
from vermont to new york to canada
don't think i'll ever compain again!

8:17

Naturally radiant girls to die
for jogging with their perfect
bods and bobbing ponytails
and vanishing somewhere
near to the remote future

all irrelevant
as all about
the moment

8:35

The very distinguished schizophrenic
stuffing his pipe like clockwork
on the bench in front of
his residence like some
country club member looking
off to the distance completely disoriented
disassociating in the emptiness of evening

everyone has taken off to the links…

9:02

Sad self-reflective nurses fading
wasting away into the evening

they tell you their whole life story
that they worked 40 years in manufacturing
in 15 minutes getting off their shift as if suggesting…

9:18

It really is so damn keen and amazing how everything
truly does come around full-circle while your grandfather
used to own his own quaint charming corner pharmacy
in turn of the century bedford stuyvescent, brooklyn

used to sell ice cream sodas and heroin over the
counter and now i'm like some secret undercover
agent dropping off painkiller for the whole damn blessed
juvenile delinquent geriatric population in the northeast kingdom

9:30

They keep on putting up american flags and condominiums
all over the place; those neat look-alike cookie-cutter self-
contained communities with *mcdonalds* and real estate
agencies and cathedrals and acupuncturists (i suppose
everything one needs to live and survive) and little
white boy wiggers who tail you in the night acting o so dangerous
and scary all with the exact same safe and secure place to reside

9:34

At the old age home on the old army base
old women are passed out in their wheelchairs
and planted in front of televisions in the middle
of the deep dark bleakness while all you hear
in the background are these bizarre sounds
of what sounds like french language tapes
repeating over and over again very loud
and articulate *au revoir au revoir* then
long gaps of silence and that repetitive
au revoir…au revoir going on forever
au revoir…au revoir as though some
eternal postmodern waiting
room for the afterworld

9:46

On the campus in the middle
of the haunted dark quad very
organized regimented firemen
are simply practicing their skills
and drill with their ladders coming out
from long red trucks extended to the stars

9:53

Bizarre how just fall in love with some young beautiful polite
demure nurse who i am delivering psychotropic meds to
at one of the stops on my rounds through the deep dark
mountains of vermont; last shot of morphine which
will knock that old lady out for good, while her
daughter just shows up as well in a pall in a
respectful deferential mood of sympathy and
support knowing it will be her last night on earth
and nothing else can be done and will share the bed
with her; there is something really silent and sacred
when i deliver the last shot of morphine to this pretty
young nurse who actually seems the most scared
and is the only one here but she's beautiful polite
and demure and what else can be said as think
she knows deep down inside how much in
one simple prepared moment have respect
and fond of her and wish her the best

10:01

God the people out here so nice and kind
and down-to-earth this beautiful blonde
at the big empty *mobile* station when i
come creeping in like some tired old
truck driver or petty thief or criminal
asking me how my job went tonight
as if she really did care and give a

damn more than any man or supposed
friend or aquaintance i have ever had
taken completely off my guard wondering
if i know her but then it just dawns on me
she's just being friendly and tell her something
stupid stumbling with my words—"it was alright" (yours?)
stumbling back out to my car with a great big dumb smile

11:15

You dream coming in off
the cold dark streets riding
up the elevator dazed and distant
and make it to the bleak nurse's station
and reaching down deep into your bag
of drugs to pull them out this radiant
young cute ivory girl dove angel devil
of a nurse suddenly reaches from behind
for my bulge and turn her around and
give her one of those long passionate
kisses in the midst of the pill room then
some time around midnight little less
misguided (a little more patient)
move on to my next destination

12:01

After getting lost all night
in the seriously deep
steep mountains
of old depressed
shattered mill towns
now haunted drug
havens, heaven
is just people
staggering
out to

the mad
brightly lit
parking lot of
the waffle house

the whole town
looking like a great big
crime scene with cops
and false witnesses
searching for some
fugitive as you felt
like the sole survivor
your expired license

mozying on through
the tv cameras

all you thought
about all night
was getting
back home
to your
wife
and
child

12:30

You finally make it back home
like some blissful desolate
revelation in the pitch-black
lit-up new england evening
high school boys hanging
with high school girls
on the corner outside
the barroom and library
trying to make their score
and score with them and get
romantic and prove themselves
worthy (which never quite will

and deep down inside eternally
existentially the whole desperate
and pathetic challenge) and just
realize all this hanging-out
is what it all comes down
to and what it's all about

1:01

Very late at night
when the whole
world and town
has shut down
young girl
walking
her wild
wolf
across
the road
no place
left to go
which
says
it all

1:14

It was a long night tonight
which seemed to never end
which was just fine and got
all the morphine and oxycotin
out to those cute young hard-working
nurses who just like you seemed like
they had absolutely no place to go

1:15

When you get home after trying to wind down
and watch some sports to try and get to bed
or even in the morning to extend your sleep
cycle just a little longer you fantasize
about that pharmacist in her sundress
who appears eternally single and eternally
responsible and that other girl with the bubble
butt you got no idea what she does but always
just seems to find excuses to show up to your aisle
while you are in the midst of the frustrating madness
of trying to figure out the anacronyms and squinting
to make sense of the rx numbers and medications
and what and what is not a controlled substance
and then have to specially wrap and secure them
as if something is going to happen on the way from
the stripmall to the geriatric and juvenile institutions

1:16

Just got home after delivering
the painkiller through the dark
country mountain roads of deer
suddenly poking their scared
and shy eyes and shot torsos
out of the deep fog which show
up in different shapes and forms

1:16

Like suddenly showing up
from behind some curtain
which separates the day
from evening separates
the climates separates
the seasons separates
meaning separates

realities to a strange
audience completely
unfamiliar unbecoming
and desperately wanting
and needing to get back
to the place they came

2:00

Last night after getting hit with torrents
of rain all i saw instead of cats and dogs
were cops and frogs! cops and frogs!
cops and frogs! cops and frogs!
splashed out all over the road
all these awful horrible cops
with their blue beamers going off in quaint
small town ghettos picking off poor souls
while frogs having the time of their life
peeping, leaping all around; some of them
already wrecked, whacked by cars in the middle
of the road and others just dancing back and forth
like some joyous festival, oblivious, blissful
from the recesses of the deep dark forest
in the aftermath of the puddles of oasis'
as all i saw last night were cops and frogs!
cops and frogs! cops and frogs! cops and frogs!

3:00

Baby, didn't get home till 3 in the morning
so don't wake me unless the house is burning
matter of fact don't wake me even if the house
is burning...fuck got stuck up and down the same
goddamn dark country mountain road all evening
you wouldn't believe and the mist and fog got me
seriously insincerely and that effeminate phillippino
nurse made the moves on me and asked me if i was
married while dispensing the medication and then

all of sudden turned cold and distant when i told him
(what the fuck happened to all that hippa shit and
so sick of the double standard and that's what you
get for just always trying to be friendly, yet what
balanced it out was those nurses with the nonstop
tourettes and really nice to me and even challenged
me every week to see who could lose the most weight
and told them i'd have to hold off on account i was
an emotional eater and do enjoy my beer and sports
when i get home) while all i could think of was people
surely do live these sad and lonely and stranded lives
candles and pillars lining the beat bleak countryside
and the farmhouses all somehow looked like brothels
with scarlet curtains tonight and the stray cats from
the ghetto were running for their lives but do love
when they turn off the stop lights when they all
go blinking when you return back to the long
lost holy empty town...reminds me of a big
old blinking railroad...it should always be
an old blinking railroad and felt like a
cuckoo who wanted to creep back into
the beddie-bye belfry of the cathedral
left some lasagna and *coors* beer
in the refrigerator for you

3:01

Leaving chocolate chip
cookie on kitchen counter
means the world in a world
which holds no meaning at all

cactus flower exploded
and dogs barking
through window
all welcoming

Some time…

In the morning feeling down-in-the-dumps and depressed and nauseous as always, dream (when real dreaming goes on) the phone reads something like "ex istential"…they put a man on the moon and down here they are working on perfecting vacuums, while somewhere in between still feeling so down on your luck and blue and finally come to conclusions that you're just not gonna be able to solve all the problems of the world and answer all the questions from your bullshit job and that is just well and good and fine and whatever happens happens who don't show an ounce of gratitude for how hard you work for them, and yesterday evening even coming in early had a sign on the time clock which read something like 'if you don't punch in for your half hour lunch you will get a warning, if done again will be grounds for termination' (and you think really?) think you gotta be kidding! this is how they treat you spending evenings driving through the crazy rough terrain of insane mountains for them to deliver bins and bins of psychotropic medication fucken bitches and bastards! when you get back some time in the whee hours of the morning you suddenly realize one narcotic box and sealed-up controlled substance slipped out the bag and gonna have to head back out to that madman institution where the alarms are constantly going off and the nurses don't even notice a recording in the background which plays over and over something like—"alarm has been activated… please turn off…alarm has been…" find yourself howling in the middle of the puddles of the parking lot not giving a fuck with those six secret cameras set on your every move and expression to try and catch you and capture you and make sure you are not ripping them off, drop off the narcs and head on back home swerving down the road somewhere between consciousness and your sleep-cycle; when you wake up once more you realize the only news you like is news you don't know and news stations you don't recognize pointing out the overall destruction from another one of those hurricanes in places like baja california and cabo san lucus of which you find you are completely able to relate to; the neighbors across the road getting another one of those great big crates delivered to their garage; think this time it might be kong…

About the Author

Joseph Reich is a social worker who lives with his wife and thirteen-year-old son in the high-up mountains of Vermont. He has been published in a wide variety of eclectic literary journals both here and abroad. His work has been nominated seven times for The Pushcart Prize.

Fomite

About Fomite

A fomite is a medium capable of transmitting infectious organisms from one individual to another.

"The activity of art is based on the capacity of people to be infected by the feelings of others." Tolstoy, *What Is Art?*

Writing a review on Amazon, Good Reads, Shelfari, Library Thing or other social media sites for readers will help the progress of independent publishing. To submit a review, go to the book page on any of the sites and follow the links for reviews. Books from independent presses rely on reader-to-reader communications.

For more information or to order any of our books, visit: http://www.fomitepress.com/our-books.html

More Titles from Fomite...

Novels
Joshua Amses — During This, Our Nadir
Joshua Amses — Ghatsr
Joshua Amses — Raven or Crow
Joshua Amses — The Moment Before an Injury
Jaysinh Birjepatel — Nothing Beside Remains
Jaysinh Birjepatel — The Good Muslim of Jackson Heights
David Brizer — Victor Rand
Paula Closson Buck — Summer on the Cold War Planet
Dan Chodorkoff — Loisaida
David Adams Cleveland — Time's Betrayal
Jaimee Wriston Colbert — Vanishing Acts
Roger Coleman — Skywreck Afternoons
Marc Estrin — Hyde
Marc Estrin — Kafka's Roach
Marc Estrin — Speckled Vanities
Zdravka Evtimova — In the Town of Joy and Peace
Zdravka Evtimova — Sinfonia Bulgarica
Daniel Forbes — Derail This Train Wreck
Greg Guma — Dons of Time
Richard Hawley — The Three Lives of Jonathan Force
Lamar Herrin — Father Figure
Michael Horner — Damage Control
Ron Jacobs — All the Sinners Saints
Ron Jacobs — Short Order Frame Up
Ron Jacobs — The Co-conspirator's Tale
Scott Archer Jones — And Throw Away the Skins
Scott Archer Jones — A Rising Tide of People Swept Away
Julie Justicz — Degrees of Difficulty
Maggie Kast — A Free Unsullied Land
Darrell Kastin — Shadowboxing with Bukowski
Coleen Kearon — #triggerwarning
Coleen Kearon — Feminist on Fire
Jan English Leary — Thicker Than Blood
Diane Lefer — Confessions of a Carnivore
Rob Lenihan — Born Speaking Lies
Douglas W. Milliken — Our Shadows' Voice

Fomite

Colin Mitchell — Roadman
Ilan Mochari — Zinsky the Obscure
Peter Nash — Parsimony
Peter Nash — The Perfection of Things
George Ovitt — Stillpoint
George Ovitt — Tribunal
Gregory Papadoyiannis — The Baby Jazz
Pelham — The Walking Poor
Andy Potok — My Father's Keeper
Frederick Ramey — Comes A Time
Joseph Rathgeber — Mixedbloods
Kathryn Roberts — Companion Plants
Robert Rosenberg — Isles of the Blind
Fred Russell — Rafi's World
Ron Savage — Voyeur in Tangier
David Schein — The Adoption
Lynn Sloan — Principles of Navigation
L.E. Smith — The Consequence of Gesture
L.E. Smith — Travers' Inferno
L.E. Smith — Untimely RIPped
Bob Sommer — A Great Fullness
Tom Walker — A Day in the Life
Susan V. Weiss —My God, What Have We Done?
Peter M. Wheelwright — As It Is On Earth
Suzie Wizowaty — The Return of Jason Green

Poetry
Anna Blackmer — Hexagrams
Antonello Borra — Alfabestiario
Antonello Borra — AlphaBetaBestiaro
Antonello Borra — The Factory of Ideas
L. Brown — Loopholes
Sue D. Burton — Little Steel
David Cavanagh— Cycling in Plato's Cave
James Connolly — Picking Up the Bodies
Greg Delanty — Loosestrife
Mason Drukman — Drawing on Life
J. C. Ellefson — Foreign Tales of Exemplum and Woe
Tina Escaja/Mark Eisner — Caida Libre/Free Fall
Anna Faktorovich — Improvisational Arguments
Barry Goldensohn — Snake in the Spine, Wolf in the Heart
Barry Goldensohn — The Hundred Yard Dash Man
Barry Goldensohn — The Listener Aspires to the Condition of Music
R. L. Green — When You Remember Deir Yassin
Gail Holst-Warhaft — Lucky Country
Raymond Luczak — A Babble of Objects
Kate Magill — Roadworthy Creature, Roadworthy Craft
Tony Magistrale — Entanglements
Gary Mesick — General Discharge
Andreas Nolte — Mascha: The Poems of Mascha Kaléko
Sherry Olson — Four-Way Stop
Brett Ortler — Lessons of the Dead
Aristea Papalexandrou/Philip Ramp — Μας προσπερνά/It's Overtaking Us
Janice Miller Potter — Meanwell

Fomite

Janice Miller Potter — Thoreau's Umbrella
Philip Ramp — The Melancholy of a Life as the Joy of Living It Slowly Chills
Joseph D. Reich — A Case Study of Werewolves
Joseph D. Reich — Connecting the Dots to Shangrila
Joseph D. Reich — The Derivation of Cowboys and Indians
Joseph D. Reich — The Hole That Runs Through Utopia
Joseph D. Reich — The Housing Market
Kenneth Rosen and Richard Wilson — Gomorrah
Fred Rosenblum — Vietnumb
David Schein — My Murder and Other Local News
Harold Schweizer — Miriam's Book
Scott T. Starbuck — Carbonfish Blues
Scott T. Starbuck — Hawk on Wire
Scott T. Starbuck — Industrial Oz
Seth Steinzor — Among the Lost
Seth Steinzor — To Join the Lost
Susan Thomas — In the Sadness Museum
Susan Thomas — The Empty Notebook Interrogates Itself
Paolo Valesio/Todd Portnowitz — La Mezzanotte di Spoleto/Midnight in Spoleto
Sharon Webster — Everyone Lives Here
Tony Whedon — The Tres Riches Heures
Tony Whedon — The Falkland Quartet
Claire Zoghb — Dispatches from Everest

Stories
Jay Boyer — Flight
L. M Brown — Treading the Uneven Road
Michael Cocchiarale — Here Is Ware
Michael Cocchiarale — Still Time
Neil Connelly — In the Wake of Our Vows
Catherine Zobal Dent — Unfinished Stories of Girls
Zdravka Evtimova — Carts and Other Stories
John Michael Flynn — Off to the Next Wherever
Derek Furr — Semitones
Derek Furr — Suite for Three Voices
Elizabeth Genovise — Where There Are Two or More
Andrei Guriuanu — Body of Work
Zeke Jarvis — In A Family Way
Arya Jenkins — Blue Songs in an Open Key
Jan English Leary — Skating on the Vertical
Marjorie Maddox — What She Was Saying
William Marquess — Boom-shacka-lacka
Gary Miller — Museum of the Americas
Jennifer Anne Moses — Visiting Hours
Martin Ott — Interrogations
Christopher Peterson — Amoebic Simulacra
Jack Pulaski — Love's Labours
Charles Rafferty — Saturday Night at Magellan's
Ron Savage — What We Do For Love
Fred Skolnik — Americans and Other Stories
Lynn Sloan — This Far Is Not Far Enough
L.E. Smith — Views Cost Extra
Caitlin Hamilton Summie — To Lay To Rest Our Ghosts
Susan Thomas — Among Angelic Orders

Fomite

Tom Walker — Signed Confessions
Silas Dent Zobal — The Inconvenience of the Wings

Odd Birds
William Benton — Eye Contact: Writing on Art
Micheal Breiner — the way none of this happened
J. C. Ellefson — Under the Influence: Shouting Out to Walt
David Ross Gunn — Cautionary Chronicles
Andrei Guriuanu and Teknari — The Darkest City
Gail Holst-Warhaft — The Fall of Athens
Roger Lebovitz — A Guide to the Western Slopes and the Outlying Area
Roger Lebovitz — Twenty-two Instructions for Near Survival
dug Nap — Artsy Fartsy
Delia Bell Robinson — A Shirtwaist Story
Peter Schumann — A Child's Deprimer
Peter Schumann — Belligerent & Not So Belligerent Slogans from the Possibilitarian Arsenal
Peter Schumann — Bread & Sentences
Peter Schumann — Charlotte Salomon
Peter Schumann — Diagonal Man, Volumes One and Two
Peter Schumann — Faust 3
Peter Schumann — Planet Kasper, Volumes One and Two
Peter Schumann — We

Plays
Stephen Goldberg — Screwed and Other Plays
Michele Markarian — Unborn Children of America

Essays
Robert Sommer — Losing Francis: Essays on the Wars at Home

www.ingramcontent.com/pod-product-compliance
Lightning Source LLC
Chambersburg PA
CBHW062031120526
44592CB00036B/1834